Reading Iconotexts

From Swift to the French Revolution

PICTURING HISTORY

Series editors
Peter Burke Sander L. Gilman
Roy Porter Bob Scribner

In the same series

The Devil: A Mask without a Face
Luther Link

Health and Illness: Images of Difference
Sander L. Gilman

Reading Iconotexts

From Swift to the French Revolution

Peter Wagner

REAKTION BOOKS

Published by Reaktion Books Ltd
11 Rathbone Place, London W1P 1DE, UK

First published 1995

Designed by Humphrey Stone
Jacket designed by Ron Costley
Photoset by Wilmaset, Birkenhead, Wirral
Printed and bound in Great Britain by
The Alden Press, Oxford

British Library Cataloguing in Publication Data:

Wagner, Peter
Reading Iconotexts: From Swift to the
French Revolution. – (Picturing History
Series)
I. Title   II. Series
704.949909

ISBN 0–948462–71–X

Contents

Acknowledgements

My first debt of gratitude is to Roy Porter. Although I had other projects at the time, he encouraged me to write this book – and I have not regretted it at all. I also want to thank Roland, an *aficionado* of representations of the Breton *Ankou* and a dedicated reader of the illustrations in Wilhelm Busch's works and in the various exciting issues of *Tintin et Milou* and of *Astérix et Obélix*. He has taught me to read pictures (in books and on television) vigilantly, and his joy has been as much of a pleasure for me as our additional enterprises. Anne-Claude gave me considerable assistance in tackling the Medusa and other mysteries in the works of Ripa and Alciati. And Marie-Laure and Odile, confronted with some of my more freakish arguments, helped me back to the safer ground of common sense.

I am also grateful to those friends and colleagues from France, Germany and the USA who participated in my symposium on icons and iconotexts in Eichstätt in 1993. Their fascinating papers gave me some exciting ideas which have found their way into this book. To Bernadette Fort, Frédéric Ogée, Ottmar Ette, James Heffernan, Roland Hagenbüchle and Catherine Cusset I stand indebted for a series of fruitful discussions that helped clarify some of my arguments. And the exchange of ideas and words with W.J.T. Mitchell in Nice persuaded me to carry on exploring what he termed image/word constructs. I thank also Paul-Gabriel Boucé, editor of *Evolutions et révolutions* (Paris: Presses universitaires de la Sorbonne, 1993), and the editors of *Dispositio: American Journal of Semiotics and Cultural Studies*, for permission to use portions of published articles. Thanks also go to Joachim Möller who made available to me several papers by contributors to his forthcoming *Hogarth in Context: Ten Essays and a Bibliography*.

Ignaz Osiander surpassed himself, once again, in producing excellent photographs, and my former colleagues at the University of Eichstätt, Jürgen Malitz (the only reader of *Private Eye* in town and for miles around) and Peter Grau (occasional art historian by volition, and decoder of emblems and frescoes), provided useful help and advice in areas where I remain an amateur.

1 William Hogarth, Detail from illus. 60, *Masquerades and Operas* ('The Bad Taste of the Town'), 1724.

1 How to (Mis)Read Prints

Whilst a man is free, – cried the Corporal, giving a flourish with his stick thus –

A thousand of my father's most subtle syllogisms could not have said more for celibacy.

Sterne, *The Life and Opinions of Tristram Shandy, Gentleman*

The image is not the expression of a code, rather it is the variation of the work of codification: it is not the repository of a system but the generation of systems.

Barthes, 'La peinture est-elle un langage?'

To exemplify the focus and the subject of this book, let me begin with a cartoon from a recent number of *Private Eye* (illus. 2), for illustrations, if we are to trust the *Oxford English Dictionary*, can bring something to light, they may elucidate, enlighten, render illustrious, and even clear the head or brain. The cartoon contains some details that, like traffic signs, help the observer to arrive at a first level of understanding: the guillotine, the sansculottes and the cart with the two condemned refer to the period of terror during the French Revolution. However, to comprehend what is really going on here, we need more information than that which is given by the pictorial signifiers, which are too ambiguous. That information is provided by the caption beneath the cartoon. Without it the image would not make sense, or rather it would be open to many interpretations or readings. Like titles, captions can generate meaning(s), serving as what Michel Foucault has termed

2 Alan de la Nougerede, cartoon, *Private Eye*, 26 February 1993.

"Things might have been worse, Marie — we might have been torn to pieces by the tabloids"

'supporting pegs and yet termites that gnaw and weaken' our interpretive constructions.[1]

As far as pictures and their titles are concerned, there is perhaps no better ironic comment on that relation than Mark Twain's saucy if splendidly apposite passage in *Life on the Mississippi*, in which he argues that paintings are actually helpless without proper labels. After seeing in New Orleans a 'fine oil painting representing Stonewall Jackson's last interview with General Lee' (Everett B. D. Julio's *The Last Meeting of Lee and Jackson*), Twain briefly launched into a spirited attack on the art criticism of his day. 'The picture', he wrote, in his usual deadpan manner,

is very valuable .... But, like many another historical picture, it means nothing without its label. And one label will fit it as well as another:

First Interview Between Lee and Jackson.

Last Interview Between Lee and Jackson.

Jackson Accepting Lee's Invitation to Dinner. . . .

Jackson Asking Lee for a Match.

. . . A good legible label is usually worth, for information, a ton of significant attitude and expression in a historical picture. In Rome, people with fine sympathetic natures stand up and weep in front of the celebrated 'Beatrice Cenci the Day Before her Execution'. It shows what a label can do. If they did not know the picture, they would inspect it unmoved, and say, 'Young Girl with Hay Fever', 'Young Girl with her Head in a Bag'.

This passage has now become a favourite source of reference for scholars investigating the relation between images and words.[2]

Inspired and encouraged by Mark Twain's irreverence, we can now return to our cartoon. One could imagine another caption for it, for instance: 'Until this morning, I always thought the death penalty a good thing', or, 'What if I told them "L'Etat c'est moi"?'. Our 'making sense' is thus ultimately determined by the legend, a term that is perhaps more appropriate than caption since its second meaning denotes 'invented story'. The text of the present caption both clarifies and limits our reading of the picture: we learn that the two persons to be executed are Louis XVI and his Austrian-born wife, Marie-Antoinette. The point of the cartoon, i.e., the message that is supposed to make us smile, is hidden in the allusion of the final word, 'tabloids'. We are urged, in this instance, to relate the killing of the French royal couple during the Revolution to the metaphorical killing of British royals by the gutter press in the 1990s.

To convey its message, then, the cartoon relies on verbal and visual texts evoked by allusions. These references to what we have already seen and read are both implicit and explicit; they suggest that we juxtapose, and indeed bring into play, our knowledge of images and texts representing the execution of Louis XVI and Marie-Antoinette as well as the present-day reporting in British and Continental papers on the intra/extramarital affairs of Anne, Charles and Diana, Andrew and Sarah, and the sorrows of Queen Elizabeth and her husband.

Meaning in the illustration in *Private Eye* thus depends on the decoding of the allusions in the picture and in its legend. Such allusions are extremely important in what since the 1970s has come to be known as *intertextuality*. This theory of interpretation insists that a text cannot exist as a hermetic or self-sufficient entity, and hence cannot function as a closed system. As Roland Barthes pointed out some decades ago, the word *text* is derived from the Latin *textus*, meaning 'tissue' or 'texture' (that which is woven). One may therefore compare the implicit (unmarked) and explicit (marked) allusions in any given text to the knots in a textile fabric or mat: such knots 'make a point' by introducing new threads into the fabric being woven.[3]

The image in *Private Eye* in turn provides a particular interpretation of an important event in early modern history, an interpretation that, although part of a witty cartoon, should make us wary of the evidence of visual material. For it suggests that Louis and Marie-Antoinette faced death together, and that the gutter press of their day did not tear them to pieces. More reliable sources concerning this event tell us, however, that Louis and his Queen did not chat together in a cart during their final hour. And although they were guillotined by the same executioner, C.-H. Sanson, Louis went to his death on 21 January 1793, while Marie-Antoinette did not mount the scaffold until 16 October.[4] This suggests that we question the *OED*'s confidence in the clarifying power of illustrations. Apparently, if images are able to bring something to light (which is the original meaning of the term illustration), they are equally able to obfuscate, distort or misrepresent. Like verbal texts they can be studied as *representations* and hence as *interpretations*.[5]

In this book I shall be concerned with two important aspects that have emerged in my brief discussion of the *Private Eye* cartoon. There is, to begin with, the fascinating and highly intertextual nature of eighteenth-century prints. I prefer to call these prints iconotexts[6] because of the interpenetration of texts and images they exhibit. Perhaps it would be useful to revive that obsolete English word 'intermedial', for, as we shall see, the allusions are more often than not to 'texts' in or from other media: images refer to novels and poems; poems and novels integrate paintings or prints; and pictures again might refer to musical pieces. 'Intermediality', then, is a particular form or area of intertextuality.[7] Some of the images under scrutiny in this book are also embedded in texts. I shall also look at the various ways in which iconotexts encode discourse and represent events. It goes without saying that in attempting an analysis of this kind I cannot ignore the role of the one who ultimately always 'makes sense' of them – i.e., the reader or observer.

Perhaps the best way to explain what is new about this approach is to recall the manner(s) in which Hogarth's prints have been used by historians, literary scholars and art historians.[8] Less interested in the semantics and hermeneutics of visual images, historians have employed Hogarth's graphic works as ancillary evidence rather than as explicanda, assuming the semantics of the engravings to be in tune with that of their own critical texts. The tendency to make Hogarth's graphic art subservient to history is especially obvious in the works of M. Dorothy George, which, although useful social histories in their own right, disregard the rhetorical power of images. Similarly, Derek Jarrett in his *England in the Age of Hogarth* (1976) reads Hogarth's popular works as if they were 'a collection of snapshots' (p. 20),[9] while

Lawrence Stone ignores the rhetoric of the graphic art of Hogarth and Rowlandson in his search for 'social reality'.[10] Paradoxically, it is the realistic aspect of graphic art that causes the greatest interpretive difficulties, and, as Peter Brunette and David Wills have argued, it is precisely this very claim of visual art 'to speak "directly" somehow, supposedly avoiding the mediation inherent in verbal language, that is most in need of deconstruction'.[11] To read graphic images as mimetic renderings of eighteenth-century reality ignores what French post-structuralist writers such as Barthes have written about the creation of realism in the reading (or viewing) process, and also turns a blind eye to the undeniable fact that visual material contains figurations of meaning; in Mieke Bal's words, 'rhetoric is as visual as it is verbal.'[12] It is only with the recent emergence in Britain and the USA of New Historicism, and partly in the wake of Hayden White's exploration of the rhetoric of history writing, and in the context of the bicentennial re-evaluation of the French Revolution, that historians have begun to realize that Hogarth's prints are partisan interpretations, and as such are signs of a larger fabric that a culture weaves around itself.[13]

Literary historians and critics have also quarried Hogarth's graphic works, mainly in search of 'the correspondences of the arts'. This approach is problematical because it focuses almost exclusively on what might be termed elite culture while tacitly assuming that Hogarth's engravings are essentially 'high art'.[14] Instead of considering the intertextual allusions to all kinds of discourse in the prints, most critics, with the notable exceptions of Ronald Paulson and Pat Rogers,[15] have worked with definitions of 'literature' that present eighteenth-century writing in exclusive, canonical, terms as seen from the twentieth century. Many literary scholars seem to be unperturbed by a fact that I find remarkable: in all of Hogarth's graphic works there is not a single scene in which somebody is shown to be reading an English novel of the Enlightenment. We see people flocking to puppet theatres, ballad operas (illus. 1) and masquerades (illus. 6), and they are depicted reading or selling ballads (illus. 3), newspapers and crime and trial reports (illus. 4) – but never a novel. And yet we continue to explore Hogarth's relationship with, say, Fielding and Smollett. In fact, Hogarth refers to a novel only once: in *Characters and Caricaturas* we find the smiling faces of the artist and the novelist and, in the caption, an explicit allusion to Fielding's *Joseph Andrews* (illus. 5). The sheet bearing the title *Moll Flanders*, which appears in plate 1 of *Industry and Idleness* (behind Tom Idle), refers to a ballad version of Defoe's work (illus. 7) And we also notice how the popular reading matter of the apprentices (ballads on criminals and successful men, and guides for

3 William Hogarth, Detail from illus. 61, *The Enraged Musician*, 1741.

4 William Hogarth, Detail from *Marriage A-la-Mode – VI*, 1745, etching and engraving (second state).

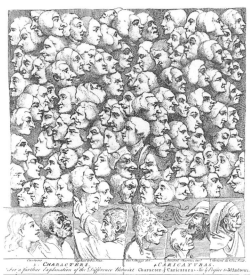

5 William Hogarth, *Characters and Caricaturas* (Subscription Ticket), 1743, etching (first state).

6 William Hogarth, *Masquerade Ticket*, 1727, engraving (first state).

apprentices) is presented here in terms of opposition. The term 'novel' (in the plural) does turn up in one of Hogarth's prints: the lady's volumes in *Before* (illus. 8) include one entitled 'NOVELS', but the plural form suggests that it contains erotic short stories and novellas, for the meaning of the expression 'novel' was rather vague in the early eighteenth century. Finally, in plate 4 of *Marriage A-la-Mode* (illus. 9), the book beside Counsellor Silvertongue is not of English origin; it is *Le Sopha*, a mildly erotic bestseller from the pen of Crébillon *fils*. An entire body of popular works consumed by all social strata, including that below the classics-reading and property-owning section of English society, has remained in the dark and will stay there if we continue to study the products of the subculture (perhaps a misnomer in the light of its influence on Hogarth) in the laundered versions presented by high art and literature.

This does not mean, of course, that literature by Swift, Defoe, Pope, Richardson and Fielding did not influence or interest Hogarth as an artist. As a book illustrator, for instance, he was obliged to deal with plays by Molière, Garrick and Fielding; he provided illustrations for Shakespeare's plays, Cervantes' *Don Quixote* and Samuel Butler's *Hudibras*. And he responded to the fiction of Swift and Fielding that

7 Detail from illus. 67, Hogarth's *Industry and Idleness – I.*

8 William Hogarth, *Before*, 1736, etching and engraving (first state).

9 William Hogarth, *Marriage A-la-Mode – IV*, 1745, etching and engraving (second state).

proved important both structurally and thematically for his graphic satires.

The best known example of this is *The Punishment Inflicted on Lemuel Gulliver* (illus. 10). Published on 26 December 1726, it was both a congenial response to the Dean's *magnum opus* and itself an allusion to the anti-Walpole satire marking Swift's work. Jocularly inscribing the author of *Gulliver's Travels* as designer of the print (spelling his name backward), Hogarth aligned himself with Swift in the role of 'inferior' engraver. Like the subtitle stating that the engraving was 'intended as a Frontispiece to his first Volume but Omitted', this was of course a pose and a joke. Although the writer and the artist had certain satirical aims in common, they depended on different media, producing effects that only at first sight are similar. Hogarth, for instance, mingles visual allusions to passages in *Gulliver's Travels* with elements from the genre of art known as *bambocciate*, a body of works by minor artists in northern Italy who created grotesque scenes of low-life that combined realism with traditions derived from Flemish art, *commedia dell'arte* figures and popular tales. The pump/clyster motif is derived from a number of Brueghel's prints and *bambocciate* (perhaps the major source) by Faustino Bocci. When the print was reissued in 1757 it was retitled *The*

10 William Hogarth, *The Punishment Inflicted on Lemuel Gulliver*, 1726, etching and engraving (first state) signed 'Nahtanhoj Tfiws'.

Political Clyster, the new caption proposing that various politicians should likewise be purged.[16]

I do not then deny the influence on Hogarth of (what we, today, see as) major fiction. But I am stating that we tend to exaggerate the role of the novel to the disadvantage of other discursive forms flourishing for the last time in the first half of the eighteenth century. We must heed Ian Watt's reminder in *The Rise of the Novel* (1957) – that the prices of novels were far beyond the means of any except the comfortably off, and that the novel was not, strictly speaking, a 'popular' literary form.

From the ostensible vantage-point of the twentieth century, which overestimates the importance of the novel for the early eighteenth century, the popular discursive forms evoked in Hogarth's prints appear to be marginal. But their peripheral position is a consequence of changes in taste as well as of the suppression that goes along with it. In the course of the eighteenth century popular discourse as practiced in the market place began to be displaced by more polite genres. It is only by deconstructing Hogarth's own iconographic satires of, say, the 1720s and early 1730s, that one discovers their contradictory nature: *Masquerades and Operas* (illus. 60) and *A Just View of the British Stage* (illus. 11), both from 1724 and discussed below, are attacks on the commercialization of culture and taste, and yet, like the later *Southwark Fair* (illus. 12), they reveal the influence if not the 'central' position of raree-shows, ballad operas, and puppet theatres.[17] I will try to show in chapter Four that Hogarth's early graphic art exhibits a Janus-faced nature: it provides satirical views of popular Enlightenment entertainments while participating in the general critique by middle-class Augustans of the hybridization occurring at the fairs and in the theatres. Offering a slanted glimpse of the fascinating cultural variety of entertainment, his prints published before the 1730s also inscribe themselves in a hegemonic ideology and give expression to a particular *mentalité* (I use the French term, as employed by the historians of the *Annales* school and Foucault).

If we are genuinely interested in retrieving the culture and the *mentalité* of Hogarth's age, we must extricate ourselves from readings of the Enlightenment that mainly serve to justify our taste and to cement traditional methodologies and boundaries. We must also admit that there was more to eighteenth-century culture than the works we have arbitrarily selected for our modern canons of Augustan art and literature. These canons may suit us very well, but they do not fit the age of Hogarth.

Hogarth's graphic art also poses considerable problems for art historians, although these difficulties have only emerged in recent

11 William Hogarth, *A Just View of the British Stage*, 1724, etching.

12 William Hogarth, *Southwark Fair*, 1733/4, engraving.

ekphrases.[18] Reading Hogarth's images is not as easy as it used to be. Over recent decades three ways of interpretation have largely dominated in this area. They resume the 'tenor' of earlier commentators in the eighteenth and nineteenth centuries. The first is Paulson's intentionalist reading. He sees Hogarth as a revolutionary *manqué*, an artist who was always on the side of the nobodies against the somebodies. This means that Hogarth's prints apparently contain a double discourse, one being superficially moralistic, and the other, intended for readers of 'greater penetration', subversive.[19] The second line of interpretation can be found in the works of Sean Shesgreen. While he also attributes a moral and political impulse to the artist, his central argument is that the realistic details of the engravings ultimately overwhelm signification. The third approach is that represented by the studies in iconography in the tradition of Panofsky that try to explore the use and the art-historical functions of emblems, icons and symbols.[20]

It is obvious that intentionalism still dominates in the criticism on Hogarth, and not exclusively in Paulson's works. In tune with 'retrieval art history',[21] the ekphrasis of Hogarth's graphic art seems to be at the stage where literary criticism found itself before the advent of New Criticism. Whereas since the 1960s authorial (or declared) intention has been considered relatively unimportant in the analysis of literary texts, a strong umbilical cord still ties (or should one say, *fetters?*) the Hogarthian prints to their producer. This is, alas, evident even in those recent studies that seem to recognize the openness and ambiguity of Hogarth's graphic art. It is typical, for instance, that in their respective articles Stephen C. Behrendt and Werner Busch first explore these issues with persuasive examples – but only to attribute the creation of ambiguity and indeterminacy to the genial creator, to a Hogarth who controls dualistic thinking and invents a new language for art.[22]

A part of what needs to be done in the study of eighteenth-century pictorial material in general, and of Hogarth's engravings in particular, is the subject of this book: an interdisciplinary analysis of the prints in the light of post-structuralist theories, particularly intertextuality and intermediality. I agree with Ivan Gaskell that 'no one profession has, or . . . should have, a monopoly over the interpretation of visual material' (p. 190). This implies a number of consequences. To begin with, I cannot write any longer as a literary historian (which is the job I have been trained for) or, for that matter, as a historian or art historian. Ignoring these traditional boundaries, I intend to visit the neighbouring fields in an interdisciplinary approach that stresses common ground rather than differences. Two exemplary, indeed trailblazing examples of such a new way of writing are Barbara Maria Stafford's *Body Criticism: Imaging the Unseen in Enlightenment Art and Medicine* (1991) and Mieke Bal's equally challenging *Reading 'Rembrandt': Beyond the Word-Image Opposition* (1991).[23]

But to assess eighteenth-century images in the 1990s also implies a consideration and critique of hermeneutics, that is in 'doing what comes naturally'[24] one should establish first what one's theoretical position is – and remain conscious of it along the way. If, in the following pages, I address the problems of reading iconotexts of the Enlightenment, I cannot deny my debt to such writers as Barthes, Kristeva and Foucault. Their pioneering works in what have come to be known as semiotics and discourse analysis will, I hope, provide useful tools in the field I intend to till. I have also profited from the selfconscious approaches of New Historicists laying bare the textuality of history and the historicity of texts, while the works of New Art Historians such as Norman Bryson, Hubert Damisch and Georges Didi-Huberman, for instance, have entirely convinced me that it is high time to replace Gombrich's account of art in terms of perception with an account of art not as sign (which would run aground because of its linguistic model) but as intermedial fabric established by allusions.[25] To apply these new ways of seeing, however, presupposes a twofold daring deed. On the one hand, the courage to replace older models of explication, such as Gombrich's approach as well as Panofsky's 'almost theological harmonizing of meaning in the visual arts' (which is ultimately derived from the hermeneutical exegesis of biblical texts);[26] and, on the other, the courage to cut the umbilical cord between author (intention) and work (as suggested by Foucault and Bourdieu) and to ignore, for the sake of one's argument, the traditional author function. More than twenty years ago Foucault sketched the prospects that await us in the world beyond the liberation of the text from its author. If we ignored those voices, he argued, that incessantly inquire about the writer of a text and analyse it exclusively in relation to the author, we might at long last be able to realize that the (distinguished) author can also obstruct access to his/her text. As soon as we turn away from the author function we will hear what the text itself has to say.[27] Applying Foucault's and Bourdieu's admittedly radical suggestion to eighteenth-century graphic 'fabrics', I want to do what A. W. Schlegel thought Georg Christoph Lichtenberg had done with Hogarth's prints, i.e., 'liberate them from the platitude of [their] genre.'[28] A practical example of this approach is my chapter Four, on official discourse in Hogarth's graphic works.

I hold that eighteenth-century prints, and especially Hogarth's engravings, can be considered as graphic equivalents, and examples of Kristeva's conception of poetic utterances in which can be identified a great variety of discursive traditions evoked by a code of familiar traces, by what Barthes has aptly termed the 'déjà lu, vu, fait, vécu' (that which has already been read, seen, made, experienced).[29] In terms of recent applications of speech-act theories to art, one might say that I study prints as 'enunciations' with iconic and linguistic backgrounds – with the stress on the 'listener' making sense.[30] Once enunciations (pictures or words) take (a) shape, spacing becomes a common ground of expression. My task, then, is both an archaeological one and an architectural one: it is not for nothing that, as recent deconstructive criticism reminds us, a work of art may be conceived of 'as a receptacle or dwelling place for meaning, one whose borders are both clearly defined and consistently repressed to provide the spectator with easy access to its centre and seat'.[31] Hogarth's engravings may therefore be studied as inhabitations, with my discourse being no more than a rethinking of the conflation of word and image in spacing/inhabitation/framing. If this works, one ought to be able to discover a fascinating universe of ambiguity and of multiple meanings behind the verbal and visual allusions that establish the 'fabric' and the meaning(s) of the prints. I am, of course, not the first to notice the (inter)textual nature of the Hogarthian engravings. Horace Walpole thought of Hogarth 'rather as a writer of comedy with a pencil than a painter'; and his affinity to language was briefly suggested by other eighteenth-century commentators, such as Jean André Rouquet and especially Lichtenberg, a post-structuralist *avant la lettre*.[32] In the nineteenth century, in his *Essai de physiognomonie* (1845), the Swiss artist and writer Rodolphe Toepffer advanced to a theoretical level when he sketched a brief theory of narrating in pictures. Comparing Hogarth's 'littérature en estampes' to literature proper, he argued that even two volumes from the pen of Richardson could scarcely express with the same force what is contained in Hogarth's series *Marriage A-la-Mode*. Stephen C. Behrendt apparently takes Hogarth to the threshold of post-structuralism when he argues that the 'elaborate visual vocabulary' of the series 'generates a potent intertextuality that expands, refines, and redefines for the viewer particular aspects of actions and character traits' and that Hogarth's works are 'in many significant ways the most profoundly intertextual visual performance of the period, assembling as they do materials garnered from portraiture, caricature, emblems, history painting, and conversation pieces, from classical mythology, music, and architecture'.[33] But since the time of Lichtenberg, Hogarth's prints have not been made the subject of a thorough semiotic and intermedial reading that focuses on the 'text' rather than on the producer; and the graphic art of the Enlightenment (especially prints and book illustrations) is just beginning to attract the interest of scholars interested in semiotics.[34]

Finally, I think that an analysis of the structural and semantic relations between the signifiers and the texts that are alluded to in iconotexts should also provide a good example of three concepts propagated by Jacques Derrida and frequently misunderstood by critics. The first of these is the notion of 'différance', the subtle ways in which meaning is never really clarified but constantly postponed and deferred from one signifier to another (say, from a biblical text serving as pretext to a Hogarthian engraving to the title of that work of art and on to the explication of title-work-pre-text). The second is the surreptitious hermeneutic construction (by the critic relying on alleged author intention) of hierachies of meaning. Finally, there is Derrida's notorious, and notoriously misrepresented, pronouncement: 'il n'y a pas de hors-texte' (there is no outside-the-text). This phrase does not deny the existence of things outside texts, but rather that all natural presences are mediated by texts or, in Derrida's own words: 'What I call "text" implies all the structures called "real", "economic", "historical", socio-institutional, in short: all possible referents'. For the Hogarthian engraving, this means that in its capacity as referent or enunciation it must be replete not with reality but with differential traces. It is the exploration of these traces and codes that is part of the subject of this book.[35]

Lest all this sound like high jinks and rhetoric, I should like to conclude my introduction with a few visual examples that will demonstrate how I read eighteenth-century prints: what makes them fascinating is not so much their ironical and naturalistic commentary on social reality but rather their rhetorical strategy in an appeal to the spectator's *mentalité* and knowledge of discourse and images. This strategy works by way of mingling and layering visual and verbal texts, and it also employs the margin(al) and the frame/framing. Various codes and sign-systems ultimately create what I have termed 'icono-texts', constructs that rely on the interpenetration of words and images. Another plastic term that could be usefully applied to such constructs is 'palimpsest'. Originally, this denoted a parchment or tablet that has been written on or inscribed several times, the previous text(s) having been imperfectly erased and remaining, therefore, visible. Gérard Genette has used the term to describe and explain the derived (allusive) nature of literature; it seems to me that it serves even better as an 'illustration' of the dense texture of an engraving in which pictures

13 William Hogarth, *A Harlot's Progress – 1*, 1732, etching and engraving (first
state).

and texts inscribe themselves in or over earlier ones.

Take the famous first plate of Hogarth's *A Harlot's Progress* (illus.
13), which depicts the Harlot's arrival in London. Meaning in this
picture depends on the way we decode a great number of sign-systems
that include not only the objects but also the people if we read them as
intertextual signifiers. Whatever 'realism' there might be in this
London scene, what is also important is the fact that almost everything
shown refers to some other text(s) or image(s). Meaning, in other
words, becomes a matter of (recognizing the allusions to) texts and
contexts.

I shall begin with the allusions to pictures. On the art-historical level
the plate, since it is part of a series, comments on and indeed subverts
seventeenth-century Continental series concerned with penitent har-
lots, such as the Italian *La vita infelice della Meretrice* (1692) by the
engraver Mitelli. In addition, the constellations of the human figures –
clergyman, harlot, bawd; and harlot, bawd, rake – echo and parody
Renaissance paintings and prints of two traditional subjects: the
Choice of Hercules (Hercules at the crossroads, between Virtue and

Pleasure), a parodic treatment of classical history painting; and the Visitation, a parody of New Testament history painting and engraving, such as Dürer's *Visitation* (illus. 14). Connoisseurs like Paulson even find echoes of Watteauesque conversation pieces in this scene.[36]

As far as verbal discourse is concerned, we encounter a similar variety of allusions to co-texts, contexts and subtexts from popular and polite genres. They reach from contemporary journalism and the reporting about the rapes committed by Colonel Charteris (the man in the doorway), and the deeds of a prostitute named Kate Hackabout, to the enormous body of erotica focusing on such bawds as Mother Needham (in the centre) and their victims; and they even include established genres like (pastoral) letters (the clergyman in the picture is reading a specimen of sorts), the whore dialogue, and verbal puns. The dead goose and the bell, for instance, help to establish an impression of realism; but they can also be read as emblems and puns: both may refer to the Harlot *and* to each other (e.g., a silly goose that will soon be a dead 'belle'). Such punning (see, for instance, the horse whose appetite leads to a minor disaster), based as it is on visual and verbal crossings, occurs in most of Hogarth's plates. As a satirical device it is indebted to earlier Dutch engravings and can thus also be seen as a Barthian trace of a (lost or absent) code. Plate I also engages intertextually and ironically with the traditional signifying suggested by such handbooks as Cesare Ripa's *Iconologia* and lexicons of physiognomy in which the

14 Albrecht Dürer, 'The Visitation', from the series *Marienleben* (*Life of the Virgin* 1511, engraving after a woodcut.

depiction of the passions was described and determined.[37] An interesting signifier in this respect is Charteris, the rapist in the doorway. His facial expression denotes lust, but it also connotes the illicit pleasure of masturbation, one of the great sexual taboos of the Enlightenment that was nevertheless discussed *ad nauseam* within the acceptable frame of moralistic paramedical treatises. The Colonel's facial expression is thus an allusion to paramedical erotica on onanism, an allusion that has recourse to texts in order to reinforce the negative characterization of the rapist.[38]

Additional dimensions of meaning emerge as we move from the exploration of the layering of the human and non-human signifiers and codes to the structural relations between the signs. The bell, for instance, is part of a sign-system Hogarth employs quite frequently (the boards or signs on public houses and other establishments);[39] yet it also comments on the two females beneath. Finally, there is also a text that leads us into the engraving: for those who might have missed the more than obvious allusions in this picture to earlier literary and sub-literary treatments of the career of prostitutes (Steele's sentimental defence of whores in *Spectator* no. 266 of 4 January 1712; Defoe's *Moll Flanders*, of 1724; and Gay's vastly influential *The Beggar's Opera*, of 1728), the title becomes a guideline in the original sense of the term. *A Harlot's Progress* again recalls other texts – the old word 'harlot' (instead of whore) suggests above all the language and the episodes of the Bible, while the term 'progress' urges the reader/observer to compare this Hogarthian series with Christian progresses as recorded in literary form, Bunyan's *Pilgrim's Progress* being the outstanding example. As with the visual pre-texts, the comparison will reveal irony and parody.

These are just a few examples of visual and verbal texts that, by way of allusions, come into play in this plate. The reader uses them to create some sort of meaning within the larger coordinates set by the satirical genre, which calls for subversive imitation, for travesty and parody, processes that rely substantially on the semiotic difference between denotation and connotation. It should be clear by now that the Kristevan metaphor of a universe evoked by references in (poetic) texts is not a fashionable exaggeration but a comparison that seems particularly useful in the case of graphic art.

My second example is Hogarth's *The Sleeping Congregation* (illus. 15). If we didn't know its title and first looked at the small print itself to find a 'central' meaning, we might come up with a whole series of alternatives: The Sleeping Beauty; The Lecherous Clerk; The Boring Preacher; and, perhaps, The Sleeping Congregation. It is here that one

15 William Hogarth, *The Sleeping Congregation*, 1736, etching and engraving (third state; 'retouched and improved' in 1762).

is immediately reminded of Foucault's observation about the constructive role of captions and titles: this one intends to make us believe that what it expresses is indeed the most important message of the visual satire. However, a closer look at the semantics and the structural relations of the signifiers reveals not one but many themes. To claim centrality for any particular subject means establishing a hierarchy of meaning, with the consequence that a great deal of visual evidence is reduced to marginal or decorative functions.

This is the case in two author-oriented readings of the picture. The Revd John Trusler, for instance, argued in the eighteenth century that Hogarth's 'piece is an excellent satire on the slovenly, indecent method of some of our modern clergy, and, the spreading lukewarmness of religion'. Trusler's ekphrasis leaves no room for the discussion of the possible functions of ostensible marginalia, such as the royal coat of arms, with 'Dieu' missing from the motto, the peculiar shape of the angel, the triangular hats, the triangle on the wall, and the objects held by the sleeping beauty, to name just a few obstreperous details that make more sense than one might suppose on first glance. In fact, a closer analysis of these signifiers in terms of intertextuality (i.e., the pictures and texts they introduce by way of allusion) proves them to be complex semantic nodes, crossings of visual and verbal texts with several layers of meaning, that finally create a fascinating palimpsest even *before* we start considering the syntax (the relation of the signifiers), a further level of meaning of which Trusler was totally unaware. One might read the lady's fan, for instance, as an unimportant decorative detail. But as always in Hogarth's allusive art, it stands for other images and texts that introduce a series of ideas. Here, we should remember that around 1735 women had a great variety of fans at their disposition. Different fans were used at such occasions as marriages, burials and daily service. More often than not they were decorated, serving as sign-systems for the ladies who employed them, even in church, to encourage or discourage male admirers. Addison, among others, attacked the fan as an instrument of immoral coquettes in *The Freeholder* (no. 15, 10 February 1716). The observer of Hogarth's image should therefore be aware of the ambivalent and polysemous nature of this signifier, for the picture plays with the denotations and connotations of the fan – as an ornamental object used by women, as a sign that refers to images and texts, and, on another ironical level, even as a sign-system (cf. the sign-boards of public houses). The fact that the fan also appears in other Hogarth prints where (illicit) female eroticism is implied (see, for instance, plate 2 of *Industry and Idleness*, illus. 16, and plate 3, 'Evening', of *The Four Times*

16 William Hogarth, Detail from *Industry and Idleness – 2* ('The Industrious 'Prentice Performing the Duty of a Christian'), 1747, etching and engraving (second state).

17 William Hogarth, Detail from 'Evening', *The Four Times of the Day*, 1738, etching and engraving.

of the Day, illus. 17) confirms its function as part of a sign language of flirtatious women.[40]

More recently, Paulson has discussed *The Sleeping Congregation* within the context of English iconoclasm and Hogarth's attack on idolatry. If we are to believe Paulson, the print contains a central 'satiric message', determined by the artist of course, namely that 'not only art but all trace of religious feeling has disappeared from the church'. Such a reading requires that all the details fit the critical view. Paulson has no difficulty with this problem since he believes in authorial intention.[41] For the polysemous triangle on the wall, for instance, this means that its multiple meanings must be curtailed. Paulson does not consider the fact that the triangle conflates its traditional use as a visual emblem (with a long artistic history that also includes 'primitive' representations of the female sex), as a religious symbol, and as a linguistic sign (the Greek letter *delta*). According to Paulson, it functions as 'a sign of the world-turned-upside-down'. And since Paulson is convinced that Hogarth 'intended' it as a masonic triangle it must 'suggest the secularization of the church into lodge'. To my recent suggestion that the picture might also present 'a comic and essentially moral juxtaposition of the absence of God and the presence of lust', Paulson responded, typically, with the insistence on Hogarth's intention, arguing that my reading 'does not correspond to the *centrality Hogarth* [my italics] gives the young Mary-substitute.'[42]

If we follow Trusler and Paulson and try to retrieve author intention we might be lucky with our speculations. Hogarth might have had such ideas – but what if he had not? And why not avoid building one's reading exclusively on such shaky intentionalist foundations?[43] As soon as, in the spirit of Foucault, we liberate the voices in the picture, we notice that the title, for instance (like the frame or the caption), is a controlling device that reduces meaning. *The Sleeping Congregation* is about many things (idolatry, iconoclasm, lechery, sexuality, the poor state of religion, church decorations, the absence of God). In terms of the Derridean 'différance', the title promises a central message that is to emerge from our reading of the print – but that reading produces not one but a series of 'messages' and 'points'. If we resist the temptation of reading for realism in Hogarth's picture, we can decode every detail on a semantic and structural level. Such a decoding will show the multiple meanings of the signs and the surprising possibilities of the constellations. (Mis)using a favourite phrase of Paulson's, one might say that the point of this and other Hogarth prints is precisely that, semantically speaking, there is more than one 'point'. In a detailed study of the semantic and structural polyvalence of Hogarth's graphic art, Werner

Busch has recently shown that the difficulties of reading Hogarth do not derive from the dualism of satirical intention; rather they are due to the collapse of the relation between signifier and signified, which thus opens the way for individual, subjective, reception.[44]

It might be objected at this point that my reading of eighteenth-century graphic images, and of Hogarth's prints in particular, yields results that are not strikingly different in kind from those in more traditional kinds of studies (e.g., Paulson's books on Hogarth). My aim, of course, is not to be different at all costs, but rather to demonstrate the possibilities of reading iconotexts in the light of post-structuralist theories. I differ from traditionalists in that I make a distinction between authorial intention or encoding (which I find interesting but unreliable as a ground for interpretation, and hence negligible) and critical reading or decoding: these are two essential stages of meaning-production which must not be confused or conflated. Furthermore, I argue that hierarchies of reading/decoding (with central messages or meanings) collapse once we approach visual art from a deconstructive angle that uncovers the strategies and 'fearful symmetries' of ekphrasis. Finally, I hope to show that such new post-structuralist readings are not destructive (all they destroy is the illusion of the critic who takes his own ideas for those of the author); rather, they produce knowledge while alerting us to the very process of production that is often denied or silenced by traditionalists.[45]

The following chapters provide practical examples of the ways in which iconotexts can be studied. Perhaps the procedure of the book needs a few words of explanation. Although my playing-ground will be the eighteenth century, I do not intend to show any sort of chrono-logical *development*. I will have no truck with teleology, whether chronological, generic or otherwise. Rather, what the book offers may be described as intermedial exercises in archaeological excavation, a search in several chapters within cultural layers or strata of the Enlightenment. In these layers, I have come across, and chosen for analysis, objects marked by fabrics of visuality and textuality; and it is these fabrics I intend to unravel, as far as the confines of book chapters allow such an enterprise.

If the objects under analysis happen to have been produced in the 1720s (Swift's text) and 1730s (Scheuchzer's *Physica Sacra*), around mid-century (Hogarth's prints), and toward the end of the century (French 'libelles' and engravings), it is all the better, and my choice will perhaps satisfy those interested in comparisons and developments. But my target is, from the beginning, a different one. I want to test the theories of that arch-archaeologist, Foucault, in order to ascertain whether eighteenth-century images are essentially marked by those lines/threads of power and discourse he saw at work in the eighteenth century. Simultaneously, I hope to be able to take Derrida at his word when I look for the eighteenth-century world as text in the iconotextual traces of images.

In *The Great Cat Massacre and other Episodes in French Cultural History* (1984), an entertaining and highly instructive study of eighteenth-century French *mentalités*, Robert Darnton argues that there is no better method to retrieve ways of thinking in the eighteenth century and to shake us 'out of a false sense of familiarity with the past' (pp. 11–12) than to wander through the archives. I found his assemblage of textual material both useful and impressive, precisely because it departed from the established modes of historical writing and thinking. I can only hope that my similar straying from the beaten path in this book, which descends into the archives of visuality and its links with textuality while keeping a critical eye on the archivists past and present, will also create the possibility of enjoying some unusual, revealing, views.

Far from being eccentric, the procedure of the book is quite simple and, to a certain extent, the consequence of the critical access to the areas to be explored. I shall begin with the frontispieces embedded in the opening part of *Gulliver's Travels*. Essentially, this part of my book (chapter Two) deals with visual/verbal simulation and the manner in which visual rhetoric is exposed as false in Swift's text through the juxtaposition of fact and fiction, words and images, re-presenting and reality, charlatans and great men. It is in this questioning of signifying practices that the Swiftean text proves almost postmodern. The chapter will also show that literary genres (e.g., travel literature) as established by literary criticism are not necessarily helpful. More often than not, they prove to be blind windows. The analysis of such inconotexts as *Gulliver's Travels* in terms of semiotics and discourse analysis promises an escape from this dilemma.

From this textual frame or access (containing pictures) I move on to iconic frames and their semantic and rhetorical functions in eighteenth-century engravings (chapter Three). Armed with tools provided by Derrida, Jean-Claude Lebensztejn and other critics who have written on the *parergon*, I will assess the margin(al) in and of prints as access, supplement, and site of meaning-making. My chief examples are some truly fantastic works by Johann Jakob Scheuchzer and an anonymous English print from the 1790s, with just a brief comparative glance at the way the Hogarthian images have been framed.

The discussion of the *parergon* will necessarily lead me into the 'ergon' and to the texts producing meaning in it (chapter Four). I analyse a selected number of Hogarth's prints. Examining merely one particular genre of writing (Pastoral Letters, laws and proclamations) and newspapers, I intend to show how the engravings comment on the reception of such discourse by the common people while subtly re-enforcing hegemonic ideologies and *mentalités*.

My way through the visual archives ends (chapter Five) in a dark corner often maligned as a smutty one, an area that Darnton and other historians have un/discovered but not fully explored in the course of the recent revival of historical writing about the period. At the centre of this section of the book are the allegedly obscene or pornographic illustrations forming an integral part of aggressive pamphlets published during the French Revolution. My contention is that these admittedly controversial works should be decoded as revolution in print, as parodic, intermedial, assaults on the *genre galant* of erotic art and the aura of holiness and greatness that had traditionally surrounded and thus protected (representations of) aristocratic bodies. Seen from this angle, even the rather crude cartoons depicting Marie-Antoinette emerge not as dirt and trash, but as discourse clad in a new radical garb which even post-modern critics find difficult to accept. At the same time, I intend to show that this new language, in its verbal and iconic varieties, does not perhaps deserve the epithet 'revolutionary', for it incorporates older discursive forms that proved highly influential in the establishment of sexual *mentalités*, precisely because they relied on clichés and stereotypes. The importance of carnivalesque elements (as rhetorical forms undermining the radical content) will also be discussed in relation to these pictures.

Finally, in chapter Six, I refuse to conclude, offering instead a reconsideration of the problems encountered along the way, with some suggestions towards the application of new approaches to the study of iconotexts.

18 William Hogarth, *The Company of Undertakers* ('Quacks in Consultation'),
1736/7, etching and engraving.

2 Captain Gulliver and the Pictures

It can be seen that the iconoclasts, who are often accused of despising and denying images, were in fact the ones who accorded them their actual worth, unlike the iconolaters, who saw in them only reflections . . .
Baudrillard, *Simulacra and Simulations*

This picture is simply what any picture is, a trap for the gaze . . . . In this matter of the visible, everything is a trap . . . a labyrinth.
Lacan, 'Of the Gaze as *Objet Petit a*', in *The Four Fundamental Concepts of Psycho-Analysis*

Before one decides what is parergetic in a text dealing with the isssue of the 'parergon' one must know what a 'parergon' is – at least one ought to know whether there is one.
Derrida, *The Truth in Painting*

Even a superficial comparison of the various extant critical editions of *Gulliver's Travels* shows that postmodern readers are offered different means of 'access' to Swift's magnificent satire. In this chapter I analyse the various parts of the 'front-matter', which is in dire need of editorial reassessment. The introductory part is, in Gérard Genette's terminology, a para-text, that is, writing surrounding the major body of a literary work. Like the frame(work) of a picture (see my following chapter), it is what philosophers from Kant to Derrida have termed a *parergon*, a by-work or extra ornament. The function of a *parergon* is to comment on the central part, to control our vision by putting things into a particular perspective. And it is this frequently underestimated, subversive function of the verbal framing (which in the case of the *Travels* includes portraits, i.e., visual material) that I want to discuss in detail. One of my guidelines is the theory that we should be reluctant to adopt prescribed perspectives precisely because they may be traps preventing a better vision.

For the general reader, and even more for the academic critic, the *Travels* can prove an obnoxious book, for it seems that the games its text plays with discourse as well as with the reader turn the reading process into a voyage. More often than not, this voyage draws the reader-traveller into an endless and inescapable textuality that, at least for those who trust the narrator and his creator, is bound to end in entrapment. From the very beginning, Swift's *magnum opus* has created difficulties for taxonomists trying to place it in neat categories. If critics can agree at all about the genre to which the *Travels* belongs, they stress its complexity and deliberate mingling of various forms of discourse, including the imaginary voyage, utopian and dystopian journeys, spiritual autobiography, picaresque narrative, the philosophical tale à la *Candide* – and a parody of all these forms. Over the centuries, as critics have attempted to come to terms with Swift's recalcitrant text, their efforts to accommodate it in a traditional genre or category ended in frustration or (which amounts to the same) in an extension of existing genres. Thus, in 1734, Nicolas Lenglet du Fresnoy put the *Travels* in his fourteenth, and last, category for fiction, 'romans divers qui ne se rapportent à aucune des classes précédentes' (various novels that do not relate to any of the preceding categories), while Northrop Frye, no less inventive in 1957, 'rediscovered' two genres for it that he termed anatomy and Menippean satire. Indeed, the history of the reception of the *Travels* is as fascinating as is the book itself. The reception shows a series of genre decisions that attempt to cope with the indeterminacy and ambiguity of Swift's text by forcing it into artificial literary kinds promising coherence and stability. Ultimately, however, these desperately created genres prove to be what Genette has termed 'blind windows'.[1]

Genette's critique of the deforming power of literary taxonomies, of the systematizing and 'fearful symmetries' of literary criticism in the face of diversity, is just one example of recent attempts to clear the way for discussions of the undeniable intermedial nature of texts and genres. While Genette, in a number of painstaking analyses that will serve as one of my guidelines in this chapter, has shown that there is no such thing as a 'naked text' and that every literary work includes or refers to earlier or other texts (Barthes's description of modern literature as a final state, a 'degré zéro', also mirrors this notion of derived texts), Derrida has argued convincingly that 'every text participates in one or several genres . . . yet such participation never amounts to belonging'. In the wake of recent critical theories, the *Travels* has been subjected to new approaches stressing the complexity of its texture, the need to consider its contexts, and the obvious play of Swift's palimpsest with reader expectations in what is now being recognized as an accreting generic or class parody.[2]

Nevertheless, recent close readings of Swift's 'Lucianic mock-traveller's tale'³ reveal travel literature to be the major genre whose forms and styles are consistently aped, imitated, parodied and, finally, subverted. Critics would seem to agree now that in the *Travels* the discourse has disguised itself as a travel book subverting the particular style of linguistic colonialism. Both the efficacity and the functioning as such of the satire in the book depend on the sophisticated use of authentic and fictional travel accounts. 'Under the broad canopy of the travelogue', F. N. Smith concludes, 'Swift discovers a remarkable number of other genres'.⁴

My effort in the following pages to deal with the subtle ways in which the front-matter of the *Travels* simulates and assails travel literature as a form of discourse is indebted to Grant Holly's pioneering study of textuality in Swift's masterwork and to Genette's analyses of intratextuality, that is the 'entrances' or accesses (the French equivalent is 'seuils') literary texts construct around themselves. Holly argues that there are several ways in which the *Travels* reflects 'mapping', one of these being embodied in the very graphics of the book, 'in its size and shape . . . the kinds of type, the table of contents, the layout of books and chapters, headnotes, engraved scenes and designs, and of course, the maps and diagrams'. I agree with Holly that, since Swift's book is concerned with 'techniques of portraying significant structures', these aspects 'have every right to be considered in an analysis of the *Travels*' (p. 149). Focusing on the framing of the book or on its *parergon*,⁵ I hope to show that the introductory parts (consisting of texts, images and iconotexts – my term for the mixture of verbal and visual signs) is very much part of a subversive strategy in which the text eventually defamiliarizes itself. What I offer in this chapter is a short guided tour through a maze. The structure and aims of the *Travels* suggest that the reader is required to make this tour as a kind of introduction to the main text. I shall demonstrate how the book lures the reader into the traps of a labyrinth by getting him or her involved in an intertextual game. But before I start, I should perhaps explain some of the terms, borrowed from Genette, used in this analysis, not least because Genette's most important book (*Seuils*, 1987) does not yet seem to be known in the Anglo-American world.⁶

Arguing that a novel, for instance, rarely appears without the reinforcement and accompaniment of a certain number of 'productions' such as an author's name, a title, a preface, a frontispiece etc., Genette calls these surrounding or liminal parts of text the *paratext* of a literary work: it serves as a threshold or, a term he adopts from Borges, a vestibule. It is a fringe that, since it presents the main or major text, controls our reading and understanding of the 'central part' to an important extent. The expression *paratext*, then, designates everything visual and textual that comes before or after the main textual body of a book. Genette distinguishes between this spatial part of a paratext, which he terms *péritexte*, and the texts that are outside the book or literary work but still relate to it (e.g., interviews, letters from the author etc.), which are called *épitexte*. As we shall see, there is an important paratext of this kind (a letter from Swift) whose function in the *Travels* needs to be discussed. Finally, three further Genettean terms are important for what follows. The *Travels* is also a generic parody. It urges us to recall various traditional forms of writing, types of speech and literary genres; these categories are, for Genette, *architexts*. In his system of intertextuality, which he labels hypertextuality, the relations between such architexts are established by *hypertexts* and *hypotexts*. This means, quite simply, that a text B, a hypertext, is derived from or depends on a text A, a hypotext. Swift's book, in other words, is for Genette a hypertext that alludes to both hypotexts (*Robinson Crusoe*, for example) and architexts (e.g., travel literature or utopian tales). These intratextual and intertextual relations will be at the centre of my interest.[7]

Despite the discovery in 1976 of the so-called Armagh–*Gulliver* (Swift's personal copy of the edition published in 1726 with corrections he made himself) there is still no critical edition of an authorized text of the *Travels*. Meanwhile, the Swift industry continues its discussions of the reliability of the extant versions, Hans Hunfeld's recent 'discovery' of yet another island being one of the more exhilarating contributions in a truly Swiftean spirit.[8]

One of the reasons for this dilemma is Swift's strategy of disguising the authorship of his work by taking great pains to occult his own relationship to the *Travels*. To some extent, the game of disguise and metamorphosis Swift played with his publisher mirrors the textual strategies of the book. Before we face the snares of the *Travels* itself we should perhaps consider the way Swift virtually staged and implicitly problematized such issues as authorship and ownership, authenticity and veracity, and textual reliability. The story of the mysterious genesis of the *Travels* begins on 8 August 1726, when the London bookseller and printer Benjamin Motte received a letter.[9] Delivered by an anonymous messenger, it was evidently composed by the Dean, although probably set down by John Gay. To make things more complicated, it was signed by one 'Richard Sympson', who claimed to be the cousin of a certain 'Lemuel Gulliver':

Sr

My Cousin Mr Lemuel Gulliver entrusted me some Years ago with a Copy of his Travels, whereof that which I here send you is about a fourth part, for I shortned them very much as you will find in my Preface to the Reader. I have shewn them to several persons of great Judgment and Distinction, who are confident they will sell very well. And although some parts of this and the following Volumes may be thought in one or two places to be a little Satyrical, yet it is agreed they will give no Offence, but in that you must Judge for yourself, and take the Advice of your Friends, and if they or you be of another opinion, you may let me know it when you return these Papers, which I expect shall be in three Days at furthest. The good Report I have received of you makes me put so great a trust into your Hands, which I hope you will give me no Reason to repent, and in that Confidence I require that you will never suffer these Papers to be once out of your Sight.

As the printing these Travels will probably be of great value to you, so as a Manager for my Friend and Cousin I expect you will give a due consideration for it, because I know the Author intends the Profit for the use of poor Seamen, and I am advised to say that two Hundred pounds is the least Summ I will receive on his account, but if it shall happen that the Sale will not answer as I expect and believe, then whatever shall be thought too much even upon your own word shall be duly repaid.

Perhaps you will think this a strange way of proceeding to a man of Trade, but since I begin with so great a trust to you, whom I never saw, I think it not hard that you should trust me as much. Therefore if after three days reading and consulting these Papers, you think it proper to stand to my agreement, you may begin to print them, and the subsequent parts shall be all sent to you one after another in less than a week, provided that immediately upon your Resolution to print them, you do within three days deliver a Bank Bill of two hundred pounds, wrapt up so as to make a parcel to the Hand from whence you receive this, who will come in the same manner exactly at 9 a clock at night on Thursday which will be the 11th Instant.

If you do not approve of this proposal deliver these Papers to the person who will come on thursday.

If you chuse rather to send the Papers make no other Proposal of your own but just barely write on a piece of paper that you do not accept my offer.

I am
Sr.
your humble Servant
Richard Sympson

Motte agreed to publish, and received the outstanding part of the *Travels*, 'he knew not from whence, nor from whom, dropp'd at his house in the dark, from a Hackney-coach'. When Swift saw a copy of the first edition, which was published on 28 October, he was extremely dissatisfied with the many misprints and with the alterations Motte had made in order to tone down those passages he considered dangerous. But despite his anger Swift did not get in personal contact with Motte. It was Swift's friend, Charles Ford, who (presumably at the Dean's request) protested at the printer's errors and the publisher's changes. The textual alterations were retained until 1735, when George Faulkner reprinted the *Travels* in Dublin as volume III of Swift's *Works*. It is again telling that Faulkner never received a corrected version of the book (although Swift did help with corrections), and the source for his edition remains obscure.[10]

What is important about Swift's shenanigans is not that he might have feared prosecution and so sought to protect himself as well as the publisher, or that he loved mystification and, in this instance, has his work stage itself, as it were. In terms of intertextuality, the *Travels*, with all its displacements and substitutions, begins with the first letter sent to Motte. As a text that is 'out of the book' and hence, in Genette's terminology, an epitext, but still very much part of the paratext, the letter anticipates the rhetorical strategy of Gulliver's 'report', for the real author, Swift, pretends that his letter, probably written down by Gay, is from the pen of a Richard Sympson. The name was chosen with care: there was a real Richard Simpson, a publisher and editor Swift got to know while working for Sir William Temple. But it was surely not a coincidence that *A New Voyage to the East-Indies*, from the pen of a fictitious Captain William Symson, had appeared in 1715. There is additional irony in these games with names, identities and texts in that Symson's book was plagiarized from an earlier travel-book. One of the points of the extensive paratext of the *Travels* is of course to equate Gulliver with the pseudonymous Symson, a liar and plagiarist. Sympson is one of Swift's poses or masks; yet the name also virtually embodies the fascinating relations between the real and the invented, between textual and authorial pretension and semantic reality, which lie at the heart of the book. Thus the name is yet another riddle to be solved by careful readers.

Every critical edition of the *Travels* ought, therefore, to include the letter to Motte, for it is in this epitext that a fictional character is introduced who reappears in the introductory material (the paratext) to vouchsafe for the veracity and honesty of Gulliver and to continue the intertextual games with various forms of writing. The paratext includes the following:

(a) A brief introduction entitled 'The Publisher to the Reader' – which is in fact signed 'Richard Sympson' rather than by the publisher – in which Sympson introduces his 'antient and intimate Friend' Mr

Lemuel Gulliver and explains the circumstances by which the *Travels* came to be published. This first appeared in the edition of 1726.

(b) An unsigned 'Advertisement', which precedes (c) – Gulliver's 'Letter' – in the Dublin edition of 1735, in which the publisher seeks to shift the blame from himself with regard to the charges made in Gulliver's 'Letter'.

(c) 'A Letter from Capt. Gulliver, to his Cousin Sympson', dated 2 April 1727, in which Gulliver, among other things, complains that on reading the published *Travels* he discovered that it differs materially in content from the manuscript he had submitted. This 'Letter' first appeared in the Dublin edition of 1735.

In view of the fact that this introductory front-matter, this paratext, deliberately undermines both generic and editorial conventions, it seems odd that modern critical editions pay so little attention to its various component parts or to its sequence. Thus, the *Travels* in the Penguin Classics Library (1967), edited by Peter Dixon and John Chalker, which draws on Motte's edition of 1726, ignores the portrait frontispiece but incorporates parts of the front-matter of the Dublin edition. The Norton text (1970), edited by R. A. Greenberg, based on Faulkner's edition of 1735, leaves out the 'Advertisement' and puts the Sympson letter and the Gulliver letter after the frontispiece and title-page. It also contains poems from the second edition of the *Travels* (1727), yet the editor places these *after* the main text of the book as things that are presumably less important or additional, when really they should serve as an introduction. Paul Turner's edition (1986) for Oxford University Press, also based on the Faulkner edition, has the front-matter (the 'Advertisement' and the letters) before the frontispiece and title-page – which are, however, those of the London edition of 1726. Clearly, in the interest of the strategic importance (for the reader) of the arrangement of the paratextual elements, a future critical edition should pay close attention to these seemingly marginal details.

Looking more closely at Sympson's letter to Motte, we notice that he writes in the same plain style that Swift allots to Gulliver. It is the style of Defoe and previous Puritan writers. When in 1727 Swift wrote to the Abbé des Fontaines, who had translated the *Travels* into French earlier that year, he commented on the readers who had obviously misunderstood his implicit criticism of this established *ductus*. Discussing the 'partisans of Gulliver', who 'number a great many amongst us', he told the Abbé:

you will no doubt be surprised to learn that [some] consider this ship's surgeon a solemn author, who never departs from seriousness, who never assumes a role, who never prides himself upon possessing wit, and who is content to communicate to the public, in a simple and artless narrative, the adventures that have befallen him and the things that he has seen or heard during his voyages.[11]

The complexity of the letter to Motte, its appropriation and subversion of style and authors, and its relationship with the paratext and hypertext of the *Travels*, demonstrate the great demands Swift's text makes on the reader. In its self-conscious sniping at the reader's poise, the *Travels*, from the very beginning, appeals to the reader's critical capacity. In fact, one might say that the extreme difficulties that are engineered in the front-matter are a condensed form of the irritations that await us like traps when Gulliver eventually seizes the word.[12]

On publishing the *Travels* in 1726, Motte could hardly keep pace with the demand. In fact, he brought out three octavo editions in that year, followed by a duodecimo and another octavo edition in 1727. If we open a copy of the first edition we are initially confronted with a portrait. Constituting the first part of the paratext, this portrait seems to be no more than a little joke. After what has been said in chapter One about the picture-text relationship, however, we should be more careful, especially since many critics still argue that pictures in literary works often 'elucidate, modify, and supplement the meaning of the verbal text'.[13] Since we know that Swift took a keen and rather critical interest in the illustrations to the *Travels*, even instructing Motte on the scenes to engrave, one can even assure those who are looking for author-intention that the Dean must have pondered the signifying potential of frontispieces. Whether or not Swift was aware of all of these aspects, however, is not my concern. I want to focus on the intermedial, ironical, relations Gulliver's portrait establishes with the texts and authors it relates to, and with the conventions of visual representation it subverts – for this is a part of the visual/verbal decoding the reader is invited to tackle.

One hesitates to believe that it is merely accidental that the portrait in the Motte editions exists in two different states. The original state, which appears only in the first issue of the first edition (the so-called 'A edition'), contains a caption, '*Captain Lemuel Gulliver*, of Redriff Ætat. suæ 58', that appears on a tablet fixed to a pedestal on which the oval portrait rests (illus. 19). The second state of the engraving (illus. 20), however (used in the so-called AA and B editions of 1726), provides the verbal (autobiographical) information round the oval frame, the tablet now bearing a Latin epigraph. The Faulkner edition of 1735 even depicts a completely different person and a new Latin 'subscriptio' on

19 'Captain Lemuel Gulliver', frontispiece of the first issue of Motte's edition of *Gulliver's Travels*, 1726, engraving (first state) by John Sturt and Robert Sheppard.

20 'Captain Lemuel Gulliver', frontispiece of a later issue of Motte's edition of *Gulliver's Travels*, 1726, engraving (second state).

21 'Captain Lemuel Gulliver', frontispiece of the third volume of Faulkner's edition of Swift's *Works*, 1735, engraving.

Captain Lemuel Gulliver, of Redriff Ætat. suæ 58.

Compositum jus, fasque animi, sanctosque recessus
Mentis, & incoctum generoso pectus honesto.

CAPT. LEMUEL GULLIVER
Splendide Mendax

what is now clearly visible as a supporting pedestal (illus. 21). With the exception of Grant Holly and Jenny Mezciems, critics have not discerned that the portrait is a prime example of the way Swift makes signifying the subject of his book. Furthermore, although the portraits have been described in bibliographical surveys of the *Travels*, the telling differences have not been sufficiently discussed. The frontispieces play with and reveal Gulliver's identity, most obviously of course because the editions of 1726 and 1735 show different persons, and more subtly in the hidden clues we are given in the versions of the portrait in the Motte editions. They may even hint at the real author, for Gulliver's face is not unlike that of Swift, while his age (58) was precisely Swift's age in 1726.

What we see in the first state of the engraving (illus. 19) is a traditional portrait of a gentleman that is placed on a plinth presumably providing some biographical information on the person depicted. In the second state (illus. 20), this seemingly factual information about the author is contained in the oval frame, while unidentified Latin verses now appear on the pedestal. The visual evidence of the apparently realistic portrait is thus surrounded and supported by verbal evidence that, for all one can tell, is also genuine. In both states of the frontispiece the name is mirrored, as it were, in the title-page facing the engraving. Jenny Mezciems has pointed out that the figure 'faces right (towards the narrative) and the direction may suggest rectitude, honesty, or any other right-facing qualities'.[14] The visual rhetoric, in other words, engages with the verbal in what emerges as a simulation of authenticity. The details in the frame and on the pedestal tell us more. The word 'Redriff', for instance, would have duped a gullible reader, for it was a real place (today's Rotherhithe in London). The wording of the frame/pedestal thus contains a telling mixture of information (Gulliver's name, his age, and his home town) that seems to be true because some of the information is verifiable. This is the first instance, if we except the letter to Motte, where Gulliver is cast as a swindler who, in the manner of Lucian's traveller in the *True Stories*, tells all sorts of lies in the most plausible manner.

If we consider the larger embedding of such frontispieces within the generic parody of travel accounts found in the *Travels*, the satirical function of Gulliver's portrait comes to the fore even more forcefully. Comparing both the portrait and the entire front-matter to earlier prototypes of the fictional traveller, Mezciems has argued persuasively that the figure we see in the portrait might be that of Hythlodaeus or Panurge, for Gulliver's engraved portrait exhibits striking similarities with the verbal portraits of the heroes we find in More's *Utopia* and

22 Frontispiece of the first edition of
Daniel Defoe's *Robinson Crusoe*, 1719,
engraving by Clark and Pine.

23 Frontispiece of a German edition
of *The Travels of John Mandeville*,
Augsburg, 1481, woodcut.

Rabelais's *Pantagruel*, both important sources for Swift. In addition,
one should perhaps compare the picture of Gulliver to the frontispiece
portrait of another daring seafarer, Robinson Crusoe, whose adventures had been published in 1719 (illus. 22). Evidently unperturbed by
the generation of illusions suggested by such pictures, one twentieth-
century critic has remarked that this illustration of Crusoe has
'outlasted several centuries of criticism. . . . It has come to be the
accepted portrait [!]; no legend is required: one knows that he is
looking at Robinson Crusoe'.[15] Such engraved portraits were a
standard part of travel books. Simulating authenticity and veracity,
portraits adorned numerous accounts of voyages and adventures, both
real and invented, from *The Travels* of that arch-liar, Sir John
Mandeville (illus. 23) down to Captain John Smith's reports and the
later works of Vincent Le Blanc and Jean Baptiste Tavernier.

To understand the extent to which the *Travels* engages intertextually
and generically with the illustrations in the literature of travel, it seems
appropriate to look briefly at the reports of John Smith, an illustrious
captain and adventurer who laced his true accounts with a few passages
that are probably fictions. Smith's various travel reports are not listed in
the inventories of the libraries of Swift or Sir William Temple (who

24 Portrait of Captain John
Smith, from his *A Description of
New England*, 1616, engraving by
Robert Clerke after (?)Simon van
de Passe.

25 Frontispiece map of John
Smith's *A Description of New
England*, 1616, engraving by
Robert Clerke after (?)Simon van
de Passe.

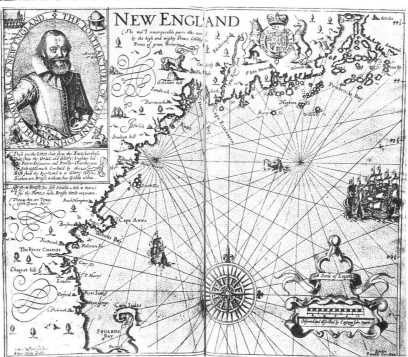

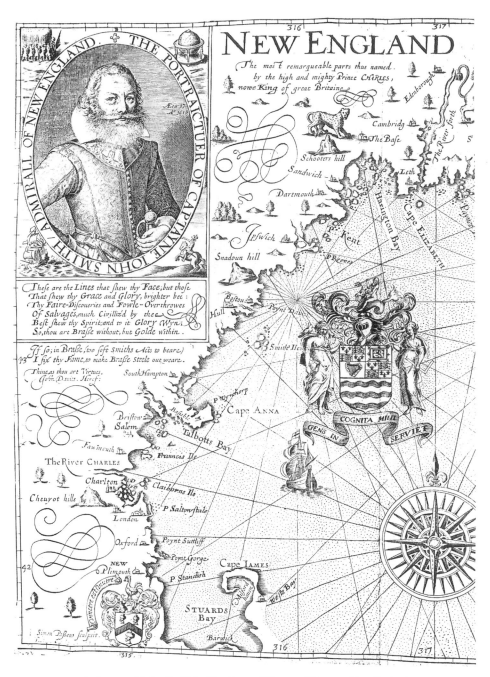

26 A map of John Smith's *The General History of Virginia, New England, and the Summer Isles*, 1624, engraving by Robert Clerke after (?)Simon van de Passe.

employed Swift for some time). This does not mean, however, that the Dean did not know the works. Just before Swift began writing the *Travels* he read Sir Thomas Herbert's *Relation*, a travel account laced with moralizing; and in July 1722 he wrote to Vanessa that he had 'read I know not how many diverting Books of History and Travells'.[16] What is important here is the manner in which the *Travels* subverts not a particular book, but rather both pictorial and editorial traditions while warning the careful reader to distrust representations claiming to depict 'reality'. It is interesting and telling, for instance, that the portrait of Smith – the 'Admiral of New England' – forms part of a map (illus. 25) in his *A Description of New England* (1616). What looks to us like a bizarre confluence of scientific mapping and artistic portraiture is nothing else but an attempt to persuade the reader with the semblance of the real in the mimetic. It also tells us something about the way maps were read in the early seventeenth century. Like the later portrait of Captain Gulliver, Smith's 'portraictuer' (illus. 24) has the traditional oval frame with name and title, and the additional information in the picture about his age ('Ætat. 37') and the year ('A° 1616'). Drawn by Simon van de Passe and probably engraved by Robert Clerke, the portrait depicts an imposing man whose daring deeds and remarkable accomplishments, in his multiple roles as adventurer, discoverer, surveyor and writer of various books and 'sea-grammars', are celebrated by the four miniature scenes in the corners outside the frame and by the verses below. Curiously, in the map-cum-portrait that was used again (illus. 26) for Smith's *General History of Virginia, New England, and the Summer Isles* (1624), we find a person with slightly different features and the name of the engraver has now been erased, while that of the printer of the map has been changed from George Low to James Reeve.

The details of the depiction of Captain Smith clearly depend not on his real features, whatever they were, but rather on both the artist(s) at work and even more on the occasion. This becomes quite obvious when we look at other illustrations of this famous adventurer. In his *General History* Smith is deliberately shown as a rather small man as he takes prisoner the 'King of Pamaunkee' (illus. 27) and the 'King of Paspahegh' (illus. 28). The idea is, of course, to underline his extraordinary courage. The layout and the characters in these engravings are again less based on 'reality' than on pictorial traditions – in this case Theodore de Bry's prints for his illustrated edition of Thomas Harriot's *A Brief and True Report on the New Found Land of Virginia*, which had appeared in Frankfurt as early as 1590. Quite a different man, it seems, appears in the plate of illustrations intended for *The True*

27 Captain Smith and the King of Pamaunkee, from 'A Map of Old Virginia', in Smith's *General History of Virginia*, 1624, engraving by Robert Vaughan.

28 Captain Smith and the King of Paspahegh, from 'A Map of Old Virginia', in Smith's *General History of Virginia*, 1624, engraving by Robert Vaughan.

29 'Captain Smith led Captive . . .', from *The True Travels, Adventures, and Observations of Captain John Smith*, 1630, engraving by (?)Martin Droeshout.

30 'Captain Smith killeth the Bashaw . . .', from *The True Travels, Adventures, and Observations of Captain John Smith*, 1630, engraving by (?)Martin Droeshout.

31 'Pocahontas', from Smith's *General History of Virginia*, 1624, engraving by Compton Holland after Simon van de Passe.

Matoaks als Rebecka daughter to the mighty Prince Powhatan Emperour of Attanoughkomouck als virginia converted and baptized in the Christian faith, and wife to the worᵗ Mʳ Joh Rolff.

Travels, Adventures, and Observations of Captain John Smith published in 1630. Probably engraved by Martin Droeshout, who is chiefly remembered today for his famous portrait of Shakespeare, the images affect to illustrate Smith's encounters with the 'Bashaw of Nalbrits' (illus. 29, 30). Again, the veracity and reliability of these portraits of sorts are a matter of occasion and artistic or authorial intention: the pictorial details are subject to what is supposed to be expressed. We find the same process at work in the portrait of Matoaka, Smith's Native American mistress, the princess better known as Pocahontas. Also designed by Simon van de Passe and engraved by Compton Holland, her portrait (illus. 31) is dominated by the same paraphernalia as that of her English lover, John Smith, who probably invented some of the details of the report that tells how the princess saved him from execution.[17]

Simulating the alleged veracity and the accepted correctness of cartography, portraiture and verbal description, the engraved title-page – as we find it in Smith's *General History* (illus. 32) – is a prime example of the traditional mixture in such travel books of fact and fiction, a mixture and a convention Swift was to use for his satiric purposes. Tellingly, in Smith's title-page it is the representation of

32 Title-page
from John
Smith's *The
General History
of Virginia, New
England, and the
Summer Isles*,
1624, engraving
by Jan Barra.

what seems most exact (cartography) that proves fictitious. The background consists of two parts: the upper half is a map, conveying what was then known of the new-found lands, but the lower half is a pastoral landscape with valleys, groves and forests suggesting illimitable wealth and a paradise to be conquered.[18]

With this tradition in mind, we may now return to the *Travels*. Appropriating the tradition of 'comely' frontispieces and engraved title-pages, the *Travels* explodes a technique of graphic representation (including cartography and portraying) by carrying it to the point where the careful observer begins to notice both the traditions and the problematics of signifying as such. Clearly, one of the functions of the image is to lend credibility to the author who appears visually and verbally, and to create the impression of authenticity for the page facing it as well as for the verbal information to come.

Yet the illusion of authenticity is merely the surface level of the intermedial relations between the engraving and the paratext and hypertext of the *Travels*. More can be discovered in the structure and texture of Gulliver's portrait (illus. 19), whose authenticity seems to be further strengthened by the presence of what, at first glance, looks like factual evidence. In the traditional contemporary manner, names are added below the engraving: 'Sturt et Sheppard Sc.' The fact that we find two names, and the letters 'Sc.' for *sculpsit*, indicates the thorough-going division that emerged in book engravings during the eighteenth century. Although some engravers also designed their own works, a distinction was made between the work of the designer and that of the engraver. The reference, in this case, is to John Sturt (1658–1730), a well-known engraver who produced a number of small portraits as frontispieces to books as well as the frontispiece to the 1710 edition of Swift's *The Tale of a Tub*. He also provided illustrations for many religious and artistic publications of the time, including an edition (1728) of Bunyan's *Pilgrim's Progress*. The other name presumably stands for Robert Sheppard (*fl.* 1725–40), an engraver who worked for booksellers and was especially known for his portraits of sovereigns and statesmen in Rapin's *History of England* (1732–7). Sturt's name in particular would lend the book an additional air of respectability.

The second state of the frontispiece (illus. 20) is intriguing because of the Latin motto, 'Compositum ius, fasque animi, sanctosque recessus / Mentis, et incoctum generoso pectus honesto'. This epigraph also appeared in the newspaper advertisement in the London *Daily Journal* (28 October 1726) announcing the publication of the *Travels*. As a framing device, it is lifted from the second satire (ll. 73–4) of Persius' *Saturae*. The Roman writer Aulus Persius Flaccus (AD 34–62), an iconoclast in his own right, probably appealed to Swift since he, too, opposed all artifice and exaggerated style in poetry. Persius attacked the literary industry of his day and age. Like the Dean he became known for his brilliant style and intertextual references to previous and contemporary authors. In Persius' second satire, con-cerned with issues of morality and proper sacrifice to the gods, the passage referred to under the engraving reads slightly differently: 'Compositum ius fasque animo santosque recessus / mentis et incoctum generoso pectus honesto'. Suggesting an appropriate manner of religious devotion, the verses could be translated as 'a heart's blend of justice and right, a mind profoundly pure, a breast pervaded with heroic virtue'. The revelatory function of the Latin inscription depends on the reader's knowledge of the classical source and on the pretentious modern (invented) author it is applied to. We are asked to consider the implications of the original text, i.e., that 'only the good man can approach the gods without fear' and that the deities are pleased only by a mind that is truly good.[19] The verses gain a new meaning in their allusion to Gulliver, a proud and conceited liar. The alert reader of the time could thus find in the epigraph a movement towards ambiguity, for the original satirical context attacks hypocrisy; in the new context, however, under a (false) picture claiming authenticity, the Latin words confirm qualities that seem to be expressed in the portrait too. Hence the Latin text can easily mislead readers.

When Faulkner published his version of the *Travels* in 1735, he tried to persuade the London engraver George Vertue to produce a portrait for the book. Although Faulkner was unsuccessful in this, the frontispiece of the Dublin edition (illus. 21) is interesting for several reasons. Grant Holly has summarized some of these:

The oval which frames the portrait is a shape common to both portraits and mirrors, thus underlining the mimetic aspirations of this kind of painting. But the image is not a portrait, pure and simple, for two reasons, both of which indicate the decay of the signified and the predominance of signifying. In the first place, it is the engraving of a portrait, which implies that it is a representation of a representation . . . . In the second place, the image cannot be considered a portrait in the usual sense because there is no such person as 'Lemuel Gulliver'. The frontispiece . . . merely exemplifies a mode of signifying . . . what we see is the sign of engraving balanced on the engraving of a sign.[20]

A number of observations can be added to Holly's close reading of the later frontispiece. For example, the fact that the portrait rests on a pedestal is as significant as the picture itself, for in the eighteenth century, portraits, usually a prerogative of the 'better sort of people' (mostly noblemen and affluent merchants), became the rage of the *nouveaux riches* in the professional class. Swift as well as Hogarth objected to this strong element of disguise in portraiture. Like Swift, Hogarth engaged satirically with the tradition of portraiture[21] when he engraved his own portrait (illus. 33). Although he Latinizes his name (William becomes Gulielmus), which can of course also be read as an ironic reference to the tradition, the 'pedestal' in his engraving is not made of stone; rather, his image rests on English satire (books by Milton, Shakespeare and Swift), and his dog, Trump, represents a slightly ironic allusion to the staunch Englishness of the artist and the customary (lap)dog in portraits. If Gulliver has such a portrait appear in his *Travels*, the implication must be that he is rather vainglorious and quite the opposite of what he wants to make us believe in his travelogue.

33 Self-portrait of William Hogarth, 1749, etching and engraving (fourth state).

Gulielmus Hogarth

As an engraved monument that might also support a bust, the pedestal is a complex sign with iconic, symbolic and indexical features. Literally and visually it alludes to several traditions in art, sculpture and writing. The epigraph it displays is a hybrid form fusing architextural and textual elements – it is, paradoxically, an iconic form held in words that invades the text. According to A. Compagnon, the epigraph constitutes the 'quintessence' of the quotation, the one that is engraved in stone for eternity, on 'arcs de triomphe' and on the pedestal of statues. In this case, in the *Travels*, the epigraph represents an iconic zone where text and image overlap and unite, commenting in their new form on what is erected above.[22] Both epigraph and pedestal elevate Gulliver to the position of an important man; they give him the solid, monumental status of the well-known people who are represented in the 'comely frontispieces' of Renaissance books and in sculptured works of art, thus reinforcing the contradiction with the text in which he claims to be plain and humble. The frontispiece may be read, then, as a facade to the book[23] and as a revelation of Gulliver's pride and pretension.

In addition, the mirror shape of the portrait needs to be considered. If what we see merely exemplifies a mode of signifying – for Gulliver is a pure fabrication – the mirror-portrait invites the reader/observer to reflect not merely on portraying as such. What is at issue here,

57

foregrounded by the interpenetration of the ideas suggested by the series mirror-reflection-reality-representation, is quite simply the nature of vision and the dependence of understanding on visuality – but in the light of scientific discoveries that preceded the *Travels*. If the mirror, 'as machine, tool, paradigm, and toy, was at the centre of all apparatus magnifying a reduced reality into a concentrated and enhanced picture', it was only a short step for logocentric critics to join the camp of iconoclasts by arguing that 'vision . . . was synonymous with swindle'.[24] Furthermore, early eighteenth-century readers would be familiar with the recent development of the mirror as an instrument of visual quackery, of seducing by simulating mimesis. Simultaneously, the mirror/portrait reminded them of older, contradictory, traditions in which the looking-glass had a central role: the 'speculum' as an instrument that may produce both reflection and reflexion; the mirror as sign for (and accoutrement of) Vanitas, Luxuria and Superbia (but also for Prudentia and Sapientia); and the looking-glass as metaphor for (mis)understanding and the world as such. By the time the *Travels* was being written, these traditions had left more than a Barthian or Derridean trace in English literature and Western art – and it is these traditions, which today have fallen into oblivion, that served as pre-texts and points of reference for the attack mounted in the *Travels* on visuality and representation as sophistic rhetoric.[25] With Gulliver we find the ordinary Englishman's reaction to recent scientific advance-ment, a reaction that is already affected by visual quackery. After all, he is conceived as the average Englishman of his period. As the allegorical representative of mankind he is Everyman, a gullible believer in surface meanings and mimesis, a dedicated scientist and pious explorer who analyses and observes but does not really understand. His picture suggests that the careful reader will detect Gulliver's pride and credulity in himself. The shape of the frontispiece, then, not only suggests a mirror, it *is* a mirror, for the person depicted (or rather engraved, an art process that is closer to the action of writing), since he does not exist, is the one looking at it.

The frontispiece we find in the edition of 1735 (illus. 21) differs from the first portrait (1726) in several significant respects. To begin with, we see a different person or 'author', a fact that must thoroughly undermine any belief in a real author called Gulliver. Although stressing the pedestal and therefore also Gulliver's pride, the second engraving does not completely abandon the sophisticated subversion of the conventions and stereotypal ideals of portraiture and travel literature. Even the hide-and-seek *vis-à-vis* the author, which had already been beautifully staged in the first edition, is continued, for none of the four volumes of Faulkner's edition of Swift's works actually contains his full name. The title-page of volume I (illus. 35) announces *The Works of J.S., D.D., D.S.P.D.*; and the page facing the frontispiece showing Gulliver refers to 'VOLUME III. of the AUTHOR'S WORKS' (illus. 34). In the preface to volume I Faulkner deliberately continues the mystification around the identity of the 'supposed author'. In addition, the new portrait bears an obvious resemblance to those of Swift made by the fashionable painter Charles Jervas (one is now in London's National Portrait Gallery; the other was formerly in the possession of the late Sir Harold Williams) and to the engraved version that appears as the frontispiece in volume III of Faulkner's edition of 1735 (illus. 35). Such (possibly intentional) similarities cause new anxieties about the separation of the narrator from the author, the confusion of identities requiring us to think carefully about the motto.

This *subscriptio* of the engraving reads '*splendide mendax*' (gloriously false). The words are taken from Horace, one of Swift's favourite authors, whose voice he frequently borrowed to mask his own. In Horace's *Odes* (Book III, 11, l.35), the two words occur in an ironic marriage hymn for a reluctant bride who is 'gloriously false to her perjured father'. At first glance, Horace's oxymoron would seem to identify the person in the engraving (a Gulliver who appears even more vainglorious than the one in the frontispiece of the earlier edition) as a wonderful liar. Another ironic function of the Latin text consists in the allusion to the conventional, ostentatious, use of such 'subscriptions' and of Latinized names: Hogarth, as we saw above, called himself Gulielmus Hogarth in the engraving of his self-portrait produced in 1749.[26] If one considers the deliberate confusion of identities created by the likeness of the portraits (Swift looks like Gulliver and vice versa), it is evident that the portrait and motto of the Dublin edition resume the play with fact and fiction while putting an additional screen around the exposed truth.

In terms of the *parergon* (to which I turn in the next chapter), the framing of Gulliver's portrait is, in the words of the *OED*, only a 'by-work, an accessory to the main subject'. But if the entire front-matter of the *Travels* ought to be understood as a network of allusions to, and subversions of, textual genres, the plinth on which the portrait rests, the Latin inscription, and the actual oval frame, are corresponding iconic allusions to be discovered and decoded. The allusions are mainly to the history and practices of framing in art, and more precisely to the frame as a parergetic part of the whole. In a sophisticated answer to Kant, Heidegger and Meyer Shapiro, Derrida has written persuasively about and around the connections between the clothes of statues, architectural columns and picture frames as similar forms of the *parergon*. They are all *hors d'œuvre*, an apposite term that in French conflates the notions of entrance/access/outside/beginning/part of something.[27] From this point of view, the framing of Gulliver's portrait constitutes an impressive *mise-en-scène* as well as a *mise-en-abîme* of manners of framing works of art.

Those acquainted with the history of frames would recognize a great many iconic allusions in the set-up of Gulliver's portrait. The architectural plinth, for instance, is both a remnant and a trace indicating the ecclesiastical, and indeed religious, origin of works of art. It is an old parergetical form long associated with holy persons and things. In fact, until the seventeenth century the sculpted frame was automatically taken as a sign for an important personality in the Church or at the Court. The frame (or at least this part of it) determined the context and, ultimately, the importance if not the meaning of the portrait. The frame-work of Gulliver's portrait constitutes a confluence of several traditions of framing works of art: the architectural/sculpted *cadre* extending back to its origin in church portals, tabernacles and altar decorations; its derivated mundane form in portraits for aristocrats; and the frame as it emerged in its modern form after 1600, when the portrait changed its role from part of the furniture to a piece marked off by its frame as a distancing device. On closer analysis of the allusive traces in Gulliver's portrait, the picture emerges not as a simple joke but as a parodic-critical engagement with artistic and visual methods of persuasion, with the mimetic attempts of art to elevate *representations* to the status attributed to saints and aristocrats. The frame creates the impression of something 'extraordinary' – which is, as Derrida reminds us, one of the meanings of *parergon*.[28] Ultimately, it is the frame or, in other words, the manipulation of perspective and vision, that persuades us of the value of the depicted. The irony with Gulliver's portrait is that the centre, the person represented, is a fiction sustained by an elaborate framework celebrating and elevating – nothing, or rather nothingness.

Together with the maps and the diagram that appear later in the text, the frontispiece portrait forms an iconic discourse which traverses the mass of the written discourse in the *Travels*. The portrait punctuates that discourse with a 'monument' that, at least for those who pay attention, raises more questions than it answers. An imitation and parody of the Grand Manner portrait, the frontispiece belongs to the order of the visible that seems to confirm the belief that, in Tina Turner's words, 'what you get is what you see'. But what the picture (and the other visual material in the book) really tells us is that pictorial

VOLUME III.

Of the AUTHOR's

WORKS.

CONTAINING,

TRAVELS

INTO SEVERAL

Remote Nations of the WORLD.

In Four PARTS, *viz.*

I. A Voyage to LIL-LIPUT.	PUTA, BALNIBARBI, LUGGNAGG, GLUBB-DUBDRIB and JAPAN.
II. A Voyage to BROB-DINGNAG.	IV. A Voyage to the COUNTRY of the
III. A Voyage to LA-	HOUYHNHNMS.

By *LEMUEL GULLIVER*, first a Surgeon,
and then a CAPTAIN of several Ships.

――――――――― *Retroq;*
Vulgus abhorret ab his.

In this Impression several Errors in the *London* and *Dublin*
Editions are corrected.

DUBLIN:

Printed by and for GEORGE FAULKNER, Printer
and Bookseller, in *Essex-Street*, opposite to the
Bridge. MDCCXXXV.

34 Frontispiece and title-page of Volume III of Faulkner's edition of Swift's *Works*,
Dublin, 1735.

THE

WORKS

OF

J.S, D.D, D.S.P.D.

IN

FOUR VOLUMES.

CONTAINING,

I. The Author's MISCELLANIES in PROSE.

II. His POETICAL WRITINGS.

III. The TRAVELS of Captain *Lemuel Gulliver.*

IV. His Papers relating to *Ireland*, consisting of
several Treatises; among which are, The
DRAPIER's LETTERS to the People of *Ireland*
against receiving *Wood's* Half-pence: Also,
two Original DRAPIER's LETTERS, never before published.

In this Edition are great Alterations and Addi-
tions; and likewise many Pieces in each Volume, never before published.

DUBLIN:

Printed by and for GEORGE FAULKNER, Printer
and Bookseller, in ESSEX-STREET, opposite to
the Bridge. MDCCXXXV.

35 Frontispiece and title-page of Volume I of Faulkner's edition of Swift's *Works*,
Dublin, 1735.

discourse can be as mendacious as any other form of rhetoric: what we see is, in Jeanne K. Welcher's words, 'the very realistic portrait of the very imaginary "Capt. Lemuel Gulliver"';[29] we perceive the depiction of a fiction, and as such it merely anticipates on the iconic level what is to be enacted in the text of the *Travels*.

This game of misleading the reader on the pictorial level with apparently realistic representations continues on the verbal level. As our glance moves from the frontispiece to the title-page of the edition published in 1726, we discover that the real title of the book is not *Gulliver's Travels*, under which it has gone down in literary history, but '*TRAVELS* INTO SEVERAL *Remote Nations* OF THE *WORLD*' by Lemuel Gulliver, with two words in full capitals (illus. 36). Simple and self-explanatory as it may seem, the title is a prime example of the palimpsests Swift continually creates in his book. As an interpretative key, a title can bait, influence and seduce readers. Discussing the typographic and iconographic information contained in book-titles and sub-titles, Genette distinguishes three main functions: identification, description and seduction; he also points out the hermeneutic import-ance of the reader who ultimately relates the title to the contents of the book.[30] The title of the *Travels* would confuse readers, for by Swift's time travel tales were gaining increasing authority as reports of a new reality. Swift's *Travels* designates an ambiguous architext (the trav-elogue) but does not disclose the exact nature (the form, the genre, etc.) of the text that follows. The early eighteenth-century reader would therefore have wondered whether he or she had bought an authentic travel report, a work of fiction such as the imaginary voyage, a Robinsonade or one of the many nautical versions of spiritual biography. The contemporary literary background was far from being helpful in this case. During the seventeenth and early eighteenth centuries, works of fiction, particularly first-person narratives, mixed all kinds of elements. The *Travels* clearly plays with the reader's generic expectations while mocking literary systems and taxonomies. The book creates a puzzle for the critic who prefers the comfort of neat categories.[31]

Baiting the reader with the apparently familiar, Swift's iconotext conducts him or her through the entrance ways of the paratext (the front-matter of the book) into the main section, where the confusion becomes even more intense. The title-page offers another example of this misleading, a further step as it were towards the reader's total puzzlement: the sub-title claims that the *Travels* is written by one 'Lemuel Gulliver, first a Surgeon, and then a Captain of several Ships'. The first name, Lemuel, means 'devoted to God'. It is a subtle, ironic

36 Title-page of volume I of Motte's edition of *Gulliver's Travels*, London, 1726.

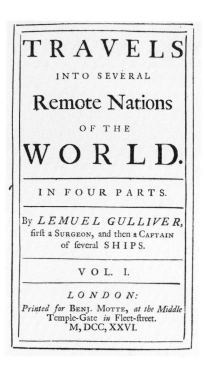

TRAVELS

INTO SEVERAL

Remote Nations

OF THE

WORLD.

IN FOUR PARTS.

By *LEMUEL GULLIVER*,
firſt a Surgeon, and then a Captain
of ſeveral SHIPS.

VOL. I.

LONDON:
Printed for Benj. Motte, at the Middle
Temple-Gate in Fleet-ſtreet.
M, DCC, XXVI.

hint at dissenting authors like Daniel Defoe, and it underlines the narrator's veracity in a Lucianic manner. The family name offers additional ambiguity. 'Gulliver' is, on the one hand, a typical Swiftean pun that connotes such meanings as the verb 'to gull' and the adjective 'gullible'; on the other hand, Richard Sympson confirms in his letter following the title-page that 'Mr. *Gulliver* was born in *Nottinghamshire* . . . yet . . . his Family came from *Oxfordshire*. . . . I have observed in the Church-Yard at *Banbury* . . . several Tombs and Monuments of the *Gullivers*'. If a literal-minded reader wanted to verify this information, his confusion would have increased on finding that a Gulliver family actually lived at Banbury in Oxfordshire where, in the church-yard of St Mary's, several tombstones bearing the name Gulliver can still be found. Furthermore, an educated reader would have discovered an intertextual dimension in the collocation 'Lemuel Gulliver', which recalls a similarly contradictory name, namely that of the fictional traveller and physician Raphael Hythlodaeus (meaning 'God has healed' and 'dispenser of nonsense') in Thomas More's *Utopia*. Significantly, Hythlodaeus was also an experienced ship's captain, his first name suggesting the medical profession.[32]

The information the sub-title provides about Gulliver's professions is again a telling mixture of allusions to travel literature (i.e., to familiar reading matter) and a subtle warning about the alleged author's reliability. To a contemporary reader, the word 'surgeon' would suggest quite the opposite of what the term denotes and connotes today. As a ship's surgeon, Gulliver is a good candidate for a picaresque tale, for surgeons had already figured as rogues and narrators in picaresque fiction, such as Vincente Espinel's *La vida de Marcos de Obregon* (translated into French in 1618) and Simon de Patot's *The Travels and Adventures of James Massey* (first published in French in 1710). The reference to Gulliver's profession, then, suggests picaresque fiction, one of the genres or hypotexts the *Travels* incorporates; but at the same time it connotes the unreliability of the mendacious picaro. This was further strengthened by the bad reputation surgeons and doctors had in the early eighteenth century. In popular discourse they were generally mocked as charlatans and quacks, and even novelists and artists such as Fielding and Hogarth usually draw on the stereotypal image of doctors as cheats and mountebanks. In Hogarth's *The Company of Undertakers* (illus. 18), for instance, one can detect the conflation of various forms of predominantly pejorative discourse (mostly satire) about doctors.[33] The allusion to Gulliver's second profession – 'Captain of several Ships' – functions in the same way, suggesting both the works of previous authors of travel literature and the fact that some of them, including More's Raphael Hythlodaeus, were liars and plagiarists.[34]

Examining the variety of literary genres and familiar forms of discourse we discover as an integral part of the paratext of the *Travels* (e.g., travel literature, the imaginary voyage, the picaresque tale, and memoirs), one might say that the front-matter of Swift's palimpsest simulates. Above all, it simulates a travel book. The television reporting by CNN on the Gulf War (Operation Desert Storm) gave us daily and nightly examples of the manner in which simulation eventually abolishes the difference between the true and the false, between the real and the imaginary or imagined, substituting as it does signs or icons of the real for reality itself. Having learned a lesson from TV coverage made during the Vietnam War, the American military machine only allowed clean images to be screened: instead of screaming children and women, bleeding bodies and howling soldiers (on both sides), we were given something to see that resembled fireworks and festive events. In the *Travels* such simulation is exploited as a satiric strategy for two reasons. First because the Swiftean text implies that its author always found it much too simple, indeed too primitive, to adopt the blunt instrument of straightforward condemnation. He preferred appropriating the ideas and language of those who were to be attacked and lampooned. Second, the text also proves that the Dean was a radical iconoclast who saw clearly the danger of simulation in religion, especially in connection with icons and the simulacrum of divinity. Although he adopted simulation as an effective rhetorical device in his own works, Swift rejected it in art and literature because, in his opinion, it was liable to produce iconolaters who mistook the signifier for the signified, thus adoring and deifying the (visual or verbal) image of a woman, for instance, instead of being sensible.[35]

As we move further into the front-matter of the *Travels*, the simulation of authenticity continues. In the first page after the title-page in Motte's edition and in the title-page of Faulkner's we see how Swift's text adopts the simulation of certain kinds of discourse – but only to hoist it with its own petard. If we accept the critical view that Gulliver, in his role as observer who fails to understand, is one of Swift's satiric targets, the layout of both pages appears in a new light. The Motte edition lists the four parts of the *Travels* in an orderly, sequential form, with the sections identified by Roman numerals (illus. 37). And the first impression of Faulkner's new arrangement of the sub-title ('In Four PARTS') is also one of order: the voyages are now arranged in two columns, again with roman numerals listing Gulliver's four travels (illus. 38). We know that Book IV, the voyage into the country of the wise horses, was written before Book III. Swift had his reasons for rearranging the sequence in which the travels finally appeared in book form.[36] To an eighteenth-century reader, however, the spatial layout of the title-page would have immediately suggested the similar order of a scientific treatise. What the ordering of the page simulates is the very simulation of the scientific discourse of the Enlightenment, which pretended to discover or uncover ultimate truths by sticking to precise observation and formal logic. Gulliver travels from the world of small things to that of giant creatures, and then on to more complicated and 'more perfect' worlds. His 'progress', in other words, is from the simple to the complicated, and from the familiar to the unknown. Simulating an ordered discourse according to the 'scientific' principles of the day, the sub-titles of the editions of 1726 and 1735 thus try to lend credibility to the text that follows while simultaneously mocking the obsession with order that we find in abundance in the discourse of Enlightenment scientists and natural historians. Barbara Maria Stafford has summarized the relations between the wish to perceive/understand and the stylistic change in Swift's time:

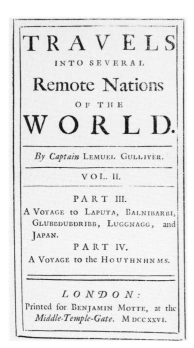

37 Title-page of volume II of Motte's edition of *Gulliver's Travels*, London, 1726.

38 Title-page of volume III of Faulkner's edition of *Gulliver's Travels*, Dublin, 1735.

The dictum that on a deep level the functioning of natural philosophy was the impartial imaging of nature readily allied itself with a verbal and visual style of recording. The pairing of these representational concerns – which the ambitions of science raised to an aesthetic level – occurred in Bacon's *Advancement of Learning* (1605) and in Hobbes's *Leviathan* (1651), where it was asserted (inverting the message of Quintilian's *Institutes*) that words were but the images of matter. This asseveration was matched by the growing desire of the Royal Society – and, by extension, all other scientific academies – to make words and pictures (that is, any artificial constructs) match things in order to make concrete a true model of the physical world.[37]

It is important to recall that the Royal Society gave instructions to its members and to travellers with regard to how they should record their *visual and verbal* observations. The satire on the style and content of the *Philosophical Transactions of The Royal Society* and on Thomas Sprat's history of that institution thus begins not in Book III of the *Travels*, but in the sub-title that both apes and undermines the alleged logic order of Enlightenment reports on scientific discoveries and experiments.

The title-page of Faulkner's edition of the *Travels* (illus. 38) contains a motto 'Retroq; / Vulgus abhorret ab his' – whose functions have not been sufficiently explored. Borrowed from Lucretius' *De rerum natura*, the epigraph is much more than a bait for the reader.[38] We can assume that Swift was very well aware of the importance of this part of the paratext. In his satirical, tongue-in-cheek *A Letter of Advice to a Young Poet* (1721) he admonished his addressee:

> You must not fail to dress your Muse in a Forehead-cloath of *Greek* or Latin, I mean, you are always to make use of a *quaint Motto* to all your *Compositions*; for besides that, this Artifice bespeaks the Readers Opinion of the Writers Learning, it is otherwise Useful and Commendable. A bright Passage in the Front of a Poem is a good Mark . . . and the Piece will certainly go off the better for it. . . . Words are but Lackies to sense, and will dance Attendance, without Wages or Compulsion.[39]

This passage indicates both the Dean's knowledge of epigraphic conventions and his iconoclastic strategy in the use of mottoes. Recalling Foucault's point about author intention, however, we may go further and consider what a motto achieves within the paratext of a literary work. Genette distinguishes four main functions of the epigraph in books:[40] it comments on and, to a certain extent, explains the title; it provides a sort of critique of the text; it draws our attention to the author of the epigraph; and it constitutes what Genette terms 'an epigraphical effect' and 'a sign of culture' (Swift's reference, in the passage quoted above, to the 'Writers learning'). The motto from Lucretius in the title-page of the *Travels* fulfils these functions. Titus Lucretius Carus (97–55 BC), an advocate of Epicurus, must have been congenial to Swift because he tried to make poetry subservient to his didactic aims. Guided by logic and humanitarian ideals, Lucretius turned his major work into a drama of recognition or enlightenment, and it is this aspect of *De rerum natura* which appealed to eighteenth-century writers. Both the text and the context of the source are important, for the original contains a different pronoun (*hac*), reading 'retroque / volgus abhorret ab hac' (the people shrink back from it). It occurs twice in *De rerum natura* (see I, ll.944–5; and IV, ll.19–20): in each case Lucretius compares himself to a physician who, trying to administer distasteful medicine to a child, coats the rim of the cup with honey, to trick the child into taking the helpful dose. The word *hac* refers to a doctrine (*ratio*) on which Lucretius' passage comments thus:

> Since this doctrine commonly seems somewhat harsh to those who have not used it, and the people shrink back from it, I have chosen to set forth my doctrine to you in sweet-speaking Pierian song, and as it were to touch it with the Muses' delicious honey, if by chance in such a way I might engage your mind in my verses, while you are learning to see in what shape is framed the whole nature of things.[41]

Since *hac* becomes 'his' (from them or with them) in the paratext of the *Travels*, it must be related to 'travels', to Gulliver's report. This link opens a variety of new significations, including Swift's imitation of Lucretius (dressing up his 'doctrine' in the garb of the travelogue) and the warning to shrink back from Gulliver's lies. The motto here subverts a literary convention that was extremely popular in the age of Enlightenment and beyond. The epigraph from Lucretius comments on the real and fictitious authors of the *Travels*, and it addresses an educated and attentive reader. The reader is supposed to notice not so much the traditional learning of the author conveyed by the classical source, but rather the epigraphic effect in that the paratext plays with a convention. To understand the point of this play one must identify the convention and recognize its subversion, surely not an easy task, which depends to a large extent on the difference between *hac* and *his*.

As we turn to what might be called the preface of the Dublin edition of 1735, we notice that the *Travels* again simulates not merely the different parts of prefaces in works of fiction but also their very techniques. Even the earlier Motte edition apes the conventions: the letter from 'The Publisher to the Reader' is followed by the title-page of part I and two pages of chapter summaries. Like the frontispiece and the title-page, the preface (the 'Advertisement' and the letters from Sympson and Gulliver) is a highly treacherous entrance-way to the main text. Genette defines the preface as 'every sort of liminal text, by the author or another person, consisting of discourse about the text that follows or precedes' the main text.[42] In the *Travels*, the three parts of the preface refer to one another while trying to simulate authenticity; they comment on Gulliver's text; and they contain hints and clues about the real nature of Gulliver and his allegedly true travels. Since the reader is to be persuaded of the author's 'veracity', the special types and functions of prefaces must be imitated. Thus the editor or publisher of the *Travels* explains how he received the text; there are remarks about corrections and changes as well as some information about the author's (Gulliver's) life. Gulliver, in turn, comments on his text in the manner of writers of autobiographies. The point of all this aping, however, is the ultimate assault on conventions of writing, for the fictional preface is a framing device that reflects and stages itself.[43]

The 'Advertisement' begins with a sentence that seems to contain a mistake: 'Mr Sympson's Letter to Captain Gulliver'. In his edition of the *Travels* Paul Turner notes that this is 'a mistake' for 'Captain Gulliver's Letter to Mr Sympson'.[44] But it is hardly imaginable that the corrected edition of 1735 should contain such a howler. Since Swift, after some initial hesitation, gave Faulkner real assistance in the preparation of the *Travels*, the 'mistake' may also be a clue. If it is, it throws some light on the fictional nature of both Sympson and Gulliver. The rest of the text of the 'Advertisement' mocks various conventions of prefaces in travelogues. Thus Swift practices the traditional satirical art of writing a preface by claiming that he will not write one when he has the publisher of the Advertisement declare that Sympson's letter (which is really Gulliver's letter) 'will make a long Advertisement unnecessary'. We also find the conventional *excusatio propter infirmitatem*, which, paradoxically, is intended to boost the literary work as such and serves as what Lichtenberg once termed a lightning rod:[45] admitting that the *Travels* contains 'many Alterations and Insertions', the advertisement blames 'a Person since deceased', a ghost-writer, who was to have made the alterations but did not comprehend 'the Scheme of the Author, nor . . . his plain simple Style'. The ghost-writer is also held responsible for the ticklish political allusion Gulliver complains about in his letter. The final part then comments on the corrections for the Dublin edition, constructing a mystery about the origin of the *Travels* and the handling of the manuscript.

One of the functions of these ludic and seemingly genuine references to 'real' persons (Sympson, Gulliver, a ghost-writer, a friend, a publisher) is of course to create an impression of authenticity.[46] This is also the case with the text following this piece, which is entitled 'A Letter from Capt. Gulliver, to his Cousin Sympson'. In this angry epistle, added in the edition of 1735 and perhaps even written for it, Gulliver writes as hero and author. Along the way he voices some of Swift's criticism of the edition and, more importantly, gives himself away unwittingly as we get information about the genesis and true aims of his book. There are some intertextual allusions to the 'Interpolator' (the ghost-writer) and dangerous political passages mentioned in the 'Advertisement', which is to boost the truthfulness of both texts. Important hypotexts for the *Travels* are also mentioned; for example, 'my Cousin *Dampier* and his *A Voyage round the World*', which had appeared in 1697, and More's *Utopia*. Since the pirate and explorer William Dampier (1652–1715) copied many parts in his book from other writers, this is one of the initial instances in which Gulliver unmasks himself. We notice, for instance, that he wants to appear honest and humble. Insisting on his 'veracity', he points out the fact that he was able 'in the Compass of two years . . . to remove that infernal Habit of Lying'; and he complains to Sympson that his cousin 'prevailed on [him] to publish a very loose and uncorrect Account of [his] Travels', and that because of unauthorized alterations, he made him 'say the thing that was not'. Simultaneously, Gulliver emerges as a hypocritical Puritan (his style and choice of words give him away) with such an immense pride in 'mine own Work' that he will neither thank Sympson nor pardon him his mistakes.

By having Gulliver unmask his pride and pretension, the paratext of the *Travels* indicates that the narrator must not be trusted and that he is in fact one of the targets of the satire. We are given the most obvious clue when the narrator, sticking close to the tradition of autobiographical prefaces, talks about the real, moral, aims of his book (which the title places among travel books). Gulliver tells Sympson that in publishing the *Travels* he intended to see 'a full Stop put to all Abuses and Corruptions, at least in this little Island' and that he expected 'a Thousand other Reformations . . . as indeed they were plainly deducible from the Precepts delivered in my Book', but that even 'after Six Months Warning, I cannot learn that my Book hath produced one single Effect according to mine Intentions'. Forgetting that the title-page of his *Travels* declared him 'first a Surgeon and then a Captain', Gulliver wants the 'physicians banished' and expects a sound reformation of morals and manners in England.

Gulliver's letter is a brilliant example of the constant simulation of literary practices and conventions that is at work in the book. Gulliver is allowed to seize the word in what, initially, looks like a traditional literary device. But those who read with care will discover both the true nature of the hero's character and the limits of the paratext that is here undermined. This simulation continues in Sympson's 'The Publisher to the Reader', which apes the claim for authenticity that we find in the similar pieces that were a standard part of travelogues. Masterfully hidden in stylistic allusions of a text that unveils its mendacity by the very insistence on Gulliver's 'veracity' and the 'Air of Truth' in his report, the intertextual references in this section are to Lucian's *True Stories* as well as to Dampier's *Voyage* and similar travel books. A telling mixture of fact and fiction, of true and false, predominates again; and the textual play with generic conventions and reader expectations culminates in the final sentence: it refers the sceptical reader to Gulliver himself (the liar) whose text will provide 'satisfaction' about the author's identity.

In the *Travels* the preface becomes a kind of dramatic act that eventually reflects and mimes itself. Recalling the tale of Narcissus, who fell in love not with his own countenance but with its reflected image, Genette has argued that prefaces in general reflect a 'self-consciousness' (he uses the English word) that is both disturbing and playful; it is a self-representation in the mirror that comes close to dramatic enactment.[47] With its narcissistic aspect, the preface must be considered as one of the most typical literary practices. It is hardly coincidental that the myth of Narcissus, which structures and inspires the comedy and satire in the *Travels*, is again evoked in the usual Swiftean, tongue-in-cheek manner on the very first page of Gulliver's text. In this instance, the innocent narrator becomes involved in a pun on 'Master Bates' and the verb 'masturbates'.[48]

Many of Swift's works transcend and undermine conventional frames of seeing and writing. The preface of the *Travels*, if preface it is, is one such magisterial example of the ironic questioning of imaging, self-images, and describing 'reality'. Taking the place of the debate structure in the works of Plato and Thomas More, the prefatory material tells the careful reader to beware of simple judgements and to recognize the essential differences between the signifier and the signified. The paratext of the *Travels* often requires the reader to recall the similar paratexts we find in More's *Utopia* and in the opening sections of Lucian's *True Stories*, where the narrator-liars insist on the veracity of their discourse. It seems that Swift adopted the ludic framing strategy of *Utopia*, for instance, which opens with two letters excessively concerned with veracity, a (fictive) map followed by a 'Utopian alphabet', a poem and further letters. In fact, it might be argued that the front-matter and the entire Book I of *Utopia* form a kind of introduction to Hythlodaeus' description of the utopian island in Book II. Conflating generic and rhetorical forms of fiction and historiography, Swift's *chef-d'œuvre* constructs semiotic worlds only to question and to destroy them. The *Travels* ultimately refers the reader to a problem that is central to both Swift's works and 'travel literature': the reliability of verbal and visual systems of representation and the fictitious nature of reality that depends on such unreliable forms of discourse.

It is a matter of discretion to decide where the paratext ends and where the 'main' text of the *Travels* begins. For the editions published by Motte and Faulkner contain two further parts that are, strictly speaking, not attributed to Gulliver, the narrator. Like the final chapter of the *Travels*, in which the hero reflects again on his own writing (in Genette's terminology, this constitutes a peritext), the table of contents as well as the first map still belong to the paratextual corpus of the book. In view of the work to be done for a future critical edition of the *Travels*, I should like to point out very briefly what remains to be analysed in the front-matter of Swift's magnificent palimpsest.

First of all, there are the chapter summaries. They are listed in one

39 *Map of the Island of Utopia*, frontispiece woodcut map by Ambrosius Holbein from Thomas More's *Utopia*, Basel, 1518.

group before the map and the first page of text, as if they were a text to be considered apart. Their very position immediately reminded the reader of similar arrangements in novels and travel reports. This textual part of the book deserves more attention, not least because its allusive and structural functions play an important role in the general undermining of Gulliver's text, which Swift orchestrates by simulation from the very beginning of the book. These are, of course, real chapter summaries and headings, yet at the same time they mock this form and its tradition while revealing a lot about the narrator and his style.

This is also true for another important visual part of Gulliver's travelogue – the maps that precede the four books. If the oval portrait of Gulliver subverts the grand manner portrait in its very use of it and suggests a 'true' reflection of a mirror while showing an Everyman or nobody, the maps pretend to replicate the world, offering verifiable facts (genuine coast-lines, for instance, known to eighteenth-century readers) and fictional dystopias. Indeed, the maps urge us to read them as another sign-system and to compare them to earlier (false) maps, such as the frontispieces used in the editions of More's *Utopia* (illus. 39).[49]

In addition, Motte's corrected edition of the *Travels*, published in May 1727, contained five poems ('Verses on *Gulliver's Travels*') as yet another part of the opening matter of the *Travels*. Excepting the Norton edition of 1970, these parodic poems – probably written by Pope, Gay and Arbuthnot – have not been adopted in critical editions; nor have they been assessed in view of their hermeneutic value. Imitating the mingling of discursive forms that distinguishes the *Travels*, the poems are held in a variety of poetic genres and evoke different contexts of the book. Both the formal and intertextual functions of these partly bawdy poems ought to be explored within the larger frame of the paratext of the *Travels*.

This brief discussion of some important visual and verbal parts of the front-matter of Swift's best-known text should demonstrate the literary sophistication of a work of fiction that makes real demands on the reader. As a highly self-reflexive book it stands in a line of remarkable, pioneering fictional texts extending from Cervantes's *Don Quixote* to Sterne's *Tristram Shandy* and postmodern examples, such as Thomas Pynchon's *V* (1963) and Umberto Eco's *Il Nome della rosa* (1980), which use paratexts, framing devices and intermediality in a similar manner that is both ludic and revealing. Pynchon's latest novel, *Vineland* (1990), may be compared to the *Travels* in its incessant appeal to a special form of *déjà vu*, the reader's experience of (American) television. If Swift's *magnum opus* plays with travel literature, Pynchon's novel creates similar difficulties with its repetition and aping of the virtual reality created by mass media. In fact, critics have misjudged the aims of *Vineland* as much as eighteenth-century critics misjudged the *Travels* – both books are dangerously close to the originals they parody and attack.

Simulating the iconotexts and contexts of travel literature, the front-matter of Swift's book, although only an accessory or *parergon* to the book as such, proves to be a fascinating if tricky entrance-way to a maze. The attentive reader must find the hidden clues to escape entrapment and to avoid misreading. As Richard Nash has argued recently, 'to read Swift is to experience entrapment', for his game of simulation 'requires the reader to participate actively in the text's creation of meaning in a manner that conforms to the meaning being created'. Approaching a Swiftean text, one will therefore be well advised to take cognizance of Genette's caveat: *attention au paratexte!*[50]

40 Luca Signorelli, *Empedocles, c.* 1503, fresco, Cappella della Madonna di S. Brizio, Orvieto Cathedral.

3 Frame-work: The Margin(al) as Supplement and Countertext

Look at the Harbour of La Rochelle *with a field glass that embraces the field of the picture but* excludes the frame. Forgetting *that you are examining a painted work, you will exclaim* . . . *'O the fine vista!'*
Diderot on Vernet's 'Le port de la Rochelle' ('Salon de 1763')

But that which has produced and manipulated the frame will make every effort to efface the effect of the frame. . . . Deconstruction must neither re-frame nor dream the downright absence of the frame. . . . There is a frame, but the frame does not exist.
Derrida, *The Truth in Painting*

From the paratext or framing devices of a work of fiction I now turn to the framing of pictures to demonstrate that the production of meaning in illustrations is also substantially determined by what philosophers from Kant to Derrida have called the *parergon*. Literally meaning 'by-work', this term designates (in art) something that is subordinate or accessory to the main subject (and also, tellingly, a work apart from one's main business). The term 'accessory' contains the noun 'access', which reminds one immediately of the access to texts discussed above. In this chapter I explore to what extent the supplementary or parergetic aspect of the frame assumes a rhetorical function that is at least as important as the so-called content of a work of art.

The pictures examined in this chapter are to illustrate the frame-work (I use the hyphen with intention) of visual representations. Rhetorically and epistemologically, pictorial liminality is part of an iconographic strategy that allows the subversion of what is allegedly more important or central. This strategy of questioning the purported message of an image by calling attention to its framing – to the work of the frame generating perspective, sense and evaluation – may be compared to the way the fiction of Swift, Sterne and, to a lesser extent, Fielding, relies on framing devices.

Works of art, whether they are verbal or visual in kind, apparently also need frames to produce additional effects. For instance, to set themselves off from their surroundings (the context) and to establish their own space, to draw the observer's attention to their artful (framed) nature, and, sometimes, to celebrate framing at the expense of the framed. In this latter sense the eighteenth-century pictorial frame is what Nycole Paquin has termed a 'site of paradox' (*lieu de paradoxe*), threatening the internal image by bordering it with a hybrid area whose physical expansion indicates and marks the common ground shared by painting, sculpture and the mirror.[1]

For a long time, artists have been aware of the effects and the functions of the frame. Medieval illuminators, for instance, often allotted more space to the decorated margins or borders of images than to the 'central' subjects themselves. And the parergetical area on these pages is at times the site of visual commentary, of a counter-text giving voice to the obscene or the taboo. Witness the rather mundane figures, and the worldly occupations, represented in the frame of 'The Visitation', a miniature illustration by the Limbourg brothers for the *Très Riches Heures de Jean, Duc de Berry* (illus. 41). The holy subject – Mary's visit to Elizabeth – finds a counter-text in the burlesque ornaments of the frame-work: a woman chasing butterflies with a sword; a knight resisting the attack of a snail; an old man carting away a bear playing the bagpipes; and a clergyman trying to catch birds with a ladder, the whole signed as it were by the *seign* (the white swan) of the Duc de Berri.[2] In his detailed analysis of such subversive 'images on the edge', in which similar visual examples have been reproduced, Michael Camille has argued that 'medieval artists created marginal images from a "reading", or rather an intentional misreading, of the text'.[3]

The artists of the Renaissance were heirs to a tradition that knew how to play with liminality. When Luca Signorelli, for instance, produced a picture of Empedocles for a fresco in Orvieto, the excessive border was both ironicized and foregrounded through the painted metaphor of the window (illus. 40). An equivalent of the window, the eye, and the mirror, the representation insists on its own framing, on an astounding accomplishment that fascinates even the one who is being depicted.[4] Whereas late fifteenth-century Tuscan artists like Signorelli evidently enjoyed playing with the frame as limit between art and nature, fiction and reality, a playing that went as far as Antonio Fantuzzi's framing of the empty space in art celebrating the *cadre pour cadre*,[5] some artists of the Enlightenment tried to play down the role of framing devices. Thus Nicolas Poussin even gave specific instructions to his patrons concerning the framing of his paintings. The frame, he

41 Paul, Jean and Hermann Limbourg, 'The Visitation', *c.* 1416, illuminated page from *Les Très Riches Heures de Jean, Duc de Berry*. Musée Condé, Chantilly.

wrote, ought not to be too elaborate. While it should set off the painting from surrounding objects it must not attract too much attention itself. As J.-C. Lebensztejn has shown, these remarks are echoed in Kant's insistence on the frame as mere ornament, as a *parergon* (in the *Critique of Judgement*), a by-work that 'wrongs true beauty'. Indeed, Poussin defines a classical conception of representation that claims its own specific space *separated* from natural space – while simultaneously claiming that the separation is given, not constructed. As one of the *motti* to this chapter tells us, Diderot was to develop such a view into an illusionistic theory that ignored the frame.[6]

Given the undeniable importance of frames, it seems odd that museums issue slides or photographs of paintings without their original frame. Some museums even 'normalize' frames or, worse, reframe works by Old Masters, putting, say, *French* framework from the sixteenth century around the works of Vermeer, Rembrandt and Steen.[7]

But my aim here is not to retrace the history of the frame in art, a subject that now is just beginning to receive attention.[8] Nor is this the place to explore the equally fascinating aspect of the gendering of frames (in the widest sense) and, by implication, the glance or gaze (masculine) and the work of art (feminine).[9] Rather, intrigued by the silence about, and the latent opposition to, the *parergon* in philosophical and ekphrastic discourse (where Diderot's attitude marks only one instance), I intend to inquire into the *parergon*'s signifying potential. If philosophical writing has always been against the frame, as Derrida has argued, could it be precisely because the importance of the *parergon* is to be denied and effaced because it presents a menace? It threatens not the picture but the vision of the one making meaning of/with it. I shall pretend for a while that I simply do not know what is essential and what accessory in a picture; and since framing has been deliberately neglected in critical writing (for strategic reasons, one suspects), it will be my *ergon* for a few pages. Even if the frame only helps to make sense, it has every right to be examined within a theory or a practice that is interested in semantics and signifying, all the more since hermeneutics, semiotics and phenomenology have always insisted that meaning resides in the picture.[10]

The *OED* defines the *parergon* as 'an extra ornament in art', derived from the Greek 'by-work' or 'subordinate business'. In painting, it denotes something 'accessory to the main subject or an addition'; it is a 'work apart from one's main business', even (in an obsolete form) a 'supplemental work'. The frame of a picture, then, as *parergon*, may be considered as a supplement that is at the same time an introduction or an accessory which, as Derrida puts it in a telling punning phrase, 'one has to accommodate at the border, on board; it is above all access' ('Comme un accessoire qu'on est obligé d'acceuillir au bord, à bord. Il est d'abord l'à-bord': *La Vérité en peinture*, p. 63). A *parergon*, which (in French) also denotes the exceptional or extraordinary, 'comes up against, beside, and in addition to, the *ergon* . . . but it does not fall beside it', rather, like an *hors d'œuvre* or a remnant, it 'touches and co-operates', supplementing and making up for a lack in the centre of the work (p. 63).

I shall begin my archaeological search in the parergetical area in early eighteenth-century Augsburg, with some engravings produced at the behest of the Zürich-based natural historian Johann Jakob Scheuchzer (1672–1733), whose herculean attempt at a kind of scientific theology led to the production of a monumental encyclopaedia conflating sacred and natural history. From these Swiss/German framing practices I will move on to France and, in turn, to England.

In 1731 Johann Andreas Pfeffel, a reputable Augsburg publisher and master engraver to the Emperor, brought out the first volume of what came to be known in German-speaking countries as *Die Kupfer-Bibel* (the engraved Bible). A magnificent example of late Baroque/early Rococo book art, this is a most fascinating communal product that has been primarily if unjustly associated with the Swiss scientist Scheuchzer, whose contribution consisted in a scientific commentary to the Bible. The four volumes of the 'Copper-Bible' published in 1731–5 in German and Latin editions went down in history as the *Physica Sacra*. Its 753 illustrations were impressive enough to persuade the Benedictine monk German Cartier to use them again, a few years later, for his *Biblia Sacra*, whose success was undoubtedly due to the engravings. Dutch and French translations of Scheuchzer's *Physica Sacra* were marketed even before the completion of the original German and Latin editions.[11]

Confirming once again the rule of writing over the visible, Scheuchzer's *ekphrasis* has overshadowed the contributions in this wonderful palimpsest by other writers and, more importantly, artists. The pious Scheuchzer was one of those eighteenth-century 'universal' scholars interested in science, medicine and theology. In the year of his death he was appointed physician to the city of Zürich, which, for all we can tell, had been his ultimate aim in life. What makes the *Kupfer-Bibel* interesting for postmodern readers is, first of all, Scheuchzer's commentary, which uses illustrations of biblical episodes as pretexts (in the double sense of the word) for propagating scientific lore from medicine, biology, zoology, astrology and other *natürliche Sachen* (natural things). Scheuchzer's understanding of 'natural' comprehended the phenomena of nature as much as the things created by man, with the implication that there was indeed a natural *and* divine origin to every thing (in 1715 he had published a treatise proving the existence of God by natural phenomena). The *Physica Sacra* was to show that scientific knowledge did not contradict the tenets of theology: it revealed the correspondences between the truth of the Bible and the 'natural' world as apprehended by Enlightenment science. This intention produced the most bizarre combinations of text and image. Plate DCXXXIII, for example (illus. 44), is supposed to be an illustration of, or for, Ezekiel 27:6, a passage commenting on ship-building ('Of the oaks of Bashan have they made thine oars; the company of the Ashurites have made thy benches of ivory, brought out of the isles of Chittim'). But the image we see in the *Physica Sacra* is not the beautiful vessel made of cedar and ivory as described in the Old Testament. Johann Georg Pintz, the artist who, under Pfeffel's supervision, engraved this picture for Scheuchzer, reproduces the outlines of an English man-of-war as seen from two angles. The perspective is a result not of a close reading of the passage in Ezekiel but of the practice of contemporary shipwrights. Diderot would hardly have appreciated the subversive framework of this 'vista': it is a double frame, one being a traditional Rococo wooden frame capable of being gilded that could also be used to contain a mirror, and the other a sort of background, or even backdrop, consisting of the parts of a man-of-war, with two blueprints at the bottom. One almost gets the impression that the ships inside the frame have grown out of the frame, that they are there to celebrate the business of the framework – shipbuilding. In his prose commentary to this palimpsest Scheuchzer quickly abandons the Bible after a few philological and etymological explanations in order to launch into an introduction to the 'Engl. Kriegs-Schiff vom ersten Rang'. Ezekiel's words do not interest him anymore than they had the artist. As with all the other plates, the commentary closes with a couplet from the pen of Johann Martin Miller (1693–1747), a clergyman who advised Scheuchzer on things theological and 'summed up' the message of the iconotexts:

> *So weit hat Menschen-Kunst im Wasser es gebracht,*
> *Und solche Vestungen zum schwimmen ausgemacht.*

> Man's art on water has advanced thus far,
> Selecting such fortresses and making them float.

It would indeed be interesting to analyse Scheuchzer's commentary in view of the constrictions (or the framework in a manner of speaking) under which he had to work without knowing it. One finds (both Barthian and Derridean) traces everywhere of 'conceptions' imposing themselves on his discourse: the implicit fear of offending the Church as well as the concomitant fear of finding transgressions of 'natural' laws in the Bible. But that is not my concern here.[12] I am alerted by the fact that Scheuchzer's prose commentary is merely one stone in a mosaic or a thread in a fabric made up of several series of texts, images and frames – Scheuchzer's production being itself one verbal frame claiming to explain the image in each case. As Hans Krauss notes (p. 10) in his abbreviated edition of the *Physica Sacra*, that commentary deserves as much of our attention as the illustrations. It is important to know, I think, that Scheuchzer did not make the images and that, irony of ironies (and unnoticed or ignored by critics like Stafford, for instance), the frames were in turn the brainchild of a different artist.

Here are the facts that need to be considered.[13] The engravings were all designed by the Zürich painter and engraver Johann Melchior Füßli. As Scheuchzer explained in the preface to his monumental work, Füßli worked under his direction, 'aber zugleich aus eigener

Invention' (simultaneously out of his own invention). And this 'invention' has left its traces – in the landscapes, for instance, which are more Alpine than Oriental. Plate DCLXXXII (illus. 42) is one of many examples: Hebrew figures harvesting wheat(!) are set in Swiss or south German scenery, the whole surrounded by European weeds that grow from the picture into its frame, serving as a decoration of sorts.[14] All the plates for the *Physica Sacra* were then engraved in Augsburg, where Johann Andreas Pfeffel employed more than twenty artists, most of them from Augsburg or Nuremberg: Johann Georg Pintz (208 plates), Georg Daniel Heumann (167), and Jakob Andreas Fridrich the Elder (113) were the more prolific members of this group that contained specialists for all subjects, such as Johann August Corvinus, who engraved forty-two illustrations of an architectural kind. If there was an artistic brain behind the plates, the one who designed the frames was perhaps even more gifted and certainly more inventive: this was Johann Daniel Preißler (whose name Scheuchzer mentions immediately after that of the designer of the plates), who provided all the decorations and frames to the illustrations, an astonishing achievement not least because every frame is different. Apart from Scheuchzer (the main author) and Pfeffel, who took pride in his artistic creation, there was another *spiritus rector* – Johann Martin Miller, the clergyman who shared with Scheuchzer an almost obsessive interest in the biblical Flood. It was Miller who corrected and enlarged the text of the Swiss scientist; it was Miller who supervised the printing in Augsburg; and it was Miller who wrote the poetic part, a theological *ekphrasis* in verse, for the *magnum opus*. The clergyman contributed a poetic introduction cum summary and provided each plate with a couplet allegedly summarizing the illustration.

I have provided this detailed information for two reasons. First to demonstrate that the *Physica Sacra* is not the work of Scheuchzer alone; and second to refute critical attempts to read either the pictures or the texts accompanying the illustrations as unified entities. What we find in the *Kupfer-Bibel*, then, are palimpsests marked by both intertextual and intermedial relations that call for clarification *before* we subject the iconotexts to our critical concerns. Specifically (and to make things even more complicated), the relations to be explored comprehend entire series of texts, images and iconotexts: from the biblical quotations wrenched out of context to serve as verbal pre-texts for pictorial illustrations, on to engravings again that pretend to comment on the Bible while really illustrating phenomena from natural science as seen by Scheuchzer and/or his helpers (drawing on anatomical and other scientific collections), and, finally, the additional intermedial step from picture to verbal (Scheuchzer's text) and poetic (Miller's verses) *ekphrases*. It should be obvious by now that I cannot undertake an analysis of these relations within the confines of a brief chapter. But I shall try to show the difficulty of the subject-matter at hand by focusing on the tension between the frame and (the subject-matter of) the plates, on what seems to be a relatively unimportant part of that chain of transposition, translation and (mis)representation that even post-modern critics tend to underestimate.[15]

Plate DXXX (illus. 48) is Scheuchzer's visual pre-text meant to illustrate the wonders of the miniature natural world recently discovered by chemistry and physics. The biblical Ur-text here is a passage in Job where Jehovah refers to his 'treasure chambers' of snow and hail awaiting the day of fight and battle:

Hast thou entered the treasures of the snow? or hast thou seen the treasures of the hail, which I have reserved against the time of trouble, against the day of battle and war?

The verses stress the negative qualities of winter as a punishment and a tool of God's power used against the enemies of the Israelites. But the engraving is concerned with the beauty, not with the terror, of what Scheuchzer terms 'Schnee-Schätze' (*Thesauri nevis*; i.e., snow treasures) in two 'Eisblumen' that he had seen on a window shutter. Like the parergetical plants growing out of the snow at the bottom, the entire image is in praise of life and the beauty of nature. Death and punishment are totally ignored by the engraver Pintz. The frame, in this case, is threefold: a traditional small, rectangular frame is supported by an ornamented, sculpted background that uses *trompe-l'œil* to efface the limits between representation, allegory and reality. If the inside of the frame and the framed, like a mirror (Scheuchzer uses the word *spiegeln* on occasion), reflects what Scheuchzer thought he had perceived, the small frame foregrounds the aspect of seeing and reflection while the additional framing area underneath conflates motifs from sculpture, emblems and biology to suggest the universe of life. The winter wind blows (emblematically) below, and hence 'outside', but paradoxically, the ice and snow it produces turn into aesthetic harmony, which even includes the well-balanced icicles at left and right.

It is, however, the third part of the frame I find most fascinating (it is far from being *nüchtern* – austere or plain – as Krauss argues, p. 178) because it introduces a true palimpsest: the upper part of the picture and frame is covered by a torn parchment or scroll (both suggest the ideas of something religious, old, and valuable for the 'holy' message it contains); the nails that fix it to the frame are still visible. This parchment, then, literally imposes itself on the (artificially represented) natural world below. The 'hieroglyphics' on the parchment represent the 'Schnee-Schätze' promised in the Latin/German epigraphs. And yet the ice crystals are more than a decoration. As a text of sorts, they allude to the discoveries in optics made and published around 1715; and as a visual *mise-en-scène* they are also a *mise-en-abîme* in that they not only invade the pictorial representation in the frame, they even hide it. The optical look at the world, the scientific eye, is more important than what the layman's eye sees on window shutters. The microscopic vision equals and finally displaces natural sight. Both uncover, according to Scheuchzer's commentary, a 'most wondrous art-work' (*ein höchst verwunderliches Kunstwerk*). Although Scheuchzer finally returns to the biblical passage, which refers to snow and hail as a punishment of God that may lead to death, the tension between the frame and the framed in the illustration says the very opposite – we see a harmonious 'natural world' recorded by the communal efforts of artist and scientist. The scientific outlook (symbolically represented by the paper with the ice crystals nailed across 'nature') undermines the biblical text. In the competition between the frame and the framed, Preißler's elaborate framework seems to win both over Pintz's engraving and the words at the beginning of this chain of texts, images and inappropriate explications.

This is indeed a 'wondrous' example, reminding one of Derrida's seemingly innocent question: Where does the frame begin, and where does it end? The frame, in any case, is the site where meaning is being produced that eventually overpowers the allegedly central text and its ill-fitting illustration.

More often than not, the frame in the illustrations of the *Physica Sacra* functions as a battleground on which biblical legends (serving as title and guide for the picture) are displaced by the perspective of natural science. Physics and optics provide a new sight replacing natural sites/sights. Thus in plate CCCLIII (illus. 45) the frame, at first glance, seems to be in harmony with Deuteronomy 28:38–42, where locusts and worms as the messengers of God's vengeance invade cultivated fields and vineyards. Once again, however, the image has rather a different story to tell.[16] Instead of biblical settings and victims of plagues we see an early eighteenth-century park, engraved by M. Tyroff, with amateur natural historians pointing out species of insects to one other. The frame is slightly less decoratively worked than those in other illustrations, with just the usual framed mirror/image on a sculpted second board. What pretends to be an illustration of 'land-verderbliche Ungeziefer' (land-destroying vermin) based on the Old Testament verse, becomes an iconotextual allusion to the wonders of modern zoology and entomology. Beautifully rendered and marked A (at bottom, and below at the left), B (top and at right) and C (on the frame-board below), various species of insect are shown invading the landscape within the frame, not in order to recall their role in the Bible (God's vengeance) but to remind the reader of their recent first scientific and visual recording. The larva marked A comes straight out of a collection of images of insects entitled *Metamorphose Surinamischer Insekten* by Anna Maria Sibylla Merian (1647–1717), a painter of flowers and insects; figures B and C have been lifted from an illustrated book, *Metamorphose und Naturgeschichte der Insekten*, which the entomologist and engraver Johannes Goedart (1620–68) had published in Latin in 1662. Inspired by these works, the Enlightenment perspective of nature literally enters plate CCCLIII, changing its meaning to such a degree that even Miller's pious accompanying verse remains helpless. Miller's didactic summary is again another story, relying as it does on other biblical passages (Genesis among them) to impose a religious meaning on a plate that both the frame and the image deny.

In plate XCVII (illus. 43) it is again a series of frames that disrupt and destroy whatever meaning is suggested by the scene in the centre. It is significant that this image is, for Scheuchzer, also a *mirror* framed by the parts of the hip which are to illustrate his subject. The caption or title, 'Lucta cum Angelo / Der Englische Zweikampf' is, as such paratexts go, a misleading summary of the framed and its *parergon*. In the biblical text that allegedly serves as a starting-point for the image (Genesis, 32:24–32), Jacob wrestles with an angel/God and suffers a lame thigh, which Scheuchzer turns into a hip.[17] Scheuchzer exploits the text and the occasion for a brief lesson in anatomy. Set around the picture, anatomical parts of the human hip provide a third frame, completely dominating the interior scene engraved by Heumann. Once again the work of Preißler, the sculpted frame and its superimposed details try to conflate allusions to things sacred and scientific. The artwork of the second frame can hardly hide its religious origin, reminding one of the sculptured tabernacles, icons and pictures decorating churches.[18] This ecclesiastical frame is in turn invaded by the anatomical parts of the hip, arranged in an order (letters A and D, a–f) which (visually) sets up a new frame and recalls books of anatomy.

Indeed, the *Physica Sacra* finds one of its best illustrations in this picture – a science apparently rendered sacred because it lists and shows the 'natural' things in Holy Writ. Imposed as it is upon a sculpted frame, one associates it with *religious* art; the third, outer, frame illustrates only itself, that is the ultimate, hierarchical, rule of the representation of human anatomy. The entire frame-work urges us to believe in the series of transpositions and translations – from the verbal to the visual, and from the frame to the framed – made in front of our eyes. The observer is shunted into the perspective of a sacred science which dominates representation and vision and attempts to efface the essential differences between word and image, fiction and reality. This violent enterprise is crowned, and again exemplified, by Miller's poetic effort, a couplet that ignores all differences in a summary that is (as in many similar cases in the book) unintentionally comic:

> Triumph, Victoria! Wird gleich die Hüffte lahm,
> der Sieges-Crantz ersetzts, den Israel bekam.

> Triumph and Victory! The winner's crown, which
> Israel received, makes up for the lame hip.

The botanist's viewpoint affects the representation in a series of plates (illus. 46, 47) showing idyllic landscapes that dwarf two human wanderers (an allusion to a fashionable topic in eighteenth-century literature). Again, the biblical verses only serve as a starting-point, relating merely superficially (through a word, for instance) to the subject of the engravings. These plates are remarkable, I think, because they draw our attention to the artful nature of framing. In plate CXXXIX (illus. 46) the illusion of a natural landscape is disturbed by the presence of a mathematical code: the Roman numerals indicate that which is important in the scene, i.e., the plants and their names. As if to underline the primary role of botany, and of identifying and rubricating, the plants grow out of the picture and into the decorative frames. Nos. II and III (*Endivien* and *Wegwerter*) visually negate the framing (in the German edition, fig. I is missing, and the captions of plates CXXXIX and CXL have been wrongly attributed), underlining Scheuchzer's deep interest in botany. In fact, his commentary likens plants to human beings, praising botanical wonders in the manner and role of what he terms a 'preacher experienced in nature', although his summary of 'bitter herbs' finally expresses the opposite of what his friend Miller, the theologian, says in verse. Miller's violent attempt to produce harmony between different media and meanings ends once again in unintended irony.[19]

A struggle between the scientific urge of the illustrator Heumann, instructed by Scheuchzer, and the framing of the natural scenery by Preißler, also governs the semantics of plate CXXXIX (illus. 46), in which 'Herbae amarae, Endivium et Cichorium' challenge the frame and thus confirm the rule of science through a new perspective.[20]

MATTH. Cap. XIII. v. 25.
Zizania inter Triticum.

Matth. Cap. XIII. v. 25.
Unkraut unter dem Weitzen.

GENESIS Cap. XXXII. v. 24. 25. 31. 32.
Lucta cum Angelo.

I. Buch Mosis Cap. XXXII. v. 24. 25. 31. 32.
Der Englische Zweykampf.

42 Plate DCLXXXII

43 Plate XCVII

EXODI Cap. XII. v. 8.
Herbæ amaræ. Endivium et Cichorium.

II. Buch Mosis Cap. XII. v. 8.
Weisser Andorn, Zwetsch Kerbl Kraut.

EXODI Cap. XII. v. 8.
Marrubium album, Gingidium.

II. Buch Mosis Cap. XII. v. 8.
Endirten, Wegwarten.

46 Plate CXXXIX

47 Plate CXL

42–49 Eight plates from Johann Jakob Scheuchzer's *Physica Sacra*, Augsburg and Ulm, 1731–5.

TAB. DCXXXIII.

EZECH. Cap. XXVII. v. 5.
Navis bellica ex maximis.

Krieg-Schiff von ersten Rang.

44 Plate DCXXXIII

TAB. CCCLIII.

DEUT. Cap. XXVIII. v. 39. 42.
Insecta Regnum infesta.

Und verderbliche Ungeziefer.

45 Plate CCCLIII

IOB. Cap. XXXVIII. v. 22. 23.
Thesauri Nivis.

Schnee-Schätze.

48 Plate DXXX

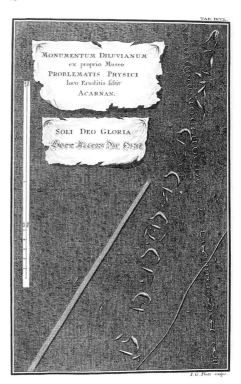

TAB. DCCL.

MONUMENTUM DILUVIANUM
ex proprio Museo
PROBLEMATIS PHYSICI
loco Eruditis sistit
ACARNAN.

SOLI DEO GLORIA

I. G. Pintz sculps.

49 Plate DCCL

The final plate in Scheuchzer's truly monumental collection is an attempt to master even the most arcane and *natural* (i.e., disorderly) things to be found in nature (illus. 49). If it has no frame it is because what constitutes the *parergon* in the other illustrations (the perspective of a 'religious science') is already part of the picture itself. The ruler is the most obvious sign of a code (geometry and measuring) that has left its traces. As I mentioned above, Scheuchzer, like Miller, was obsessed by the biblical Flood. It occupied him throughout his life. He claims that this illustration is based on a 'true remnant of the Flood' (*ein wahrhaftes Überbleibsel der Sündflut*) from his own private collection. The stone plate, 'polished and flattened by Nature herself', shows figures arranged in 'the same direction, position, and order', the 'designed characters' forming a straight line and, with the hieroglyphs, two angles. This is clearly the jargon of mathematics. It introduces the perspective of geometry (lines and angles) in order to grasp a mystery of nature or God. Two scrolls (we saw them in other plates above, as a sign of that which is already sacred, holy and of great value) both sanctify and explain the hieroglyphics. The upper one reads 'Arcanan poses as a mystery of nature for the knowledgeable a memorable piece of the Flood from his own collection'. Arcanan, a physician to Alexander the Great, was Scheuchzer's *nom de plume* as a member of a scientific society.[21] The scroll below yokes the proclamation of scientific analysis (as indicated by the ruler, the line and the scroll at top) to religion: 'To the sole honour of God' (*Gott allein zur Ehre*) maintains that even these strange 'characters and birds' are, according to Scheuchzer, 'beyond doubt a monument of the ancient Flood, whether their creator was an artist or artificial nature'.

Typically, Scheuchzer is not at all interested in the meaning of this fascinating iconic writing (which Paul Klee, for one, revived in one of his works). As a 'play of nature' (*Naturspiel*), it has to be a sign of a God manipulating seemingly unimportant mysterious phenomena. In the face of a *physica sacra*, a science that claims *a priori* that God rules in the worlds known and unknown to us, such mysteries need no solution. It is the frame inside the picture, the paraphernalia of measuring and collecting sanctified by religion (the ruler beside the scrolls), that tries to impose this view on the observer.

Let us now move to France to take a brief look at the framing of eighteenth-century French engravings of the 'genre galant'.[22] I begin with *Le Carquois épuisé*. Does the frame make a difference in meaning, perhaps even a Derridean *différance*? I think it does. The framework of *Le Carquois épuisé* (illus. 50) consists of two parts, the inner frame

50 Nicolas De Launay, *Le Carquois épuisé*, engraved after a painting by Pierre-Antoine Baudouin.

51 Nicolas De Launay, *Le Chiffre d'amour, c.* 1787, engraving after a painting by Jean Honoré Fragonard.

suggesting the rich, gilded, if unobtrusive, edge of the frame of the oil painting by Pierre-Antoine Baudouin on which this engraving is based. To the knowledgeable observer, this type of frame immediately suggested a particular subject and context: the private amusements of aristocrats.[23] The lower part of the *parergon*, a supplement to the gilded frame, establishes a connection between framing and sculpture (the escutcheon and the crown seem to be taken from a bas-relief). The written information tells us that the engraver, De Launay, copied the scene from Baudouin's original canvas. If we had only the title of this engraving, our reading would indeed be forced into the line of interpretation discussed in the chapter below, that is, the triumph of unlimited female sexual power over the limited potency of the male who has 'exhausted his quiver', as expressed in the caption/title. But the engraving is specifically dedicated to 'his Highness the Prince of Guémenée'; and the dedicators, 'les Gendarmes de la Garde du Roi', would hardly have made a present of an image in which the Prince appears as an impotent lover. Like the royal arms, a sign of possession and rule, the supporting text tries to dominate and reduce the semantics of the picture, affirming that if the Prince is the man on the sofa, he is certainly not impotent or unable to act. If the title is already an illegitimate summary of the complex picture (for, after all, the gentleman might also invite the girl to sit down beside him; and she might step forward to comply with his wish), the spirit of the dedication below the frame contradicts the title and the pictorial evidence. The central part of the engraving does not warrant the reading or view implied in the framework which, once again, surpasses its supplemental function.

This clarification of sorts by a supplementary frame, an interpretation that both dominates and abolishes the semiotic complexity of the pictorial representation, is at work in most engravings of this erotic genre. In *Le Chiffre d'amour* (illus. 51) for instance, the names of Fragonard and De Launay, as painter and engraver, highlight what Derrida has described as the function of signatures – the creation of the illusion of a presence at some time in the past as well as the continuing presence or importance of that 'signifier'.[24] Here, the names of Fragonard and De Launay already elevate the conventional scene (*qua* signature in absence) to the status of art. But there is a second text competing with the creators' trace – the arms of the Vicomtesse de Polastron disrupts the framing dedication below, and the latter establishes a reading/meaning that again tries to win the upper hand in the framework. The supplement claims logocentric importance again, limiting and deferring meaning and obstructing the development of pictorial ambiguity.

The original function of the frame as what Claus Grimm terms a 'mise à distance significative', as a device separating the space of art from natural space,[25] is a feature most of these engravings have in common. Take Greuze's famous *La Cruche cassée* (illus. 52), engraved by Jean Massard in 1773, in which the elaborate frame-work literally forces disparate notions into one central meaning: we find, in the *parergon*, allusions to the sculpted work of art (in a church or at Court), to the window and the mirror showing reality, and, in the lower part, the written supplement as an assertion of ownership and status. Due to the framework, the simple country girl loses her rustic charm (which is, anyway, a stylized pretension), since Mademoiselle Arnould, an actress, is the one to whom the picture is dedicated. But the dedicator, Greuze himself, will not easily relinquish his authorship/ownership expressed in a double signature: his name spelt in letters and his initials in an iconic sign that apes aristocratic escutcheons. At the base, three supports to either side further uphold the illusion of a sculptured monument. Greuze mounts his own work and asserts his authorship.

52 Jean Massard, *La Cruche cassée*, 1773, engraving after a painting by Jean-Baptiste Greuze.

53 Nicolas De Launay, *Les Hazards heureux de l'escarpolettes*, c. 1768, engraving after a painting by Jean Honoré Fragonard.

The parergetical signs and texts suggest that it is not to be overlooked, despite the name of Mademoiselle Sophie Arnould. Indeed, the size of the letters in the lower section give it away: the title is held in the smallest characters, surpassed by Greuze's signature at bottom right which in turn is dwarfed by the name of the actress; but, finally, Greuze's initials in the would-be-arms dominate the 'text' in every respect. His signature, in a Derridean manner of speaking, overpowers the framework which thus becomes a counter-text decentring the title and the inside of the 'mirror' above.[26]

The signature, however, is as false as the picture, claiming presence in absence while effacing the differences between originality and reproduction, reality and representation. For Greuze did not execute this print: it is the work of Jean Massard, one of the four engravers employed by Greuze.[27] The subscriptions distort the facts. They establish false authorships and deny the series of transpositions that have been at work to make sense – from painting to engraving, and from one great artistic name to another. The 'real' signature of the artist, his product, is overshadowed by a signifier replacing an absence.[28]

Finally, this principle may also be seen at its subversive work in the engraving of Fragonard's *Les Hazards heureux de l'escarpolettes* (illus. 53), whose faulty title (it should be *de l'escarpolette*), foregrounds the semantic function of this type of *parergon*. I have chosen this second state of the print intentionally, for it draws our attention directly to this paratext in a way a correct title could never achieve. The image has no traditional frame: the grey background, prolonged at the bottom to accommodate the title and a vignette, is simply a feature the image needs in order to be noticed. Although Fragonard is celebrated in the design at the bottom, this part of the print was not devised by him but by the engraver Pierre Philippe Choffard. It serves as supplementary image: a putto paints the artist's initials on what alludes both to the shape of a canvas and a coat of arms.[29] Ordered by a customer, the oil painting on which this engraving is based has its own story to tell,[30] yet we see how the absent painter, once again, asserts his importance and presence in the frame. Ironically, this assertion works with a false signature, for it is Choffard (an engraver known for his ornamental work and certainly as well-known as De Launay or Greuze) who hides behind Fragonard's name, for Choffard was the real executor.

This is an excellent example of the power relations in the hermeneutic struggle for dominance and control of meaning in a network of codes that includes the signature (and the long history of signatures and *seigns* as verbal/visual assertions), the frame, the title and other 'words in painting/engraving' (Michel Butor).[31] Words mingle with and turn into iconic forms in order to restrict and contain the dangerous potential, the indeterminacy, of the helpless visual image that cannot speak for itself.

From France, on to England. I have shown elsewhere that in Hogarth's graphic art such marginal figures as the African and Punch are part of a semantic playing with liminality, and hence centrality and hierarchy, both in the pictures and the society they depict. In plate 4 of *Marriage A-la-Mode* (illus. 54), for instance, Punch (on the left panel of the screen behind Silvertongue) literally walks into the scene, taking the role of observer and commentator. As the traditional punisher of evil and the personification of good sense, he embodies part of the popular *mentalité*. His importance for both children and adults can be gleaned from Swift's 'Mad Mullinix and Timothy' (1728), in which Mullinix argues that Punch was more in demand than any other theatrical figure of the day:

54 Detail from illus. 9, Hogarth's *Marriage A-la-Mode – IV*.

Why, Tim, you have a taste I know,
And often see a puppet-show.
Observe, the audience is in pain,
While Punch is hid behind the scene,
But when they hear his rusty voice,
With what impatience they rejoice.
And then they value not two straws,
How Solomon decides the cause,
Which the true mother, which Pretender,
Nor listen to the witch of Endor;
Should Faustus, with the devil behind him,
Enter the stage they never mind him;
If Punch, to spur their fancy, shows
In at the door his monstrous nose,
Then sudden draws it back again,
O what a pleasure mixed with pain![32]

Hogarth's Punch reminds the observer of the clear dichotomy of the puppet show, with its good and bad characters, while suggesting an analysis of the 'high society' in this picture from the moral point of view of such shows. In a similar context Paulson has discussed the subversive function of two truly marginal figures, the Samaritan Woman and Sancho Panza, who appear opposite one another (nos. 74, 75) in the actual frame of plate 2 of *The Analysis of Beauty* (illus. 55), casting doubt on the moral rectitude of the dancing couples between them as well as on the aesthetic harmony of the dance performed in this scene.[33]

In Hogarth's prints, the marginal and the very frame are thresholds which, like the titles and the prefatory matter in novels, are there to be scrutinized as part of the entire picture. In *Industry and Idleness*, for instance, framing the action of the series becomes an elaborate rhetorical exercise, a substitute for the verses that had accompanied *A Rakes's Progress*. Made up of words and images that are themselves framed again, the frames of this series foreground the framing of the pictorial sign to such a degree that the irony becomes more than obvious. In the first plate of the series (illus. 56), the master's staff extends into the shaft or handle of the Lord Mayor's mace in the frame; everything around the apprentices is solid, fixed and framed. One might say that they have been framed (in the modern sense of the term) or that they are caught in a frame (made up of language and images) that is both liminal and limiting. The observer would be well advised to read this marginal text as a commentary on what is going on in the images. As a text that is both an introduction and a supplement, the symbolic cornucopias and skeletons, the coronets with maces and the

55 William Hogarth, *The Analysis of Beauty – II*, 1753, engraving.

56 Detail from illus. 67, Hogarth's *Industry and Idleness – 1*.

The R.? Hon. LADY ANN FOLEY, and the EARL of PETERBOROUGH Playing together in Stoke Park, Herefordshire——the Post boy Watching them.

Published by J.Gill Aug.ᵗ 9 1796.

57 'Lady Ann Foley and the Earl of Peterborough playing together in Stoke Park', engraving from *A New and Complete Collection of Trials for Adultery; or a General History of Modern Gallantry and Divorces*, 1, London, 1796.

whips with fetters in the frames, seem to militate against the simplicity of the naïvely explicit titles and the biblical quotations.[34]

A particularly interesting case of framing the sign can be found in the erotic illustrations contained in collections of trial reports that were the rage in the market of erotica flourishing in late eighteenth-century London. Published mainly for the prurient and those interested in the 'Private Life, Intrigues, and Amours of many Characters in the most elevated Sphere', such reports from the Courts of Doctors' Commons were mostly concerned with adultery among the high and mighty. What makes the collections interesting is the attempt of the editors to dress their potentially pornographic texts in a garb of morality. Thus the prefaces usually bemoan the flagrant 'violation of the marriage vow' in England, and the juicy passages (excerpts from trials for adultery, incest, cruelty and sodomy) conclude with 'suitable Reflections' that are to render the works 'more worthy the Attention of Youth, even of both Sexes', who will find them '*in the end*, moral and instructive'.[35] The hypocritical and essentially contradictory rhetoric of such collections, with their mixture of pornographic detail veiled by sanctimonious editorial commentary, can be traced to the very frames of the illustrations. They reflect the double-faced rhetoric of such publications. Thus the print showing Lady Ann Foley and the Earl of Peterborough 'playing together in Stoke Park' (illus. 57) has a frame that suggests a mirror. In that respect it refers to the title-page of the book promising an 'elegant set of plates *representing* [italics mine] the most striking scenes'. In an age that still believed in mimetic artistic imitation, the visual is here supposed to recall the real. But the mirror, showing a real event in seemingly realistic terms, is surrounded by a curtain or cloak that has been drawn back to reveal something that, perhaps, ought not to be shown.

This curtain/cloak is, in fact, a trace or an allusion with a long history in iconography. Until the sixteenth century, a frame made for a painting often included a horizontal rod along the edge; this supported a curtain that protectively hid the picture from general view. The curtain suggests the original religious or devotional use of artworks as well as their taboo character. We find it as a trace throughout the eighteenth century – in some of the engravings of Scheuchzer's *Physica Sacra*, discussed above, and in the obscene illustrations marketed in the French Revolution. Hogarth's graphic art, too, provides a telling example of the use of the curtain: in plate 2 of *Marriage A-la-Mode* (illus. 58) one can see a half-drawn curtain in front of one of the paintings in the dining-room (to the left beyond the arch). The curtain permits just a glimpse of a naked foot, suggesting that the image it hides

58 William Hogarth, *Marriage A-la-Mode – II*, 1745, etching and engraving (first state).

is indelicate and, furthermore, that the lady and her company probably inspected it earlier that night.[36]

In the English engraving showing the erotic encounter between Lady Foley and the Earl of Peterborough, the cloak suggests the histrionic nature of the book of which this image is an important part, for the collection presents acts of adultery as if they were being enacted on a stage. It is interesting, in this respect, that eighteenth-century travel reports claiming scientific correctness for their verbal and visual representations often contained illustrations (mostly engravings) bordered by such curtains. The 'artful' frame, reminiscent of the artificial world of the stage and the theatre, thus undermines the claim to reality made by the visual rhetoric of the image itself.[37]

The illicit nature of this revelation of sorts is embodied by the peculiar and highly ambiguous character that, from above, watches the scene with a smile. This emblematic head, we notice, is associated with details (a devil's ears, twigs, ear-trumpets or even muskets, and serpents) that remind one immediately of two figures: Satan (and the association of sinning and the forbidden) and the Medusa, who, since the Renaissance, had been used as a decorative emblem for the arches of portals and doors. Our emblematic head is a watchful guardian; yet the mythological texts that stand behind it, as well as the texts the head seems to smile at, suggest sexuality, separation, horror and death. Like the curtain, this head can be read as an allusion to both texts and images that include, for instance, Andrea Alciati's representation of, and Latin commentary on, the 'caput Gorgonis' in his *Emblemata cum commentariis* (1621), and the painterly treatments of the severed Medusa head, with the versions of Poussin and Caravaggio as outstanding examples. One could even construct an admittedly daring if ironic connection between the head at the top of the print and the subject of the picture (illicit sexual acts), for one version of the Medusa myth (Ovid's *Metamorphoses*, IV, 790–803) reports that the Gorgon maiden was raped by Neptune in Minerva's temple; and Minerva punished Medusa by transforming her hair into serpents.[38]

The frame of this picture then embodies the insincere rhetoric of the texts in the book: it promises titillating details of illicit sexual acts while simultaneously warning against what is being revealed. Published in 1796, this print is a telling pictorial example of the emerging Victorian *mentalité* that was to dominate the discourse about sex in nineteenth-century England.

As these examples from eighteenth-century Germany, France and England demonstrate, the framing of pictures is an act and an artful device that can be compared in many ways to the framing of texts. 'Marginal, fencing, framing, liminal or januarial', the *parergon* may contribute to or, more often than not, block the creation of meaning.[39] The paratexts of novels (their prefaces, introductions and epigraphs) and the frames of engravings are attempts to use the parergetical area as a means to control what might get out of hand in the 'centre' – if centre there is. Indeed, the frame has a long history that goes back to the religious shrine. A shrine (the related German word *Schreiner*, incidentally, denotes carpenter or cabinet-maker) protects something or someone thought to be holy or sacred. It is the shrine as sign that in fact establishes this meaning, for it signals *a priori* that its content is of great value and must therefore be cherished. Before we even enter the 'arcanum', its frame/shrine has already created meaning and 'presence'. To conclude with one of those innocent Derridean questions in *The Truth in Painting* – and if there were nothing but the frame?[40]

59 Detail from illus. 62, Hogarth's *A Harlot's Progress – 3*.

4 'Official Discourse' in Hogarth's Prints

It is even probable that there exists one single rhetorical form *shared by the dream, literature, and the image.*
Barthes, *'Rhétorique de l'image'*

Let us go back to the fundamentals of image-making and this time examine it from the other side – from the viewer's gaze. . . . And from the inside – the social formation is inherently and immanently present in the image and not a fate or an external which clamps down on an image . . .
Bryson, 'Semiology and Visual Interpretation', in *Visual Theory*

What does it matter if I have added thoughts to the work of a great artist – so long as I have not subtracted or explained away such as are patently present?
Lichtenberg, *Hogarth on High Life*

After the excursions in the preceding chapters into the framing areas of texts and pictures, where we found that meaning is already being shaped, I want to move into the work of art itself, turning from the *parergon* to the *ergon*. The subject for my investigation will be select examples of Hogarth's graphic art. As I indicated earlier, a Hogarthian engraving is not, for me, a closed system or a repository that contains ultimate (and aesthetically appealing) truths we 'have merely to discover. Nor do I believe in the great master encoder, the genial artist, whose ideas and intention we must re-establish. In fact, I will argue that, more often than not, Hogarth's works contain traces of powerful lines of discourse and *mentalités* that were probably beyond his control. My aim, however, is not to find out what Hogarth thought about or intended regarding his prints. Rather, I wish to provide an exercise in what the French would call *interprétation d'iconotexte*. Given the intertextual and intermedial nature of Hogarth's graphic art, I shall be working with the assumption that his prints contain marked (and probably even more unmarked) allusions to various forms of contemporary discourse.

What follows is an example of an intertextual critical reading of some engravings in the light of ideas and theories developed by Foucault and Althusser. Better known as discourse analysis, this theory is interested in the power relations expressed in the discourse that is generated by the 'state apparatuses' (e.g., Government, School, Church, Mass Media, etc.) in their attempts to address and interest the individual in society, with the ultimate aim of making people conform to pre-established patterns of behaviour and thinking. If Hogarth's prints may be studied as fabrics in which the lines of past and present verbal and visual discourse establish fascinating knots and nodes, they should also contain traces of those power lines that lie at the heart of each society and mingle with *mentalités* – so much so that we find it extremely difficult to separate one from the other.

In February 1724, Hogarth, then a young engraver, published his first independent graphic satire. Uncommissioned, it bears the title *Masquerades and Operas* (illus. 60) and, together with *A Just View of the British Stage* (illus. 11) produced in the same year, constitutes Hogarth's conservative attack on 'the bad taste of the town', which is the sub-title of *Masquerades and Operas*. According to the artist's own words (always an interesting, though unreliable, commentary), 'the then reigning follies were lashd [sic]' in this picture.[1] The print shows, in the foreground, a man who calls for 'waste paper for shops' while carting away master-works of English drama. Carelessly heaped together in the wheelbarrow of this pedlar, book editions of Shakespeare, Otway, Congreve, Dryden, Addison and (in the second state of the engraving) 'Ben John[son]' are on their way to 'Pastem', a trunk-maker. The sheet bearing the title *Pasquin No. XCV* refers to a journal dedicated to art and literature. The potential readers for these works seem to be interested in the other attractions surrounding the books on all sides. These popular forms of drama and opera (including hybrid versions such as ballad operas, pantomimes and harlequinades) and the puppet theatres and masquerades were then flourishing; but they were soon to be displaced by more 'polite genres'.[2]

In the left part of *Masquerades and Operas* a satyr and a fool lead the crowd into the Haymarket opera house, where they are already expected by the famous impresario John James Heidegger (shown looking down from a window). A well-known magician by the name of Faux is also giving performances in this building, and his name serves as a polysemous sign (a sign-board, a name, a warning in French), as a form of the visual and verbal punning that Hogarth almost always integrates in his graphic satires. Similarly, the showcloth above the

Could new dumb Fauftus, to reform the Age,
Conjure up Shakefpear's or Ben Johnfon's Ghoft,
They'd blufh for fhame, to see the Englifh Stage
Debauch'd by fooleries, at so great a coft.

What would their Manes say? should they behold
Monfters and Malquerades, where usefull Plays
Adorn'd the fruitfull Theatre of old,
And Rival Wits contended for the Bays.

Price 1 Shilling 1724

60 William Hogarth, *Masquerades and Operas* ('The Bad Taste of the Town'), 1724, etching and engraving (first state).

entrance arcade is yet another ambiguous sign: although implicitly mocking the way aristocrats waste their money on Italian stars, it advertises operas.

On the other side of the street additional signs and figures vie for the attention of the audience. Here, in the theatre of John Rich, the trailblazer in the highly successful new genre of pantomime, a harlequinade entitled 'Dr Faustus' is to be performed. The whole iconography of Hogarth's print suggests that some people must be held responsible for the evidently bad, perhaps even dangerous, taste of the general public. The culprits can be found in the background where, in front of Burlington Gate, three aristocrats adore the figure-topped structure. The rhetoric of the print argues that it is the aristocrats, with their preference for Italian and French art and ideas, who have brought about the deplorable state of English culture depicted in this scene.[3]

The rhetorical means employed in this engraving urge us to believe its message. There is, to begin with, a sophisticated mixture of visual and verbal signs with multiple meanings, including those providing a realistic effect (a 'real' scene in London, 'genuine' people such as Fawkes/Faux, Heidegger etc.), which create what Genette terms 'vraisemblance'.[4] The paratext (i.e., the verses accompanying the first and second states of the image) supports this reading. Like the visual rhetoric, the verses of the second state argue that the precious and useful classics are no longer read, having been replaced by the superficial entertainments of commercialized culture:

> O how refin'd how elegant we've grown!
> What noble *Entertainments* Charm the Town!
> Whether to hear the *Dragon's* roar we go,
> Or gaze surpriz'd on *Fawke's* matchless Show,
> Or to the *Opera's* or to the *Masques*,
> To eat up *Ortelans* and empty Flasques
> And rifle Pies from Shakespeare's clinging Page,
> Good Gods! how great's the gusto of the Age.

But the conservative, if not reactionary, argument of Hogarth's print is not new. And if we look more closely at the satire of the time, we notice that the artist merely repeats a stereotype (classical works now only serve as waste-paper) that had already been in vogue around 1710 and was used a few years after that for similar purposes (a critique of popular culture) by Swift and Fielding. Hogarth's *Masquerades and Operas* is thus part of the bourgeois discourse in early eighteenth-century England that first conquered the organs policing public taste (for instance, periodicals such as the *Tatler* and *Spectator*) and then launched an attack on particular forms of entertainment in modern mass culture.[5] The guardians of the rising bourgeois aesthetics were especially concerned with what Pierre Bourdieu terms 'la distinction', that is, the attempt of social groups to create distinctions by trying to prove the superiority of (their own) specific tastes over other, and especially neighbouring, ones. This usually works through the establishment of highly exclusive canons. As the fair and the theatre became interfused, the moral fear of contamination grew among the new journalistic arbiters of taste, such as Addison, Steele and, a little later, Dr Johnson. Looking for 'distinction', the speakers for the rising middle class tried to define what separated high from low culture. Canons of literature was one means. Putting down popular entertainments was another. Beginning in the later part of the century, the grotesque related to the culture of folk humour as well as carnivalesque forms were denied the status of polite entertainment. Gottsched's

61 William Hogarth, *The Enraged Musician*, 1741, etching and engraving (second state).

demand in Germany that the character of Harlequin be expelled from what he termed the 'serious and respectable stage' found open ears in England; it was merely a symptom of the gradual exclusion of popular forms of entertainment, including reading-matter for plebeians, from public life. The term culture was redefined by the middle class; this meant that popular culture became branded as merely the occupation of the vulgar in contrast to the more purely intellectual pleasures that characterized the refined and educated.[6]

It seems to me that during the celebration of the rise of the novel, literary criticism has been ominously silent about the dark sides that accompanied that act of liberation of the middle class within the larger matrix of cultural consumption. A suppression and then a loss of cultural forms of entertainment occurred in the so-called Age of Enlightenment; it is in the early part of the century especially that we can find these forms. Hogarth was initially on the side of the conservative guardians of bourgeois taste and morality. Like many other artists he looked for a camp to join, starting out as an emulator and imitator. But his graphic work displays a growing awareness of the negative, repressive, development in the discursive policing of cultural consumption. If in 1724 he still voiced the arguments of bourgeois elite culture, the engraving *The Enraged Musician* (1741) provides a radically different evaluation of popular culture (illus. 61): ballads and Gay's *The Beggar's Opera* appear together with a representative of high culture (the musician in the window), and the rhetoric of the picture now scrutinizes and criticizes both forms of entertainment, giving preference to neither one of them.[7]

The commercialization in the eighteenth century of art and literature as part of cultural consumption is undeniable, but it is also the case that people continued to read Shakespeare and other high cultural works.[8] If Hogarth's prints from the 1720s and early 1730s take a stand both ideologically and rhetorically on the issue of what is acceptable in cultural consumption, we must resist the temptation to believe the visual rhetoric of the pictures. They are not illustrations of socio-cultural phenomena that can be used as 'objective' historical evidence; they are tendentious palimpsests or visual re-presentations of pictures and texts that must be analysed as interpretations.

Therefore, when I read Hogarth's prints it is not their socio-cultural background that I find most interesting, but rather their partisan encoding in a new satirical form of other verbal and visual discourse. What makes Hogarth's graphic art fascinating for me is not its ironical commentary on eighteenth-century life, fascinating though that may be. I am intrigued by the sense-making arrangement of signifiers, the incorporation of texts, and the seductive appeal to *mentalités* harbouring stereotypes, fixed ideas and prejudices from popular thought and art. Conflating verbal and visual signs, low and high forms of art and literature, and allegorical elements from what is beyond doubt an iconoclastic (if occasionally conservative) viewpoint, Hogarth's graphic satires can be a paradise for the semiotician. Unfortunately, this paradise also contains mazes in which one can easily get lost. Exploring the allusive signs and complex sign-systems in Hogarth's prints, I am also interested in an archaeology of *mentalités* as suggested by Foucault,[9] in the exploration of what is never said (and perhaps cannot be expressed) but is always present.[10] I want to uncover not merely the hidden texts in the pictures but especially their semantic (progressive and/or repressive) functions, for it is precisely in the thorough exploitation of the semantic potential of ambiguous signs, and not in authorial intention, that I perceive the value of Hogarth's art.

Complementing what I have written elsewhere on the function of reading-matter in Hogarth's prints (e.g., the Bible, crime literature, ballads, conduct books, and erotica),[11] I now want to focus on Hogarth's depiction of what I call 'official' discourse. This is a generic term for publications intended for a large audience: the Pastoral Letters and the Acts of Parliament, including the organs in which they were sometimes advertised (the newspapers). These publications can be understood as attempts by the Church and the State to exercise control with the help of texts.

As a distinct and widely known form of discourse, the Anglican Pastoral Letter assumes a semantic function that, particularly in *A Harlot's Progress* of 1732, must not be underestimated. There is sufficient historical evidence to prove the importance of the Pastoral Letter for the eighteenth century. Thus the Letters of the then Bishop of London, Edmund Gibson, who turns out to be one of the victims of the satire in the *Harlot's Progress* series, were boosted to reach a wide public. Frequently announced in newspapers, they appeared in large editions, they were reprinted and, more often than not, reappeared in 'neat Pocket Volumes' that were again heavily hyped in contemporary periodicals. The fact that the Pastoral Letter, being an extremely well known if not necessarily 'popular' form of 'official' discourse, also became the butt of satire, only contributed to its publicity.[12] Alluding to it in his graphic art, Hogarth could be sure that everybody knew this particular form of writing.

In plate 3 of *A Harlot's Progress* a Pastoral Letter lies on the stool, between the servant and the heroine who is to be arrested (illus. 62). The addressee(s) of the Letter cannot be identified (the text ends after 'to'). We might read this as an empty sign that has something to tell about the effect of the Bishop's Letter on two of his flock. In the open drawer, on the right, appears another letter that may serve as a continuation or even as a key to the 'unfinished' Pastoral Letter, for in this second epistle the addressee's name is mentioned: M[ary or Moll?] Hackabout is of course a telling name that denotes a person and connotes a profession. Hogarth's image does not make clear what the Pastoral Letter is actually concerned with. We are told, however, that it is very useful – it serves the Harlot as a wrapper for her butter. Since Moll could have availed herself of the letter (from a lover or client?) in the drawer for this purpose, the misuse of the Pastoral Letter constitutes an important semantic message. However, it is again typical of Hogarth's subversive art that the signifier (the Letter from the Bishop) creates indeterminacy rather than clarity when we explore its relations. We cannot doubt that Moll Hackabout could read the Letter if she wanted to, for the series makes clear repeatedly that the Harlot has achieved at the least a rudimentary level of literacy (in this scene, for instance, a paramour has written her a letter; and in plate 1 she (or

Plate 3.

62 William Hogarth, *A Harlot's Progress – 3*, 1732, etching and engraving (first state).

someone in her family) has addressed a note, now attached to the neck of a goose, to her 'Lofing Cosen in Tems Stret in London'). Perhaps she has even read the Pastoral Letter. But her misuse of the paper, and the discourse the sign stands for, surely indicates that the contents of the Letter are of no interest to her.

As far as the subject of the Letter is concerned, it is relevant to know that the Bishop used Pastoral Letters as a polemical and ideological weapon against the writings of Thomas Woolston, a Deist he pursued and sued.[13] Armed with this information we can recognize that the Pastoral Letter on the harlot's stool has not one but several functions. As a visual sign it refers to the attempt of the Anglican Church, or rather the Bishop, to exert discursive influence; as a sign representing a text (and the contents of that text), it also indicates the uselessness of the Letter for the addressees in the image (Moll and her servant). The disdainful use of the Pastoral Letter can therefore be interpreted as a reaction of the poor, as an indication of the irrelevance to the underclass of the theological controversy between the established

Church and Deists such as Woolston.[14] Finally, the Bishop's Letter is also a signifier designating a genre or corpus of texts produced by Anglican churchmen.

What this scene shows, then, is an unsuccessful attempt on the part of the Church to influence a (lower) part of society with the help of an established form of discourse. There is an implicit criticism here of the absence of the writer/author of the Letter, who should be looking after his sheep ('pastoral' recalls the role of the shepherd). But Bishop Gibson, who supported Walpole, engages in theological disputes that serve not his sheep but his own career. As an inactive writer of useless letters the Bishop is, ultimately, also responsible for Moll's tragic failure: from this scene, we can look backwards and forwards in the series, and in each case we discover clergymen, especially Anglicans, who fail in their capacity as shepherds because, like the Bishop, they are driven by self-interest. Like the doctors, lawyers and judges, clergymen constitute merely one of the many social groups that are branded as parasites in Hogarth's art. Thus, in plate 3 of *A Harlot's Progress* we also find a portrait of another theologian (at the left) on the wall (illus. 59). This is Henry Sacheverell (1674–1724) who, despite his inflammatory anti-Government sermons given in 1709, managed a lucrative career. In his usual 'accidental' manner, Hogarth shows Sacheverell beside the portrait of another 'great' man, the highwayman Macheath from *The Beggar's Opera*. The position – one might even say constellation – of the pictures on the wall invites a comparison between the highwayman and the theologian and also between the clergymen to whom the visual and verbal signifiers allude (the portrait and the Pastoral Letter). Selfishness and cruelty is the hallmark of the clergymen in Hogarth's satires. In the final plate of the series on the Harlot, for instance, a representative of the Church of England marks the dramatic high-point of egoism around the dead Harlot (illus. 63). Entirely ruled by sexuality, he masturbates another harlot near the coffin.

Looking back through the series we recognize that the Bishop of London's Letter and person also contribute to the meaning of plates 1 and 2. Moll's arrival in London (illus. 13) is depicted as the exploitation of an innocent girl by a corrupt society, which is one of the series' major themes. In terms of signifiers or emblems in the picture, one could also read her fate as that of a silly goose (in the foreground at right) trying to find her 'Lofing Cosen'. Behind Moll Hackabout, another selfish parson neglects his office because he is more interested in deciphering the address on a letter of recommendation to the Bishop than in the life of the girl next to him (illus. 65). The address of the letter promises a

63 William Hogarth, *A Harlot's Progress – 6*, 1732, etching and engraving (first state).

64 William Hogarth, *A Harlot's Progress – 2*, 1732, etching and engraving (first state).

65 Detail from Hogarth's *A Harlot's Progress* – 1.

career. With his eyes fixed only on his letter, the clergyman does not notice the impending catastophes nearby: the symbolic tumbling of the buckets and (to come) the more tragic fall and death of the innocent country girl who is already surrounded by human vultures. The parson will prevent neither fall. Again, the implication is that the discourse and the person of the Bishop of London, marginal though they may seem in this and other cases, generate fatal consequences.

One might of course also construct an author-oriented theory in the case of the Pastoral Letter. Always concerned with Hogarth's intention, Paulson, for instance, is of the opinion that the artist's satirical allusions to the misbehaviour of the Anglican clergy are an indication of 'something obsessive' provoked by personal motives. It is indeed tempting to read *A Harlot's Progress* in view of the fact that, shortly before 1690, Hogarth's father probably came to London in the company of Edmund Gibson. Whereas Gibson rose to the most powerful position in the Anglican Church, Richard Hogarth, an educated but poor man, attained the less attractive position of inmate in the debtors' prison.[15] But reading Hogarth's graphic art primarily under such biographical aspects (trying to explain authorial intention, motives and themes with recourse to allegedly important events in the artist's life) seems to me to be both speculative and reductionist. As I indicated in chapter One, I want to stick to what is expressed in the engravings, to an analysis of the signifiers and their arrangement. As far as the Pastoral Letter is concerned, it can be stated that the series on the Harlot plays with the meaning and importance of the Letter as a form of 'official' (Anglican) discourse.

66 Detail from illus. 64, Hogarth's *A Harlot's Progress – 2*.

Sometimes the allusions to this reading-matter and those that produced it are less obvious than in plates 1 and 3 of the *Harlot's Progress*. The Bishop of London, for instance, also makes an appearance in the second plate (illus. 64), although it is rather difficult to identify him in the paintings of Moll's keeper. To a large degree, meaning in this scene depends on the relations we establish between the pictures on the wall and between the pictures and the people. It is not quite clear whether these are real paintings or part of the tapestry: the door cuts into a 'painting', suggesting that the pictures are merely a *trompe-l'œil*, which opens another fascinating dimension for the understanding of the entire scene. The painting on the right, if painting it is, represents a biblical scene from 2 Samuel 6 (illus. 66). In the Bible, which Hogarth frequently introduces with such pictorial allusions, it is Jehovah who kills the impious Uzzah (who is not a Levite) when the latter reaches out to steady the Ark. But in Hogarth's scene a mitred Anglican bishop has been substituted for Jehovah's vengeance. In the painting on the wall, the bishop stabs Uzzah in the back. Beneath and beside the biblical scene, two small portraits are attached to the wall. These have been identified as the portraits of two Deists, Thomas Woolston and Samuel Clarke. I have already mentioned that Gibson attacked Woolston in his Pastoral Letters. As a result of these diatribes, Woolston was found guilty and went to prison where, lacking the money to buy his way out, he eventually died. This contemporary background allows us to make the relation between the 'killing bishop' (a Levite in the original text) and the impure (Deist) Uzzah-Woolston.[16]

In this second picture of the series, the Pastoral Letter and its author play a marginal, though not unimportant, part in the relations between objects and people, relations that we must recognize and pursue to make sense of the details. Moll is surrounded by works of art. They are the property of her Jewish lover. But neither she nor he are alert to the iconotexts on the wall – to them both they are decorative, like furniture,[17] i.e., signs that count not for their content or meaning but rather for the social status they indicate. If Moll or her lover could understand the meaning suggested by the signifiers in the paintings, the scene tells us, they might escape their individual destinies. Moll's life ends in disaster (suggested in the next plate), and the fate of the Jewish merchant is indicated by the cuckold's horns which the tapestry (or rather the perspective we are given in the image) places above his head.

Summarizing the functions of Hogarth's graphic treatment of the attempt by the Church to influence members of the lower class with the help of the Pastoral Letter, one notices several ironic levels. We witness how a powerful ecclesiastic tries to propagate his opinion with what is surely a repressive form of writing, for Gibson uses the Letter to warn against Deist ideas. At the same time, however, the relevant pictures in *A Harlot's Progress* also show that the attempt fails miserably. It fails because the potential readers of the Letter are not interested in its discourse or ignore it (perhaps because they feel that these texts ultimately serve the purposes of those who write them), and because the readers are instinctively opposed to the aims of the text: they do not want to be conditioned and socialized in the prescriptive ways outlined in the Letter. Hogarth's prints discussed above thus dramatize and comment on a ticklish political problem in the society of his day and age – the relation between power and its exercise or upholding through specific discursive forms. The prints probe the question whether such writing can at all address specific social strata or groups in order to keep them within predetermined limits. The rhetoric of the prints seems to suggest they could not, at least as far as the lower echelons of society were concerned.

The contemptuous attitude of lower-class readers towards the 'official' printed word is also a typical feature in Hogarth's depiction of other discursive forms produced by the state apparatuses. Conduct books, for instance, as well as laws and proclamations (in the form of broadsheets) share similar aims with the Pastoral Letter; newspapers, however, are a special case. Before turning to Hogarth's graphic commentary on the treatment of printed Acts of Parliament by the common people, I must at least mention the artist's most persuasive depiction of the conflict between the individual and the repressive discourse of society. It is in *Industry and Idleness* that success and failure in English society are closely associated with the behaviour of the reader. Throughout the series the Industrious Apprentice appears in the role of the diligent and pious (but also hypocritical) reader, whereas Tom Idle's tragedy is a partial consequence of his rejection of society's prescriptive discourse. To the very hour of his death he refuses to read and honour the written word in conduct books, indentures and the Bible. As with the Harlot, it is not a question of Tom Idle's ability to read: what Hogarth (who gave Idle his own facial features) stresses is the apprentice's refusal to obey commands and to agree to the (written) demands of society as expressed in what I term 'official' discourse. In the first plate of the series (illus. 67) Tom neglects *The Prentice's Guide* (by comparison his colleague's copy is in mint condition); later on, he defiantly throws his indenture into the water (illus. 68). Finally, when he becomes a reader (of the Bible) on his way to the gallows (illus. 69), we see how society subjects and takes possession of the penitent victim by delivering him into the hands of a fanatic Methodist and by exploiting the story of his life: the ballad sold in the foreground indicates that the tragic life and death of the rebel from the lower class will now serve as a moral warning. Ballads and similar texts will mythologize him for didactic reasons. He has finally returned to the fold of society, but at the cost of his freedom and life.

One tends to forget sometimes that *Industry and Idleness* dramatizes two kinds of tragedy. To be sure, there is the fate of the one who tries to preserve his personal liberty by rejecting all forms of writing and the obeisance it implies. But the success of the Industrious Apprentice, Francis Goodchild, a keen reader of Bibles and 'prentice's guides and laws, is a success only at first glance. It speaks for the artistic quality of Hogarth's series that the series also suggests a kind of tragedy for Goodchild, for it is precisely because of his reading and the concomitant acceptance of hierarchic social order that Goodchild becomes a prisoner of conventions. He is, finally, also a victim, caught in his seemingly powerful position: the last plate (illus. 70) presents the prisoner in the Lord Mayor's coach while the ghost of his 'prentice friend hovers in the corner – represented by a broadsheet, i.e., writing/ discourse.[18]

Members of the lower class in Hogarth's graphic art show extreme

67 William Hogarth, *Industry and Idleness* – *1* ('The Fellow 'Prentices at their Looms'), 1747, etching and engraving (second state).

68 William Hogarth, *Industry and Idleness* – *5* ('The Idle 'Prentice turn'd away, and sent to Sea'), 1747, etching and engraving (second state).

69 William Hogarth, *Industry and Idleness – 11* ('The Idle 'Prentice Executed at Tyburn'), 1747, etching and engraving (second state).

70 William Hogarth, *Industry and Idleness – 12* ('The Industrious 'Prentice Lord-Mayor of London'), 1747, etching and engraving (second state).

disrespect for any kind of written law. This rejection of repressive discourse is perhaps best depicted in *Strolling Actresses Dressing in a Barn* (illus. 71). With the Licencing Act of 1737 Walpole had finally succeeded in silencing the theatre as a forum and medium of political criticism, in which Fielding had been poised to reach the summit of his career as a dramatist. Excepting Drury Lane and Lincoln's Inn Fields, all theatres were closed down. (This action proved to be the spring for Fielding's new career as a novelist.[19]) Henceforth, theatre companies had to meet in private houses or they had to invent 'social' pretexts ('tea and coffee') to perform plays. In *Strolling Actresses*, a copy of the Licencing Act – the 'Act against Strolling Players' – lies on a crown in the left foreground. The fact that it is shown with a crown may suggest regal approval of the Act.[20] The manner in which it is treated, however, establishes a semantic parallel with the 'useful' function of the Pastoral Letter in plate 3 of *A Harlot's Progress*. In this barn, the Act has been entirely deprived of its intended function as a repressive text (illus. 72). Like the Pastoral Letter, it serves a new, practical purpose. Those for whom the actual text of the 'Act against Strolling Players' was written thus resist in their own way, accepting the *paper* but not the text it bears: the mother feeding her child uses a sheet as a bib. Additional signifiers support this satirical message. The visual arrangement in the engraving of the Act and the crown, and of the crown beside a chamber-pot, invites a comparison between these details. For instance, we can see that structural similarity (two receptacles beside each other suggest likeness) identifies the fecal contents of the chamber-pot with the legal-'royal' contents of the crown. At the same time, this seemingly accidental and (in political terms) rather daring constellation expresses the opinion of the actors *vis-à-vis* the 'official' discourse of the state and Crown.

In Hogarth's *An Election Entertainment*, published in 1755, irony becomes more intricate in the playing with signifiers, indicating both the uselessness and ineffectiveness of another legal text (illus. 73). In the right foreground, one visually marked text lies on a platter with pipes and a tobacco bag marked 'Kirton's Best'. Significantly, the title of the 'Act against Bribery and Cor[ruption]' is 'corrupted' in itself (illus. 74). The iconography of the picture indicates that at this election meeting the Act is supposed to be hidden or ignored. But like the Pastoral Letter and the Act against the players, it is put to a rather useful purpose that again comments on the refusal of potential readers to honour the textual injunctions on the paper. The paper of the Act, not its contents, is accepted, here serving as a pipe-lighter.

In each of the prints discussed above Hogarth presents his satirical

71 William Hogarth, *Strolling Actresses Dressing in a Barn*, 1738, etching and engraving (second state).

72 Detail from illus. 71, *Strolling Actresses Dressing in a Barn*.

73 William Hogarth, 'An Election Entertainment', *Four Prints of an Election – 1*, 1755, etching and engraving (fourth state).

74 Detail from illus. 73, *Four Prints of an Election – 1*.

view of merely one legal text, and especially of its effect upon the common people, who prefer the paper to the text. In the different states of *Beer Street* (1751, third state in 1759), Hogarth juxtaposes 'official' discourse in several forms and in various texts; they all vie for the attention of the reading public (illus. 75).[21] At the right, we see some books. Destined 'For Mr Pastem the Trunk maker in Pauls Ch[urch] Y[ar]d', they remind us of the classics in the wheelbarrow of the pedlar in *Masquerades and Operas*. There is a difference, however, in that the iconography of *Beer Street* implies the opposite of the earlier print; *Beer Street* argues that the literary and critical works depicted in this scene are really of no value, pleading for their use as wastepaper. The books – in a pun on their use and destination, Lichtenberg calls them 'corpses', or remains of brilliant ideas[22] – are labelled 'Modern Tragedys Vo. 12'; 'Hill on Royal Societies'; 'Turnbul[l] on Ant[ient] Painting'; 'Politicks Vol: 9999'; and 'Lauder on Milton'. For Hogarth's contemporaries, these titles were self-explanatory. 'Dr', or Sir, John Hill (?1716-75) wrote pseudo-scientific treatises; his *A Dissertation on Royal Societies* (1750) was the result of the Royal Society's refusal to make the illustrious would-be doctor a member. George Turnbull's *A Treatise upon Ancient Painting* (1740) praised the Old Masters of painting, based almost entirely on surviving descriptions of lost works. And William Lauder (d. 1771) wrote *An Essay on Milton's Use and Imitation of the Moderns in his 'Paradise Lost'* (1750) to prove that the great English author had plagiarized *Paradise Lost* from seventeenth-century Latin poets. Lauder's fraud was exposed by John Douglas, who was to become Bishop of Salisbury.

The decoding of the other texts in the picture poses greater difficulties that reflect the hermeneutic problems critics still have with the explication of the print.[23] Meaning depends on the structural relations the reader establishes between the texts (and the persons). One general 'message' or point may of course be found in the very juxtaposition of these publications. It is the simultaneous presentation of the King's Speech, visually 'supported' as it were by *The Daily Advertiser* beside the fat craftsmen, and the ballad that fascinates the fishmongers, which suggests comparison and, ultimately perhaps, similarity. The easily readable excerpt from the speech of the monarch urges his British subjects to boost trade and commerce: 'Let me earnestly recom[m]end to you the Advancement of Our Commerce and cultivating the Arts of Peace, in which you may depend on My hearty Concurrence and Encouragement'. Those depicted at the left will certainly profit from this positive speech. Therefore, they do not have to read the text, nor will they (mis)use it.

In contrast to this treatment of a (semi-) legal text, the ballad finds eager readers. It is from the pen of one of Hogarth's friends, John Lockman. In his famous and popular 'Herring' poems Lockman (as secretary of the Free British Fishery) compared the honest profits of the fishing industry with the illusory and empty promises of investors and swindlers advertising for South American gold-mines (see, for instance, Lockman's *The Shetland Herring and Peruvian Gold Mine* of 1751). In this respect there is a difference between the Kings's Speech and the ballad, although both can be considered as forms of advertising, that is, economic discourse.[24] Nevertheless, they do constitute a form of discourse that addresses the common people and intends to allot them a role in the commercial sphere.

If one reads the texts from this point of view, one immediately discovers a series of details that form a sort of counter-argument in the picture, disturbing the superficial expression of satisfaction and pride. What disturbs the impression, visually and ideologically, is, for instance, the pawnbroker's house at the right. A decoding of this dilapidated building in dualistic terms of the good (beer drinking) and bad (gin consumption) dichotomy, or in terms of cause and effect, would of course contrast the house of 'N. PINCH, PAWN BROKER' (in *Beer Street*) with that of 'S. GRIPE, PAWN BROKER' in *Gin Lane* (illus. 76). But it is precisely such thinking in dualistic terms which the print of *Beer Street* foregrounds and finally explodes. In fact, one could argue that, especially in conjunction with *Gin Lane*, it 'turns on the tension created by the presence or the operation of opposites'.[25]

Take the pawnbroker's house in *Gin Lane*. How are we to associate it with the other signifiers in the print, and with those in *Beer Street*? Is it merely accidental that the perspective of the image, in a kind of *trompe-l'œil* effect, appears to force us to associate the pawnbroker's sign with the statue of George I whose head it seems to 'crown'? And what is the relation? The ways critics have answered these questions demonstrate both the semantic richness of Hogarth's work and the fallacies of readings based on author intention. Barry Wind, at one extreme, believes in the 'establishment tenor' of the print and maintains that the statue of George I 'emphasizes Hogarth's sympathies with Hanoverian ideas and brewer interests', but then concedes that the 'motif may be only an allusion to well-known Hanoverian greed and tightfistedness'. He reads the distance of Church and state in this image as a positive contrast to the dissipation of the gin drinkers. At the other extreme, Paulson believes that the pawnbroker's sign above the monarch's head is an ironic halo commenting on the collusion of Church and state. Paulson tells us that the prohibitive Tippling Act that increased the

75 William Hogarth, *Beer Street*, 1759, etching and engraving (third state).

76 William Hogarth, *Gin Lane*, 1759, etching and engraving (second state).

price of gin was modified in 1747, when the distillers petitioned for the right to retail. As a consequence, gin consumption rose substantially, and in 1750, in some parts of London, one in every five houses was a gin shop. But Paulson does not want to support his reading with social evidence; rather, he trusts in authorial intention, arguing that 'whether or not Hogarth had this information, he assumes some such situation when he includes the spire of St George's in *Gin Lane* and juxtaposes with this print of the emaciated gin drinkers the prosperity of the fat merchants and the royal urge to greater commerce in *Beer Street*'.[26]

But why obstruct one's reading of the print with Hogarth's intention, even though Hogarth's own commentary on the series, in *Autobiographical Notes*, seems to confirm a dualistic reading?[27] Listening to the voices in the picture, *qua* signifiers, we must admit that the visual arrangement of the pawnbroker's sign above the monarch's head is not accidental. It is a consequence of perspective. Perspective in art is what rhetoric is in writing (as recent art historians, in particular Mieke Bal and Hubert Damisch,[28] have shown). Perspective urges, even forces us, to take a particular viewpoint. The problem with perspective is that in images with realistic details, such as Hogarth's prints, one tends to take it for granted, when as a matter of fact it is the most powerful sign for the real in modern art, a sign we frequently overlook precisely because it is so obvious. Hence, on the basis of the perspective in *Gin Lane* one can argue that we may indeed connect the (sign of the) pawnbroker's shop with (the architectural sign representing) George I, and, by implication, the left side and its semiotic 'connection' with the left side in *Beer Street* and its verbal connection with the monarch. Such a decoding will indeed come close to Paulson's reading – but *sans* authorial intention.

Similarly, the ostensibly happy man painting the signboard represents not one but several messages, depending on how we relate him to the signs (including the human beings) of which he is a part. He has been employed by the fat merchants and artists as a gesture of generosity on their part; but the emaciated painter, apparently even content with his new role, is not an artist anymore, he has become a simple painter of signs. This society has no need for real art.

'Official discourse', which appears here in conjunction and collaboration with the self-satisfied burghers, is further subverted when one considers that *Beer Street* is not a single picture. Together with *Gin Lane* it forms a set. More often than not, meaning in Hogarth's graphic art is created by the serial aspect, by what Frédéric Ogée has aptly termed 'les parcours sériels' that invite the eye to wander, to compare and to err (Ogée plays on the meanings of the French term *erre*, which like the English equivalent implies going astray, to be wrong, and, in its obsolete sense, to ambulate).[29] The serial aspect brings to the fore parallels (e.g., the church that stands far away in both of the prints) that undermine the meaning suggested by the titles and the verses accompanying the pictures. These parallels point out to us that the engravings do not merely comment on the consumption of good and bad kinds of alcohol; they also treat of the presence and absence of the state apparatuses (the Church, the Crown, the Government) represented by texts and architectural signs (the church spire, the statue of the monarch). In this respect one can agree with Paulson's reading of the series, when he argues that 'the basic cause and effect relationship would be understood by the poor: not that beer drinking leads to prosperity and gin drinking to want, but the reverse. Rather, beer drinking is a product of prosperity and gin drinking of want'.[30] Therefore, what at first glance looks like a praise of commerce and the acceptance of the discourse supporting it proves to be highly ambiguous in the serial context.

As a set, *Beer Street* and *Gin Lane* comprise an iconotext that can be read as an ironical comment on the paratext. This paratext is made up of the caption and the titles. In fact, the moral verses on the plates were written by Hogarth's good friend the Revd James Townley. Together with the seemingly obvious titles they do not complement the prints, as even recent critics still maintain;[31] rather, they should be seen as a first attempt to provide a comprehensive verbal explanation, an explanation that works with its own stereotypes derived from popular writings and mythology. The texts also appeal to dominating *mentalités* – the prejudiced view of France and French customs, the association of England with beer and liberty, and the glorification of things English:

> Beer, happy Produce of our Isle
> Can sinewy Strength impart,
> And wearied with Fatigue and Toil
> Can chear each manly Heart.
>
> Labour and Art upheld by Thee
> Successfully advance,
> We quaff Thy balmy Juice with Glee
> And Water leave to France.
>
> Genius of Health, thy grateful Taste
> Rivals the Cup of Jove,
> And warms each English generous Breast
> With Liberty and Love.

The caption to *Gin Lane* runs:

> Gin, cursed Fiend, with Fury fraught,
>   Makes human Race a Prey;
> It enters by a deadly Draught,
>   And steals our Life away.
>
> Virtue and Truth, driv'n to Despair,
>   It's Rage compells to fly,
> But cherishes, with hellish Care,
>   Theft, Murder, Perjury.
>
> Damn'd Cup! that on the Vitals preys,
>   That liquid Fire contains
> Which Madness to the Heart conveys,
>   And rolls it thro' the Veins.

The imagery here is also interesting in that it establishes relations less with misery and death (as in the print) but rather with Christian ideas of Satan, sin, and Hell.

These ekphrases of the two prints ignore indeterminacy while promising us clear meanings and messages. The polysemous signs as well as their syntax in the pictures militate against the simple meaning of the verbal text beneath the prints, a text that tries to impose dichotomy, based on dualism and hierachies of meaning, upon constructs that are far more complex than the Revd Townley and contemporary explicators such as Barry Wind would have it.

Indeed, if the Hogarthian visual forms harbour 'a greater potential for doubleness – or openness – of interpretation'[32] than, say, eighteenth-century fictional texts, we should preserve that openness in our reading by focusing on the semiotics of the prints and their reception.[33] Such an approach would allow at least two possibilities even for the eighteenth-century audience. As Paulson writes: 'the poor as well as their betters . . . can go to the visual image and take away the aspects they see through their particular preconceptions. But what the rich will see as peripheral irony, the poor will see as central'.[34] It is the complex referentiality of the iconography of the Hogarthian image that works directly against the conditioned expectation of simple dualistic interpretations. This 'shading' of meaning by introducing signs and constellations of uncertainty makes the viewer's task a difficult one.[35]

For those who still care about this issue, the differences between the first and subsequent states of *Beer Street* may tell us something about Hogarth's changing satirical intentions. More important, however, they also throw some light on the interchangeability of specific signifiers. Take the stout blacksmith at the left, for instance. In the first and second states (illus. 77) he is lifting a Frenchman into the air while

77 William Hogarth, *Beer Street*, 1751, etching and engraving (first state).

brandishing a jug of ale. In the third state of the print (illus. 75), the Frenchman has been replaced with a huge loin of meat (and a pavior making advances to a girl next to a basket of vegetables). One can assume, therefore, that in terms of signifying, the stereotypal, spindly Frenchman serves a satirical function that is similar to that of the meat: the aim is to invite the observer to identify with English patriotism (as a potential spy is being caught) or with Englishness (eating beef or mutton) as such.

But what kind of meat does the blacksmith hold up? In tune with earlier commentators such as Lichtenberg, Paulson believes that it is 'a shoulder of mutton' – and the lower part of the rather small leg would seem to confirm such a reading. Barry Wind, however, has recently argued that the metamorphosis is from a Frenchman into a loin of roast beef, since popular attitudes linked roast beef – and especially roast beef and beer – to 'Englishness'. I think that in this case Wind has a point, for if Englishness is to be expressed here, what better image than a huge chunk of beef.[36] After all, it is roast beef which serves as an *ersatz* for England in Hogarth's *The Gate of Calais* (illus. 93). In any case, both mutton and beef indicate the richness of the country (as opposed to France's *soupe meagre*). In the semantic and structural context in the left-hand corner of *Beer Street*, it seems that roast beef is the more persuasive 'reading'. For the loin of roast beef (assuming that it is beef and not mutton) and the jug of ale are sign types which, in terms of Peircean semiotics, are multifunctional, serving as they do as icons, indices and symbols.[37] I would argue that it is impossible to maintain that one of these categories dominates in the print, and it is precisely this fickle nature of the sign (type) in Hogarth's art that makes it simultaneously realistic, parodic, rich in meaning and deeply fascinating.

The same principle governs the altering of the reading-matter on the table that seems to be wedged between the butcher and the blacksmith. As far as the various genres of 'official' discourse are concerned, it is important that the first state presents two newspapers, *The Gazette* and *The Daily Advertiser*, whereas in the second and later states the King's Speech has been substituted for *The Gazette*. This is, I think, telling: it suggests a connection between these two types of reading-matter. Since they are interchangeable, the satirical and rhetorical function of the newspaper seems to be rather close to, if not identical with, the royal Speech. Although the Speech of the monarch introduces a new, more obviously political, aspect, the fact that his words can and do replace a newspaper should alert us to the common denominator of these forms of discourse. This common ground is their status as rhetoric aiming at the dispersion and sedimentation of an ideology that serves the Government as well as the obese burghers represented in the picture. On the textual level, then, these 'papers' (the Speech and the newspapers) are nothing else but organs of those state apparatuses (as Althusser terms the influential, discourse-producing social institutions) that *seem* to appeal to, and thus create (the illusion of), the relevant subject. Ultimately, however, their aim is the subjection of the subject through an 'appealing' discourse that is coercive rather than liberating or enlightening.[38]

Time and again, Hogarth's graphic works dramatize the ambivalent role of journalistic writing. In fact, for *A Harlot's Progress* and other series, the artist himself was inspired by scandals and sensations reported in the newspapers, and many of his prints cannot be adequately understood without a thorough knowledge of the personal and political feuds fought in the contemporary press.[39] A particularly influential medium of writing, the papers were thus a tool for the 'official' discourse to shape attitudes and *mentalités* in the world of eighteenth-century social consumption. It speaks for the artistic value of Hogarth's *œuvre* that this journalistic discourse is presented for us to ponder, in view of its social and ideological impact. Whenever we see people carrying or reading a newspaper in Hogarth's prints, the papers are more than decorative details or signs creating (the illusion of) quotidian reality: they are essentially signifiers of powerful forces. As with the other forms of potentially coercive discourse discussed above, it is the consequences of its consumption that matter. More often than not Hogarthian prints demonstrate the noxious consequences of this form of consumption. I shall restrict my discussion of the phenomenon to three examples.

In *A Midnight Modern Conversation* (illus. 78), which parodies the two denotative meanings of 'conversation' (a 'conversation piece', a genre of group portraiture, as well as an exchange of words or ideas) in a satire on the different stages of inebration, the man at the far right is characterized by his reading-matter.[40] One conclusion that can be drawn from the minor catastrophe about to occur in this corner is of course that it is precisely the preoccupation with political papers that literally sets the reader on fire. Perhaps he is a politician: the *London Journall* and *The Craftsman* sticking out from his coat-pocket support this interpretation, for they were propaganda organs of, respectively, Walpole and the Opposition. Politicians, the visual rhetoric argues, are not only impractical and unreliable, they are downright dangerous because their 'deep' thinking leads to fatal consequences. These are indicated by the candle put to unintended use by the absent-minded 'politician', and by the sword that menacingly protrudes directly from the papers. Always attentive to such seemingly marginal details, Lichtenberg pointed out that the papers 'rest meaningfully' on the sword while the open mouth of the man beside the 'politician' resembles a crater that is about to erupt in a 'revolution'.[41]

The visual rhetoric of the picture likens the effect of reading political

78 William Hogarth, *A Midnight Modern Conversation*, 1733, etching and engraving (first state).

79 William Hogarth, Detail from *The Times – 2*, 1763, etching and engraving (first state).

80 William Hogarth, *The March to Finchley*, 1750, etching and engraving (eighth
state, retouched by Hogarth, 1761).

papers to the intoxication produced by the consumption of tobacco,
wine and spirits. The 'politician' setting fire to his shirt-cuff instead of
the tobacco in his pipe is a signifier referring to pictures and texts that
readers of the time would have recognized. Hogarth's earlier painting,
The Politician (c. 1730), for instance, employs the same device in that an
absorbed reader's hat is catching fire. Later on, in plate 2 of *The Times*
(illus. 79), Wilkes's anti-Government *North Briton* is nearly ignited by
the candle of 'MS FANNY', the Cock Lane Ghost, suggesting the danger
of journalistic defamation and political journals. The inattentive
'politician' in *A Midnight Modern Conversation* whose sense and senses
have been numbed by the papers also constitutes an allusion to
Fielding's 'Mr Politic' in *The Coffee-House Politician* of 1730, for this
gentleman's dedication to the political press leads to the loss of his
daughter. Becoming absorbed in partisan newspapers, Hogarth's print
argues, is tantamount to drunkenness. Newspapers of this kind are like
alcohol or poison.

   The individual as a potential victim of journalism emerges most
forcefully in Hogarth's *The March to Finchley* (illus. 80) of 1750,
retouched in 1761. One could argue that the young soldier – here an
emblem of England in trouble – in the centre is importuned both by

two women (a pregnant girl and an old hag) and the texts each carries. In tune with the pictorial 'architext' of this detail of the picture (Rubens's painting of *Hercules between Vice and Virtue*), Virtue, here a sutler (a servant or victualler) and ballad singer, carries a portrait of the Duke of Cumberland and the ballad 'God Save our Noble King'. In an equally telling manner, Vice is associated with newspapers. The old woman is a newspaper vendor and a papist (indicated by the cross on her shawl). She is selling three opposition papers: *The Jacobite Journal*, the *London Evening Post* and *The Remembrancer*. The first was actually a satire on Jacobite propaganda (Hogarth's engraving implies that it was read by Jacobites, but it did not appear until 1747) and *The Remembrancer* is both a paper and pun.[42] It is obvious that Hogarth's satire is based on the juxtaposition and association of newspapers and political journalism with vice, danger (Catholicism) and corruption.

A Midnight Modern Conversation and *The March to Finchley* thematize the dispersion of political rhetoric. They depict the individual, the reader, as a highly contested target of noxious journalism that, in turn, is the product and vehicle of social groups and institutions: the Government, the Church, political parties. Both prints incorporate this contest (by way of discourse) for the reader and the attempt to subject him/her to socio-political norms, albeit in terms of satire. Yet journalistic discourse has another function that is perhaps even more important than its role in the contemporary arena of politics. Hogarth highlights this function in his typical 'marginal' manner, almost *en passant* as it were, in the second state of plate 4 of *A Rake's Progress* (illus. 81). As with the different states of *Beer Street*, it is again interesting to note that which has been changed, or rather exchanged: in the second state the group of seven boys on the pavement, in the lower-right corner, occupy the place of the single boy in the first who had his hand on the Rake's cane (illus. 82). There is, then, a semantic relation between the Rake and the boys. One could read this (in the first state) as the taking away of support or, in the revision of the picture, as a comparison of the ways in which the Rake and the boys support themselves. Like the man getting out of his sedan chair, the boys are gamblers, cheats and drinkers.

In a series of astute comparisons between the 'black' boys and the 'white' gentleman (a contrast also suggested by White's gaming-house, at the left, and the sign 'black' at the right), Lichtenberg throws light on the satirical relations in this scene. The chimney-sweep at far right, he points out, does not seem to refer to the Rake, but the latter – like many another gentleman with a white wig – also works his way up by 'creeping through dirty channels'.[43]

81 William Hogarth, *A Rake's Progress – 4*, 1735, etching and engraving (second state).

82 William Hogarth, *A Rake's Progress – 4*, 1735, etching and engraving (first state).

Matthew Chap: XXV. Ve: 21.
Well done thou good and faithfull
Servant thou hast been faithfull
over a few things I will make thee
Ruler over many things.

83 William Hogarth, *Industry and Idleness – 4* ('The Industrious 'Prentice a Favourite, and entrusted by his Master'), 1747, etching and engraving (first state).

Within the small scene in the corner at right, a newspaper adds additional, ambiguous, meaning to the engraving: the left-most boy, probably a bootblack, like his comrade beside him, is smoking a pipe and reading *The Farthing Post*, a cheap, piratical paper. Vending gossip, news and politics, this was the eighteenth-century equivalent of today's *The Sun* newspaper. Whatever conclusions may be drawn from its depiction here (including the allusions to the issue of piracy and to contemporary politics and the Excise Bill of 1733),[44] one cannot ignore the embedding of the sensational paper in the larger matrix of corruption, intoxication and immorality, which is foregrounded in this section of the print. The little reader is also a little politician;[45] like his colleague in *A Midnight Modern Conversation* he is characterized by the fact that he does not notice what is going on. Instead of alerting him to the problems, politics (in writing) absorbs his attention. Although only a minor visual detail, the newspaper nevertheless establishes semantic relations between the boys, the Rake and newspaper consumption.

In terms of journalistic discourse *vis-à-vis* society, however, there is more at stake here. The poor bootblack, we must remember, has nothing else but his paper to read. Indeed, *The Farthing Post* is to him what the cheap, didactic *London Almanack* is to the frugal merchant, Mr West, in plate 4 of *Industry and Idleness* (illus. 83): in each case, the particular reading-matter replaces literature and art. From the bourgeois, educated, point of view, it is *ersatz* reading (both in the German and more derogatory English meanings of the word) – the 'literature' of the common people. If one message that emerges from *Industry and Idleness* is that the diligent reader, Francis Goodchild, is always easy prey for coercive 'official' discourse, one may argue that in plate 4 of *A Rake's Progress*, the bootblack, visually and literally at the bottom of society, will stay there as a result of the thoughtless consumption of tobacco, spirits and an equally noxious journalistic discourse promising information while providing useless entertainment and sensational slander. The poor boy will remain at his lowly social position (a level the Rake has yet to reach) because his reading-matter contributes to the sedimentation of a state of mind, a *mentalité* even, that makes him yearn for gossip while preventing enlightenment.

It would of course be convenient at this point to summarize the functions of 'official' discourse that I have merely touched on here. This is impossible, for the simple reason that such an attempt would crudely simplify the concepts that create sense in Hogarth's graphic art (intertextuality and intermediality) in order to make them applicable to my critical concern. Intermedial readings as I have practiced them imply an undeniable paradox: they arise out of the fact that intertextuality provides meaningful insights into the variety and contradictory nature of discursive systems but also leaves open spaces and unexplored terrain. Jonathan Culler has suggested that 'theories of intertexuality set before us perspectives of unmasterable series, lost origins, endless horizons . . . and . . . in order to work with the concept we focus it – but that focusing may always, to some degree, undermine the general concept of intertextuality in whose name we are working'.[46] Even if, in the case of Hogarth's graphic art, one concentrates exclusively on the iconographic exploration of any single print, one will soon have to recognize that which could be termed a semantic Heissenberg-effect, i.e., the ultimate indeterminacy of such an enterprise,[47] for Hogarth's engravings are complicated constructs in which visual and verbal signifiers (with several levels of meaning), entire sign systems as well as discursive forms, produce iconotexts whose meaning unfolds within the structual and semantic relations of the elements. In this respect, it is important to recall what Derrida has said about indeterminacy. 'Every sign', Derrida argues:

linguistic or non-linguistic, spoken or written, in a small or large unit, can be *cited*, put between quotation marks; in so doing it can break with every given context, engendering an infinity of new contexts in a manner which is absolutely illimitable. This does not imply that the mark is valid outside a context, but on the contrary that there are only contexts without any centre of absolute anchoring.[48]

Indeterminacy in Hogarth's engravings arises because his works engage in playing at the level of signs as well as at that of semiotic systems (e.g., the discursive forms discussed in this chapter) by quoting and questioning texts and contexts while creating new possibilities of understanding.

Still, what can be said about the discursive forms within Hogarth's iconotexts without reducing the complexity of the issue is that the prints dramatize the socio-political use and, even more, the misuse of language and writing. Behind this dramatization lurks a satirical-iconoclastic method Hogarth shared with Swift, who also mocked and attacked the exclusive, noxious jargon developed by social groups to the detriment of other groups.[49] What Hogarth's engravings foreground in their use of such discourse is the attempt of groups and institutions to use writing as a means of gaining influence and dominance.

In this respect Althusser has suggested the analysis of such discursive forms as an expression of the ideology produced by the state apparatuses. Althusser maintains that the traditional Marxist notion of ideology is erroneous in its distinction between 'superstructure' and 'base'. He has argued that ideology is not 'false consciousness' as a result of a system of representation disseminated by the dominant classes in order to mask the capitalist control of the means of production. Rather, he has equated ideology with all systems of representation (political, religious, artistic, juridical etc.), regardless of the social class or interest group that manufactures them. Suggesting an analysis not of the manufacturers but of the systems themselves, which create the illusion of the relevant subject while trying to dominate that subject in his/her very 'interpellation', his position is thus a semiotic one. According to Althusser, who yokes ideology to representation, all sign systems are ideologically freighted. One can thus search for the structures of power within those systems rather than in the relations between 'superstructure' and 'base'.[50]

It seems that Hogarth's prints, even more than literary texts, draw our attention to the reception and the potentially repressive function of discourse. Both Althusser and Foucault perceive the origin of discourse in social institutions (the state, the Church, the school) that constitute and control the nature and knowledge of individuals.[51]

Hogarth's graphic art both shows and participates in the dissemination and sedimentation of these processes in eighteenth-century society – including the reactions of the addressees and potential targets of discourse. However, 'official' discourse as it found expression in the Pastoral Letter, in Acts of Parliament and Royal Speeches and in newspapers, is merely one thread in the intertextual fabric of the engravings. Fabric, a textile term Barthes and Kristeva have applied with much profit to literary texts,[52] is an expression that is more than apposite for Hogarth's weaving of visual and verbal texts in graphic works whose intermedial relations can still fascinate us today.

The Hogarthian image, then, can be studied as a site (with all the architectural and archaeological connotations of that word) where the partisan discourse of the eighteenth century has been encoded in the form of equally partisan artistic comments on cultural and ideological phenomena. I have argued that Hogarth's engravings hold a lot of information in store for us if we abandon the chimerical and speculative aim to reconstruct the artist's intention and focus on a goal that, to my mind, is both more rewarding and more persuasive. That goal is – to return to my archaeological metaphor – the uncovering of discursive strata or, in terms of the Barthian/Kristevan 'network', the unravelling of the woven tissue. One advantage of this approach is that it also promises insights into the schemes (pun intended) of the artist, unveiling not his intention but rather the extent to which his rhetoric depended on pre-established discursive traditions and the concomitant *mentalités*. This means, for example, that Hogarth may have been working within *mentalités* that were too powerful to be resisted. In terms of Lacan's model, one might say that he was working *sous le regard* (under the gaze), that is, in a discursive space he could neither formulate nor change. Scholars interested in the reconstruction of artistic intention will of course find such a view of Hogarth and his work wholly untenable, precisely because it challenges the idea of the genial author in command of his artistic machinery.[53]

Tous les gouts sont dans la nature.

84 Engraved frontispiece to *Les Petits bougres au manège*, (?)1791.

5 Obscenity and Body Language in the French Revolution

Doesn't the best subversion consist in disfiguring the codes rather than destroying them?

Barthes, *Sade, Fourier, Loyola*

History, then, faces the writer like the advent of a necessary choice between several morals of language; it forces him to give meaning to Literature according to circumstances beyond his control.

Barthes, *Le Degré zéro de l'écriture*

Rhetoric, by shaping meaning, constructs reality through the construction of the meanings it offers reality to work with.

Bal, *Reading 'Rembrandt'*

In a final case study, I here turn to illustrations produced during the French Revolution. My aim is not to show any sort of chronological development in image-text relations. This chapter is to be understood as another exercise in archaeological critical digging. I want to demonstrate that if Hogarthian images may be read as encoded fabrics made up of complex allusions to verbal and visual discourse, the allegedly obscene prints from the French Revolutionary period yield similarly interesting findings once we explore them with the tools provided by semiotics and discourse analysis.

Some of the illustrations I discuss in this chapter have been labelled 'pornographic' or 'obscene'. Historians and art historians have dealt with them only reluctantly, for reasons that are as interesting as are the images. Sometimes they have been described as revolutionary because their allegedly 'radical' rhetoric seems to fit historical concepts. My aim is to show that these images present fascinating palimpsests combining visual and verbal discourse borrowed from both popular and elite cultures. One of the more suprising insights I have to offer is that Revolutionary obscene imagery works with a rhetoric that only seems to be radical; my analysis suggests, on the contrary, that the apparently shocking images work with restrictive and even repressive allusions that constantly appeal to popular *mentalités* that are easily mistaken for revolutionary attitudes.

With the celebrations of the bicentenary of the French Revolution safely behind us we may now turn to what Bernadette Fort has aptly termed the 'fictions of the French Revolution', that is the strategies and explanatory models devised by the historians, art historians and literary critics who have tried to explain an event that has become hopelessly fictionalized and mediated. There are two reasons for this: first because the Revolution was extensively narrated, explained and mythified by its own actors, and because subsequent generations of commentators from various disciplines seized on these fictional paradigms while producing their own interpretations that have period-ically eliminated earlier models before being themselves replaced.[1]

What follows in this chapter is, to a certain extent, my personal comment on two recent phenomena that I take to be inextricably related. It seems to me that if the festive events in Paris over the past years were *une affaire d'état* (pun intended) orchestrated and, indeed, staged by the Government and the upper echelons of the bourgeoisie, the symbolic exclusion of the common people (expressed, for instance, in the reservation during public celebrations of several rows of chairs for the *crème de la crème*) has found an equally disturbing and (for me) distressing equivalent in the handling of Revolutionary obscenity by historians and art historians. My suspicion is that, with few exceptions, historiography in particular has been unable to deal meaningfully with an admittedly disturbing (although not necessarily revolutionary) kind of discourse, precisely because the analysts feel uneasy with radical (gutter) language and imagery and cannot escape the constrictions of their systems of taxonomy, based as they are on the aesthetic standards of traditional middle-class canons of art and literature. If Robert Darnton, whose 'model' of the Revolution has ruled the 1980s but is now being eliminated, refers to obscene pamphlets as 'dirt', and if Jacques Revel, in an otherwise useful article on Marie-Antoinette, feels obliged to defend his study of 'very mediocre literature', their judgements throw some interesting light not on the texts but on the limitations of the critical gaze in the postmodern period. The study of Rousseau is still preferred to the study of the 'Rousseau des ruis-seaux'.[2]

My subject, then, is twofold. I suggest a new intermedial reading of obscene *libelles* (and especially of their visual material) circulating in Revolutionary Paris; and the discussion of the pastiche character of these sources leads me to the fallacies resulting from both the equivocal nature of the texts and the 'schemes' (in the double sense of the word) of critical analyses. I begin with a brief description and demarcation of the field of texts and pictures to be analysed, for like Darnton I believe that before we relate libertinism and philosophy to the Revolution we should first 'identify the entire corpus of forbidden [literature] . . . examine its contents, and . . . study its reception'.[3]

The obscene (and partly anti-aristocratic) pamphlets published in France in the 1780s and 1790s are situated in a larger field of erotica. Drawing on a great variety of oral, popular, literary and semi-literary forms of discourse, pamphlet literature was produced either underground or outside France. It increased in volume in the decades before 1789 and boomed during the Revolutionary period. It is tempting, but misleading, to see the *libelles* mainly in connection with the rise of aggressive journalism (as described by Darnton) that served as a vehicle for Revolutionary ideas. The related, but more literary, *chronique scandaleuse* itself, which proved a constant and ever-flowing fountain for the virulent slander of aristocrats, was a hybrid genre with a long history, offering many shades between fact and fiction, entertainment and political attack. The common denominator of all these 'Confessions' and 'Secret Memoirs' is their indebtedness to *literary history* rather than to politics. They owe more to earlier discursive models, both in form and content, than to any sort of social protest as expressed in Enlightenment ideas. Up to the Revolutionary period there was a *chronique scandaleuse* (as opposed to the underground publications) that was apparently not deemed noxious by the censors and hence tolerated. The audience for such works was international.[4]

But there was also a substantially different and much more aggressive branch of this genre. Produced *sous le manteau* or abroad, and hounded by the censors, publications of this kind at first comprised bawdy satires but gradually gained political dimensions. While the aggressive pamphlet literature has found some attention over the last years,[5] some questions remain open: Why this sudden emergence of a frequently obscene underground literature? Who wrote it and who read it? Was it really revolutionary or rather a continuation of earlier genres of erotica and popular writings? One must agree with Revel that at this point 'we still know very little about the publishing history of that literature' partly financed by circles close to the French court; and some historians' conviction that the pamphlets fuelled 'so many beliefs' and were 'dangerously effective' lacks any solid evidence.[6] While the libertine spirit, by way of obscene erotica, surely helped to prepare the ground in its attacks on any kind of spiritual and worldly authority,[7] one must admit that the world of the printed word in pre-Revolutionary France was much too complex to be reduced to reifications of Enlightenment ideas or radical politics.

In fact, a glance at the prosecution and the policing of obscene *libelles* in Revolutionary Paris reveals some interesting facts that put into question the reading of such pamphlets in purely political terms.[8] Most of these writings were hawked and sold in and around the Palais Royal. At the beginning of the Revolution this was a kind of red-light district where prostitutes and brothels could be found and where erotica were always available, despite continuing efforts by the capital's administration to curb the commerce in licentious books and pictures (mostly prints and engravings). The police records make it clear that such erotica were confiscated because of their obscene nature, not because of any political content. Among the twenty-nine cases of police raids registered between October 1790 and August 1791 there is only one that suggests legal action was taken because the engravings offered openly in the street showed 'le Roi des Français sous diverses formes et figures indécentes, tendant à atténuer le respect qui est dû au Roi'.[9] It seems that the censors and the police intervened mostly because of the obscene nature of the illustrations in libertine fiction and burlesque ribaldry. Such pictorial material gave a visual dimension, as it were, to the obscene in publications whose texts had more to offer than copulating couples. In the case of libertine fiction, for instance, this meant that the signified was reduced to the signifier, thus turning eroticism and/or obscenity into pornography.[10]

Even during the Revolution, the publishers of erotica knew how to catch their fish. Prurient connoisseurs interested in pictures merely had to check whether the titles specified that the text was *orné de figures* or *orné d'estampes*, or again *avec figures libres*. In the telling jargon of the censor, which indicates the moral concern of the authorities, these illustrations were described as 'figures obscènes', 'estampes indécentes . . . scandaleuses', 'estampes infâmes où règne le libertinage le plus effréné' (infamous plates marked by the most unbounded libertinism), and 'gravures de la plus sale indécence'. Given the new freedom of the press, the pornographers cashed in on the demand for erotica that created a commerce which could not be suppressed.

Whatever anti-aristocratic attacks these publications may have contained, both the location in which they were offered for sale and their nature and forms suggest that they were read and prosecuted not as political writings but as erotica. In other words, the administration in Paris tried to curb an erotic discourse that seemed to be getting out of hand because it threatened civic and moral authorities, not just that of the monarch and his *ancien régime*. The records tell us that prosecutors of the erotica (who were always well informed by the prostitutes in the Palais Royal area[11]) acted because they were instructed to preserve 'le bien public' and to stamp out what Bailly, the Mayor, termed 'that corruption of manners'.[12] But the commerce of erotica in and around the Palais Royal could not be brought under control. After several raids and increased efforts in policing the sector between November 1790 and March 1791, the authorities gave up, not least because there were other evils, such as gambling, to be fought.

Such erotica, politically and sexually aggressive as they were/are, pose enormous difficulties of interpretation. Rather than being mono-dimensional and genre-specific (political or pornographic, fictional or factual), these works are 'impure' (in a literary and moral sense) and semantically ambiguous, and they cannot fully be comprehended in terms of binary concepts. Burlesquing both literary genres and political rhetoric in intertextual and intercultural allusions, the *libelles* contain a powerful parodic and ludic element that tends to subvert any sort of message, be it moral, didactic or ideological. While several critics have noticed the verbal and semantic ambiguity of the pamphlets and have stated that it is impossible to determine with any certainty how such works were read by contemporary readers, this ambiguity needs further attention.[13]

Antoine de Baecque finds in the scurrilous pamphlet literature 'a constant play on words, with lavish use of metaphor to exalt or demean', and Revel also stresses the intermedial nature of these texts when he argues that 'the pamphlets borrow much from each other, from simple allusions to whole (unacknowledged) citations', thus sharing a 'repertoire of common references' in a 'tight network of intertextuality'.[14] Both the form and the intention of this network of allusions have been ignored or misunderstood, precisely because the new radical discourse propagated by the pamphlets consists in the yoking and elision of low and elevated styles, of popular (partly oral) and elite forms of writing, of the sacred (or the literature that was sacred to the educated) and the profane.

It is remarkable that a considerable number of pamphlets are presented in the form of dramatic dialogues and theatrical scenes, thus suggesting the influence of a series of established discursive genres with strong histrionic implications that comes to the fore in the new mixed forms: the drama (of the *ancien régime*) itself, politics as a game of rhetoric practiced in the public meetings and then in the Assemblée

Nationale, and carnival celebrated in parody and travesty. *L'Autri-chienne en goguettes, ou l'orgie royale* (1789), for instance, refers to itself as an 'opéra-proverbe', and *Le Branle des capucins* (1791) is a 'petit opéra aristocratico-comico-risible en deux actes'. They insist on their histrionic (rather than theatrical) nature as much as did the *Bordel royal* and the *Bordel national*, both published in 1790. The very form of these pieces is of course an allusion to Marie-Antoinette's private theatre in the Trianon, where many a salacious play was rumoured to have been performed. Aristocrats, too, had private stages. France also knew a tradition of boisterous and burlesque erotic drama and prose whose scatalogical and obscene branches came to the fore during the Revolution. What we find here, then, is less 'political pornography' (which I take to be a contradiction in terms: pornography is always bent on a genital response, not on didacticism), as Revel and de Baecque would have it, but rather 'a rhetoric of carnivalization whose prece-dents reach back beyond the *mazarinades* to the conventionalized low style of popular literature in the Middle Ages'.[15] The pamphlets, in other words, endorse a carnivalesque vision of the Revolution and its major 'characters'.

Several pamphlets draw the reader into an intertextual game that asks him/her to identify the sources and to associate them with the political figures; in that sense the 'unacknowledged citations'[16] are part of a strategy of debunking. Thus the ribald *Fureurs utérines de Marie-Antoinette, femme de Louis XVI*, published *c.* 1791, alludes to a 'medical' bestseller of the late eighteenth century, J.D.T. Bienville's *La Nympho-manie, ou traité de la fureur utérine* (Amsterdam, 1771). This was itself read (and sold) as an erotic book because it provided ample information about female masturbators and various cures, some of them sadistic, of what was then considered to be a noxious vice.[17] The reader who recognized the source of the allusion could then link it with the Queen of France. But was this game a political one? The source suggests, above all, something forbidden; by late eighteenth-century middle-class standards, nymphomania was 'sick' because it implied a sexually active woman. This can of course be seen in terms of politics, aiming at the destruction of the public (sacred) image of the Queen; but in less serious terms Marie-Antoinette becomes a figure of fun, much like the other public figures that had been ridiculed before her. This is especially true for her husband. Since his name appears in the title, the implication must be that the King was an impotent cuckold. In the repressive discourse of popular Enlightenment erotica cuckolds were always figures of fun, whereas sexually active women were exposed to bawdy attacks. *Fureurs utérines* is characterized by ribald entertainment;

it may have a 'revolutionary' aspect in that the royal couple is ridiculed in sexual terms, but the political is clearly dominated and subverted by parody and travesty. A reading of this source in purely political terms does not do justice to its ludic and carnivalesque nature, which dominates many of the pamphlets written against the royal couple. One should also consider the fact that *Fureurs utérines* was sold, and sometimes bound, with such ribald pieces as *Le Triomphe de la fouterie, ou les apparences sauvées: comédie en deux actes et en vers* (1791).[18] With such characters as 'Marquis de la Couille, fouteur; Madame Duvagin, tribade; Moniche, nièce de Madame Duvagin; Foutine, suivante de Madame et tribade; Foutin, valet du marquis; [and] Monsieur Ducu, bougre' (Marquis of Balls, fucker; Madame Decunt, lesbian/dyke; Moniche, niece of Madame Decunt; Fuckerina, Madame's servant and lesbian; Fuckero, servant to the Marquis; and Mr Dearse, bugger), this piece mocks the genre of the comedy while exploding its own form in an obscene violation of established literary codes. What triumphs in this parodic discourse is not political attack but the sheer fun of ridiculing the high and mighty by associating them with the breaking of taboos in writing and behaviour.

I would argue that in the context of late eighteenth-century French discursive traditions (which all come into play here by way of allusion) these pamphlets were entertaining precisely because they violated the entire gamut of aesthetic norms of the high society. *Les Amours de Charlot et Toinette* (1789), for instance, uses colloquial (and hence democratic) names for the royal couple and spoofs plays as well as (upper-class) playgoing in a farce of life at the Court. The 'heroes' appear in a ribald 'pièce dérobée à V[ersailles]' (a play without clothes set in Versailles). Presented in verse that recalls classical forms while subverting them with a new obscene subject, the actual text describes Marie-Antoinette's various erotic adventures, including one with d'Artois:

> *Il baise des beaux bras, son joli petit Con,*
> *Et tantôt une fesse & tantôt un téton:*
> *Il claque doucement sa fesse rebondie,*
> *Cuisse, ventre, nombril, le centre de tout bien.*

> He kisses her beautiful arms, her nice little cunt,
> Now her buttocks and now her tits:
> He softly strikes her round buttock,
> Thigh, stomach, navel, the centre of all good.

The title-pages of such works provide ample evidence of verbal borrowings from the language of established genres – comedy, the *avis*, the *vie privée*, *mémoires* or even religious forms, such as the *catéchisme* etc. – only to ridicule them in parody that substitutes obscenity for decency and contemporary public figures for fictional characters.[19] From a traditional critical viewpoint, such mixing of genres that yokes 'classical literary conventions to puppet shows or games of verbal one-upmanship'[20] may hardly be compatible, but the point of this new *genre melé* of discourse is an attack on the old system by way of its established expressive forms. The Revolution engendered writing that was ludic, burlesque and deliberately obscene. Revel has pointed out that the discordance that often exists between (traditional if parodied) form and (new scurrilous) content provokes, 'rather than an *effet de réel*, an *effet de dé-réalization*'[21] that is the reference to a truth that was taken for granted and seems to have been created elsewhere. It is indeed rather difficult to decide with this material what was more important – the entertaining function of the pamphlets that present aristocrats in the context of farce and vaudeville or the fact that *aristocrats* were made the butt of ribald laughter.

The problems we are faced with when 'reading' these texts become most obvious as we turn to the illustrations. Their controversial nature immediately leads to a series of questions: Are they pornographic, obscene or merely ribald? Were they consumed as pornography in an age that – Restif de la Bretonne's *Le Pornographe* notwithstanding – did not know or use that term?[22] To what extent can they be considered political/ideological material? And how were they received by the French in late eighteenth-century Paris? By and large, historians have ignored them; one suspects for reasons of twentieth-century propriety: Darnton, Revel and de Baecque, for instance, have not reproduced obscene or bawdy visual material in their respective studies; the anthologies of Revolutionary obscene pamphlets (e.g., those published by Fayard in the series *Oeuvres anonymes du XVIIIe siècle*) remain silent about the function of the pictures (some of which have been included and appear dispersed throughout the volumes without editorial commentary); and the studies of Revolutionary imagery – especially those of Langlois and de Baecque – are again distinguished by their exclusion of aggressive visual evidence of the sexual variety, of pictures our *confrères* obviously find too offensive.[23]

But ignoring obscene visual representations or dismissing them as unimportant or unaesthetic ('pornographic') might be tantamount to ignoring important developments in the change of *mentalités* during the Revolution. In addition, the illustrations contained in the *libelles* are not as clear in their meaning as some historians would have it. If one avoids the pitfalls of projecting one's own twentieth-century notions into

85 'Elle a beau méditer . . .', illustration from *La Journée amoureuse, ou les derniers plaisirs de M . . . Ant . . .*, 1792, engraving.

Elle a beau méditer la perte des Français,
ses souhaits ne s'accompliront plus.

these pictures, their iconography reveals some interesting information, for they 'operate not just on the level of sexuality or the erotic but in fact are polysemous, related to multiple discourses on morality, on economics, on politics, on reproduction, on rituals such as carnivals and on a host of other areas'.[24] The piece entitled *La Journée amoureuse, ou les derniers plaisirs de M . . . Ant . . .* (1792), for instance, which mockingly refers to itself as a 'comédie en trois actes, en prose, représentée pour la première fois au Temple, le 20 août 1792', and claims to have been published 'au Temple, Chez Louis Capet', includes four prints probably produced by Louis-Marin Bonnet (1743–93).[25] One depicts Marie-Antoinette as a scheming politician (illus. 85) trying to ruin the French nation. The caption, however, states that she will not succeed: 'Elle a beau méditer la perte des Français, ses souhaits ne s'accompliront plus' (She may well plan the downfall of the French, but her wishes will not be fulfilled). The other illustrations might be termed obscene because they display sexual organs and the Queen of France engaged in sexual activities. It is not unlikely that such prints caused a genital response among eighteenth-century readers/observers. But that does

ah! gros coquin voila que tu débandes.

86 'Ah! gros coquin . . .', illustration from *La Journée amoureuse, ou les derniers plaisirs de M . . . Ant . . .*, 1792, engraving.

ah ma bonne amie ahi ahi je n'en puis plus
je me pa a ame.

87 'Ah ma bonne amie . . .', illustration
from *La Journée amoureuse, ou les derniers
plaisirs de M . . . Ant . . .*, 1792,
engraving.

88 Uncaptioned illustration from *La
Journée amoureuse, ou les derniers plaisirs
de M . . . Ant . . .*, 1792, engraving.

not mean that the pictures are merely pornography, for the three
engravings do not represent 'normal' sexual behaviour as the eighteenth century would have understood it. Louis XVI obviously needed
assistance when he wished to enjoy an erection (illus. 86). This
message and his ludicrous appearance, reinforced by the caption 'ah!
gros coquin voila [sic] que tu débandes' (oh! nasty scoundrel, there you
shrink again), must have caused snickers among those contemporaries
who enjoyed the sight of a monarch caught with his trousers down.
Since Marie-Antoinette lacks a potent husband, she too has to resort to
artificial aid. In two of the prints included here (illus. 87 and 88) she
receives it from her friend the princesse de Lamballe.

In both cases we see representations of 'unnatural' behaviour, for
according to the predominant eighteenth-century male view, homosexuality was one of the worst possible perversions, although lesbians
were treated more leniently by satirists. The use of a dildo (illus. 87)
also indicated physical corruption as well as a perverse proclivity. As
one decodes these prints, it gradually becomes clear that they appeal to
popular sexual *mentalités* in allusions to a vast body of erotica. This
includes the literature on *tribades* and *bougres*, and the bawdry
concerned with impotent cuckolds, the dildo, and other artificial aids.[26]

Although lost to us today, this entire repository of popular ribald discourse constitutes a world of its own, a world that was very real to eighteenth-century readers because it was able to create (repressive) attitudes towards sexuality that generated the subtext in these illustrations. If the texts of the pamphlets play allusive intertextual games with high and low genres of writing (including literature and official discourse), the illustrations resume this game and extend it into an intermedial level. The pictures, beyond any doubt, are still 'obscene' and in the eighteenth century they may have been sexually exciting, but by appealing to the *déjà vu* and the *déjà lu* in eighteenth-century erotica they also urge the observer to judge by the popular sexual standards that were in opposition to Enlightenment ideas.

It is significant, for instance, that in the illustrations discussed above Marie-Antoinette is associated *both* with books and with a dildo. In terms of the popular *mentalité* (expressed in a huge wave of allegedly humorous bawdry), educated and emancipated women were considered to be as dangerous and perverse as those who took the initiative in matters of sex. In that sense, the Queen's visual association with books is as telling as the one that represents her with artificial sexual devices.

What the illustrations in *La Journée amoureuse* tell us above all is that the royal couple is judged not from an objective or aristocratic point of view, but from that of the new democratic public: the sexual fictions reproduced here are perverse, and the 'actors' are both decrepit and ludicrous precisely because they cannot or will not have sex in the way ordinary folks do.

Similarly, a less prejudiced semiotics of the so-called licentious popular prints reveals the entrance of the obscene (of that which is, etymologically and literally, off-scene) into the public sphere. Such a reading would explain the frontispiece of *Les Embarras de Marie-Antoinette* (illus. 89) not as pornographic but as the irruption of democracy and a new (verbal and visual) order into the privacy of the aristocratic world. This brutal act reduces Marie-Antoinette to the simple, democratic stature of a whore penetrated by Patriotism (which is exactly what the caption, not reproduced here, says). Yet this print is as ambiguous as the texts discussed above. It employs the technique as well as the décor of the traditional erotic engraving intended for aristocrats, including the voyeuristic perspective, with the lustful nobleman now replaced by a young and potent soldier representing the people. For all its comic obscenity, the engraving also suggests that France needs regeneration through a *democratic* generation that will replace aristocratic impotence. But the new political liberty is achieved

89 Frontispiece to an anonymous pamphlet, *Les Embarras de Marie-Antoinette, c.* 1790.

at a costly price for women: what the picture establishes is a phallic representational code, a body language, that subjects women both to the male gaze and to male domination.[27]

Clearly, the illustrations are as allusive as the texts of which they are a part. They expect the reader/observer to be familiar with several verbal and visual codes that, at first sight, are hardly compatible. As far as visual representations are concerned, there is, to begin with, the code of the *iconographie galante* of the *ancien régime*, which was erotic because in its toying with taboos it veiled sexuality and merely alluded to what is or takes place 'off-scene'. Such allusions constitute the symbolic erotic code in De Launay's *Le Carquois épuisé* (illus. 50), engraved after Baudouin's painting and reproduced here (illus. 90) without its framework. The lapdog and the sword refer to sexual activities that cannot be shown, and so do the Cupid and the beckoning bed behind the curtain, the latter in turn standing for a giant, almost threatening, vulva that ironically confirms the message of the caption.[28] The new radical iconography emerging in the Revolutionary period

90 Nicolas de Launay, *Le Carquois épuisé*, undated engraving after a painting by Pierre-Antoine Baudouin.

employs this established code, but only to destroy it with obscene signs, i.e., signifiers deprived of their signifieds. Using self-sufficient signifiers (the hall-mark of pornography), this new code is obscene because it needs no veil or allusion. In this sense the scurrilous illustrations function like the parasitical texts in which they appear: old, established, forms are quoted, as it were, and supplied with new contents. This is the principle governing travesty. The frontispiece of Pierre Jean Baptiste Nougaret's anticlerical *Les Progrès du libertinage* (illus. 91), a 'short story found in the pocket of a former Carmelite', demonstrates this mingling of seemingly incompatible codes. The 'décor' is that of traditional eighteenth-century *scènes galantes* that we find even in the early work of Watteau. Lovers sacrifice on the altar of Priapus. The decorations, however, are not symbolic but straightforward: sexual activity (copulation, masturbation) is celebrated in what some observers probably consider offensive realism; and the traditional metaphors have been replaced by self-referential penes, i.e., shocking body language.

91 Engraved
frontispiece to
Pierre Jean Baptiste
Nougaret's *Les
Progrès du
libertinage*, (?)1791.

But can such pictorial parody or travesty be considered revolutionary because it ridiculed the clergy and aristocracy? The ambiguity of some of these illustrations becomes a puzzling problem where strong Enlightenment taboos are concerned. Witness the equivocal depiction of sexual acts between homosexual men in the illustrations contained in *Les Petits bougres au manège* (*c.* 1791), a pamphlet that was frequently bound and sold with *La Liberté, ou Mlle Raucour à toute la secte anandrine, assemblée au foyer de la Comédie Française*. Both works pretend to sing the praise of lesbian women and gay men, but the network of verbal and visual allusions constantly draws on popular prejudices against homosexuality to such an extent that the representations become contradictory in themselves.

One example will suffice. The frontispiece of *Les Petits bougres* (illus. 84) recalls the pastoral tradition of eighteenth-century representations in art and poetry in a ribald travesty that again substitutes obscene signifiers for allusive metaphors. Traditional figures, emblems and elements (the altar of love, the satyr and the copulating goats in the background, Venus or Diana accompanied by a Cupid) constitute visual traces of a *déjà vu*, the familiar code of Rococo eroticism. But the shocking *derrières* and the penes decorating the altar only seem to confirm what the caption expresses ('Tous les gouts [sic] sont dans la nature'), i.e., that even anal penetration (if that is the case here) is 'natural'. For the upper half of the picture ridicules the male members of the French royal family in an obscene and scatological travesty of an heraldic emblem, the Bourbon arms (usually showing the face of the sun surrounded by the Latin phrase *Nec pluribus impar*, i.e., equal to everybody, or capable of dealing with anyone). Forced into new contexts (homosexuality and scatology), the motto acquires meanings that are both humorous (or scatological) and sexual, and it urges the observer to consider additional debunking relations between the Latin text and the obscene visual detail it frames. In terms of linguistics and semiotics, for instance, one might say that the language of the state (in its iconic version in the motto) is subverted by association with popular, colloquial language, for the face of the sun (traditionally associated with Louis XIV and his successors) has become a bottom, or a moon of sorts (*la lune* is a colloquial French term for this part of the human body). The now ambiguous Latin phrase frames a visual signifier that can also be read as a popular text (*mon cul*; i.e, 'up yours') which ultimately destroys the original motto and arms and, by synecdochal implication, those they represented. A new radical text emerges, an obscene message that virtually marginalizes the great men of the royal family. This is visually expressed in the statue we recognize in the background. It is, it appears, an iconic allusion to the famous statue of Louis XIV made by François Girardon and erected by the city of Paris in the Place Vendôme in 1699. A true iconotext, the picture juxtaposes several codes associated with the *ancien régime* (sculpture, escutcheons, Latin mottoes, pastoral scenes in painting and engraving) while simultaneously wiping them out with a new, naturalistic, 'code' – the scatological, obscene laughter of the popular and oral tradition.

The curtain is a rather ambiguous sign. One can of course read it as yet another reference to the aristocratic world (the theatre of the *ancien régime* staging itself), not least because the motto and the obscene icon form a palimpsest and are thus part of that curtain. But I would argue that in terms of representation, the curtain (or backdrop) also introduces the carnivalesque note that is so often a hallmark of Revolutionary publications, precisely because it suggests that what is shown here is only a play. It is this self-reflexive, narcissistic dimension which in turn undermines the Revolutionary message, if message there is. Although there are additional codes that come into play in this print (the classical adoration of the phallus; the rediscovery of such cults in the wake of the excavations and publications of Winckelmann and d'Hancarville[29]), the entire picture must also be read against the background of the popular sexual mentality, especially of phallic representational codes, which held that homosexuals were 'unnatural' criminals. The obscenity produced here wavers between bawdy laughter, conniving acceptance, disgusted rejection and prurient interest. The comic dominates when the illustrations are interpreted as a part of the parodic text in which they appear. The liberation of sexuality thus only *seems* to be celebrated: the decoding tells us that the observer is urged to adopt age-old prejudices by remembering a repressive (masculine) code based on oral and popular traditions that works against the carnivalesque visual surface.

Seen together, the illustrated pamphlets and the separately published prints featuring aristocrats constitute an important discourse marked by its erotic and carnivalesque codes. These writings present a world that is upside down, a world in which any kind of civic and moral authority could be challenged, just as the 'normal' order is reversed during carnival. Because these works appeared at the time of the Revolution, critics tend to stress the fact that in the *libelles* morbid and physically corrupt aristocrats appear inferior to virile and healthy commoners. Such a reading ignores the fact that after 1789 anybody in public life might be made the target of ribald discourse.[30] Preferring parody and travesty, the verbal and pictorial representations of the *libelles* were themselves not serious: laughter and entertainment seem to have been the targets, with political propaganda as a secondary effect.

If the printed word and the graven image during the French Revolution are understood to be what Chantal Thomas terms 'un déchaînement carnavalesque', as one of the last if ephemeral carnivalesque explosions to take place in times of social unrest and crises since the Renaissance,[31] we must pay more attention to the entertaining side of this discourse, to its erotic and ludic nature. It seems that the authors of the pamphlets resorted to familiar forms of parody and travesty in an attempt to comment on the unbelievable events happening in reality. They looked for a tradition that was familiar to themselves and to their audience. After all, social and political reality in France was, after the fall of the Bastille, a carnival come true: the lowly *tier état* became the *état*; those in bondage and dependence found themselves in power; the Grub Street writers discovered their enormous influence; and those in power were soon to find themselves in prison and facing the guillotine.

This is not the place to inquire into the authorship of the *libelles*, but the evidence of the allusions to art and literature that are part of the parodic play of the iconotexts (Latin mottoes, for instance) would suggest that the authors were educated radicals writing for a new mass audience. One is immediately reminded, of course, of our educated contemporaries who write *for* (but surely not on behalf *of*) the audience of, say, *The Sun* in Britain, and of the *Bildzeitung* in Germany. The readers thus found/find their 'opinions' expressed by spokesmen who simply assume (pun intended) the mandate to write for a large if silent majority.

With the onset of the Terror, Revolutionary 'carnival' even gained nightmarish and apocalyptic dimensions. No wonder, then, that the literature of the time chose the carnivalesque mode as a favourite form of expression. As in a masquerade, the new language donned comic and fantastic clothing, and, of course, some of these clothes were borrowed. This masking of language served a variety of aims: it sanctioned the new Revolutionary order (the 'misrule' of carnival); it protected the appropriation of formerly restricted rights; and it suffused a new democratic discourse with euphoria. A great number of analogies of carnival/masquerade and Revolutionary pamphlets remain to be explored: both affirm the rule of libido over constraint, of promiscuity over social control; both share a power of demystification while constituting an anarchic assault on hierarchy, and both make use of images diagnosing cultural sickness.[32]

But the essential difference must not be ignored. Carnival has always been a familiar if disconcerting ritual, a limited period of 'disorder', whereas the 'misrule' of the French Revolution finally got out of hand. The ritual was turned into reality. For the discourse that had chosen the burlesque apparel of carnival and masquerade, this presented an irremovable dilemma in that the writers were finally hoist with their own petard. It may well be that, initially, they took neither themselves nor their writing too seriously. But when political reality outran the wildest fictional imagination, there was little left that could be carnivalized. Carnival itself, i.e., the Revolution, had to become the new aim of travesty – hence, perhaps, the self-reflexive and equivocal nature of many pamphlets.

Recent research suggests that Revolutionary pamphlet literature as well as the entire literary production of that period was dominated by pragmatic needs. Despite the efforts of the Jacobin politicians policing cultural expression (Grégoire, Boissy d'Anglas), cultural consumption – including reading – continued to be determined by the need for entertainment.[33] But how effective was this discourse? A part of the answer to that question can be found in the extraordinary reception of pamphlet literature. Several foreign travellers visiting Revolutionary Paris stated that it was eagerly read by all social classes. The reception even included the illiterate, who listened to pamphlets being read out loud in the streets. The German visitor Johann Heinrich Campe described these events as a 'revolution in language and literature', observing that the French now discussed the rights of kings and of their subjects in a thousand broadsides and pamphlets devoured by the nation.[34] Likewise, the obscene prints produced during the Revolution – although they create more hermeneutic and heuristic problems than the texts – appear more important in the light of recent historical evidence, suggesting a cultural influence of pictorial material. If eighteenth-century Paris households owned more prints than books (50–60% possessed one or more prints or engravings, but only 25% owned books[35]), we clearly need more studies of the role and function of popular pictorials.[36] The Revolutionary authorities were well aware of the importance of the graven image as a form of discourse, and so were the counter-Revolutionaries, such as the royalist journalist Jacques-Marie Boyer-Brun, who referred to the caricatures as a dangerous 'spoken writing' (*une écriture parlée*). Not surprisingly, in 1793 the 'Comité de Salut public' urged artists that included David to employ engravings and caricatures 'in order to wake the public spirit and to demonstrate the atrocious and ridiculous nature of the enemies of the liberty of the Republic'.[37] Such evidence of a popular art flourishing in the streets and on the walls of houses and, in the case of obscene prints, more surreptitiously in the Palais Royal district, calls for further investigation.

These investigations are invariably faced with the problems of language. What Robert Darnton has said about the eighteenth-century differentiation between licit and illicit writings applies as much to the meta-discourse of historical research, for 'the problem of demarcating forbidden literature [and pictures] appears at first as a question of language'.[38] While the archaeology of the verbal and visual discourse of the Revolution is well under way, the exploration of its historical interpretation remains a crucial desideratum.[39] Instead of forcing frequently ambiguous texts and polyvalent illustrations into ready-made categories (e.g., political, pornographic, or sub-literary) that fit the scholar better than the sources,[40] it would be more rewarding to subject pamphlet literature to a discourse analysis. Whatever its disadvantages, such an approach will at least lay bare the implicit contradictions, including the politics of the aesthetic discourse, as well as the aims of the equivocal language employed in the pamphlets. In a magisterial study of the complex intertextual nature of the *libelles*, Vivian Cameron has argued convincingly that the power of their illustrations lies in their 'intersection with the multiple discourse of eroticism, politics, rituals, Carnival, pornography, reproduction, prostitution, and the like', and that in reading the imagery too narrowly we may 'miss some of the very aspects that might account for its potency during the revolutionary period'.[41] Many of the allegedly pornographic images are, in fact, iconotexts, and their political references are a pretext (in the double sense of the term) or an addition.[42]

One may, of course, interpret the parodic textual strategies of the pamphlets in political terms, as the seizing of the word (*prendre la parole*) as it were by the lower classes in the public sphere that had been dominated by another 'style'. To be sure, the liberation of the press in 1789 also led to a liberation of obscene and erotic expression in general. Eros went public in many forms. In 1791 there was a nude life show in the Palais Royal where spectators could see (false) Africans perform coitus on stage.[43] If some recent French critics recognize in the pamphlets 'the point of view of the gutter' (*une vision ordurière*) and a 'despise of language' (*un mépris de la langue*), they underline the importance of a new radical linguistic style in the public domain that has been vastly underestimated and – given the aesthetic norms of twentieth-century bourgeois critics – misunderstood. Discussing the slanderous *Père Duchêne*, which also did not mince its words and was close to the *libelles* in style and spirit,[44] Roland Barthes, perspicacious as ever, commented on this linguistic aspect of a new radical register. Of Hébert (the editor of the periodical), Barthes wrote that he

never forgot to add 'fuck' and 'bugger' to each new number of the *Père Duchêne*. These indecencies did not mean anything – but they did indicate something, i.e., a whole revolutionary situation. This writing was not only meant to communicate or express a message, it was above all to impose another linguistic world, both that of History and the part one takes in it.[45]

One wishes that both historians and literary critics took more notice of this apposite reflection. However, as I pointed out earlier, the problem with these parodic texts is their proximity to the originals they aim to subvert. That is one of the reasons why the pamphlet literature (which was rarely written by the common people but, rather, for them by educated writers) oscillates between ribald laughter and disgust, and why the reader finds it difficult to decide whether it is meant as hostile satire or as innocuous humour.

If we address the popular and literary sides of this discourse simultaneously, we shall at some point be faced with the impact of the stereotypes that are a hallmark of pamphlet literature. Instead of comparing it to the works of Rousseau and Voltaire and, as a consequence, denying it the status of 'great' literature to be canonized, I find it more useful to study the way such allegedly revolutionary writings made use of popular *mentalités* to get their messages across. The discourse of popular erotica was extremely repressive. Women, for instance, were under constant attack because their new sexual liberty was being resented by male writers. If we apply this evidence to the obscene pamphlets of the French Revolution, we must re-examine the representation of women. Both Chantal Thomas and Lynn Hunt have argued that Marie-Antoinette, who (in the pamphlet literature) combined all the imaginable faults and vices of a woman, was in fact the victim of an antifeminist male anxiety of women invading the public sphere.[46] My analyses of the lines of discourse crossing in the pamphlets would confirm such a view. The question, then, is whether the attacks against the Queen and other (female) nobles were also, perhaps even decisively, fed by the fact that as a *woman* she did not conform to what the late eighteenth-century plebeian *mentalité* expected a woman to be and to do. Seen from this angle, many of the pamphlets are attacks against the female body as well as the new body politic that, initially, admitted women.[47] And Marie-Antoinette was, of course, the ideal target. Such issues and others relating to the impact of popular clichés (generally despised by scholars interested in high art and literature) deserve to be answered. The French Revolution, it may turn out, was not only a history of bodies elevated, put down and decapitated, it was also an event expressed in obscene body language, in a code that was/is new and radical only for those who (had) refuse(d) to accept its existence.[48]

92 William Hogarth, Detail from *Credulity, Superstition and Fanaticism. A Medley*,
1762, etching and engraving (third state).

6 In Lieu of a Conclusion

But if one wants to keep open the relation between language and the visible, if one wants to speak, not against but rather about [Foucault uses 'à partir de', which actually means 'from' or 'starting from'] their incompatibility, one must efface names/tags ['les noms propres'] and carry on with the endless task.
Foucault, *Les Mots et les choses*

It is not a question of 'applying' linguistics to painting, of injecting a bit of semiology into the history of art; rather, one must abolish the distance (the censorship) that has institutionally separated painting from the text.
Barthes, 'La peinture est-elle un langage?'

In his seminal 'Lettre sur les sourds et les muets' of 1751, Diderot sketched a programme for the exploration of the relations between poetry, painting and music. Instead of comparing the beauties of one poet to another, Diderot argued, we should look for the beauty common to all the arts, 'to demonstrate the analogies between them; explain how the poet, the painter, and the musician render the same image; seize the vanishing emblems of their expression; examine whether there would be any similitude between these emblems, etc., that is what remains to be done'. Although this was in itself an attack on Charles Batteux's *Les Beaux-Arts réduits à un même principe* (1746), in which *mimesis* was said to be the common denominator of the arts, Diderot's central assumption – that there are analogies and similarities between, say, literature and painting – has become a cornerstone in the theory inspiring 'the correspondences of the arts', or better still, 'the mutual illumination of the arts'. The theory is still in fashion, serving as a tacitly implied basis in humanist ekphrases of art works.[1]

In the foregoing chapters I have been arguing implicitly that I do not subscribe to such a view. Rather, my argument is that picture and text are dialogical, at times even polylogical and contradictory, in themselves. This means that there is, in J. Hillis Miller's words, a 'warfare' between media that is 'doubled by an internal warfare intrinsic to each medium'.[2] Before I look for analogies between the arts, an interpretive act relying on the ideas of translatability and of the work of art as aesthetic repository, entity, aesthetic wholeness – in short, and in Alastair Fowler's words, a chimera[3] – I want to focus on each medium itself. In doing this, I suggest that a picture, for instance, can be analysed with much profit if we decode it as an iconotext, as a construct that welds texts to images while appealing to the observer to activate his/her knowledge of both media. While demonstrating my theses in a few case studies of pictures and illustrations I had to leave aside a great number of unresolved problems. Therefore, instead of concluding what cannot be finished, I should like to outline some untilled areas in the intermedial exploration of iconotexts.

I suggest that we have hardly begun to study images as distorted re-activations of collective memories, of what some scholars call *mentalités*. Together with the oral tradition, and with texts and rites, images thematize and preserve that which is virtually present in the public (sub)consciousness and memory; in images, light is thrown on a 'latent memory' that is always in danger of being obscured, hidden and displaced.[4] I have no better example of this power of the (moving) image than the pupils of a school in the English Lake District who, when I arrived there in 1970 to teach German, greeted me with what they probably considered to be a jocular 'Heil Hitler'. As time went by and the shock subsided, I recognized that part of their latent memory was fed less by the oral tradition (stories from their parents and grandparents) than by war movies on BBC TV channels, by images re-constructing history in a way that I, as a young person born in post-war Germany, found irritating, if understandable. At the present time, as younger Germans attack and kill foreigners in Germany (while German intellectuals write articles and protest with candles in the streets: apologetic acts that are supposed to serve as substitutes for their own neglect of both foreigners and working-class people), I suspect that something of the power of the image and its sisters, the sign and the emblem, inspires the bored and frustrated hooligans as well as the media reporting about them. Both are attracted by the Nazi insignia and by the terrors and horrors they represent.

Eighteenth-century engravings can also be studied as visual exam-ples of pictures encoding traces of *mentalités*. Hogarth's graphic art is probably the supreme example. I have shown in a number of articles focusing on the 'popular' imagery and texts in his works that the engravings of the later period (after 1735) draw on clichés, stereotypes and prejudices. They 'make sense', but they are also there to be pondered and scrutinized by the observer.[5] My argument has been that such pictures can be studied meaningfully in an approach combining semiotics and discourse analysis with a shot of deconstruction, that is, not as perfect aesthetic products of the genial artist (whose intention must be unveiled[6]), but as partisan representations of discursive traditions and mentalities.

Let me provide an example that seems obvious but, on closer inspection, reveals the subtleties involved in the playing of the image with the *déjà lu/vu/vécu*. In my earlier discussion of *Beer Street* (illus. 75), I argued that the loin of roast beef (if it is in fact mutton, it is still meat, hence the difference is negligible) and the jug of ale, as well as the emaciated Frenchman (in an earlier state) they replace, can be decoded as signs commingling icons, indices and symbols. They are iconic because they re-present or depict things that were part of everyday life in eighteenth-century London; they are indexical in their reference to English *consumption* of food and beverages; and, finally, they are symbolical because they also serve as jingoistic allusions to a *mentalité* (fed by similar images and texts) the observer associates with English roast beef (or huge chunks of meat) and beer. My contention is that, contrary to traditional semiotic readings, which usually work with notions of dominance or hierarchy among the triad icon-index-symbol, none of the categories of the signifiers can be said to dominate. As sign, the loin can thus be described as iconic without abandoning its indexical or symbolical values.[7]

As a matter of fact, the huge chunk of meat (most commentators on *Beer Street*, from Lichtenberg on, have indeed stressed the enormous size of the loin) could be made the subject of an analysis inquiring into the functions of this polyvalent signifier in *Beer Street* as well as in *The Gate of Calais* (illus. 93). Such an investigation will foreground, on the one hand, the relations between these patriotic pictures, and, on the other, the manner in which a sign eventually develops into, or becomes part of, a code of allusions to national pride, the perennial animosity between France and England, and popular attitudes towards these issues as re-presented from the special angle of Hogarthian satire. I can only outline the steps of such a venture in a brief look at *The Gate of Calais*.

The title of this print, which dates from March 1749, is yet another of those sense-making paratexts that is apt to mislead us. In fact it has misled the authorities of the city museum in Calais, where the print is exhibited as a genuine picture of the city as it used to be! In a recent study of this print Félix Paknagel has, however, demonstrated in a most persuasive manner that, far from being a true representation of Calais, Hogarth's image is an 'anti-French tableau where all the old prejudices

93 William Hogarth, *The Gate of Calais, or The Roast Beef of Old England*, 1749, etching and engraving (first state).

against the French are present: their religion, their love of fancy clothes, their diet, their alleged poverty and slovenliness, their lack of freedom'.[8] Before I turn to the function of the roast beef (it is decidedly beef in this case!) in the print, it may be useful to consider the genesis of the picture, not least because that genesis provides some ideas about the background of prejudices ruling the visual field. In doing this, I do not intend to reconstruct Hogarth's attitudes or feelings at the time: my aim is simply the exploration of the conglomeration of signifiers, with the beef as a truly central example.

The Hogarth specialists[9] tell us that the painting (made in 1748) and the engraving are reactions to, or at least an aftermath of, Hogarth's trip to France in 1748. Later, Hogarth was to describe the incident in his *Autobiographical Notes*, which is most instructive because it teems as much with anti-French stereotypes as do the pictures. After explaining that the occasion of *The Gate of Calais* was his arrest in Calais while engaged in sketching the town's famous portal, he launches into a description of France and its inhabitants that proves, if anything, how much his vision depended on the discourse and the *mentalités* of his time:

The first time any one goes from hence to france by way of Calais he cannot avoid being struck with the Extreem different face things appear with at so little a distance as from Dover a farcical pomp of war, parade of religion and Bustle with little with very little bussiness in short poverty slavery and Insolence (with an affectation of politeness) give you ever here the first specimen of the whole country . . . fish women have faces of [. . .] leather and soldiers raged and lean . . . the Picture wherein I introduced a poor highlander fled thither on account of the Rebelion year before brozing on scanty french air in sight a Sirloin of Beef a present from England which is opposed the Kettle of soup meager my own figure in the corner with the soldier hand upon my shoulder is said to be tolerably like.[10]

Indeed, it is 'tolerably like', as a comparison with this ekphrasis of sorts proves.[11] This was Hogarth's second visit to France (his first occurred in 1743), in which he distinguished himself, if we can trust contemporary sources, by being 'clamorously rude'.[12] I tend to agree with Paulson[13] that *The Gate of Calais* is less about Calais than about Hogarth dramatizing himself as a spy caught in a comedy (note the theatrical set-up, a feature that distinguishes many of his prints). But it is also undeniable that the print derives its satirical force from a welter of allusions to texts and to images carrying age-old prejudices. Whatever personal feeling of revenge there might have been against those awful French who dared detain a person who thought himself the greatest painter of his time, the image itself contains sufficient evidence of anti-French attitudes: we get the whole range of negative images that had clustered around earlier visual and verbal satire (including Lafontaine's lecherous and obese monks); and Hogarth's reference in his commentary 'soup meager' is nothing else but the uncovering of a rather important visual pre-text, Brueghel's *La Maigre cuisine* and *La Grasse cuisine*, which were to serve him again for *Beer Street* and *Gin Lane*.

It is the sirloin of roast beef that is here literally and visually at the centre of attention. Indeed, the picture asserts that the meat – a sign for England – was exported to France for English travellers because none could be had locally. It is England's hearty fare, English well-being, and, ultimately, English pride that the beef signifies, and these qualities are juxtaposed with the shortcomings of the French, a point that is again taken up by the caption. 'O the Roast Beef of Old England etc.' is taken from a song in Fielding's *Grub Street Opera* (1731), which makes similar comparisons between the two countries, starting with a comment on French politeness and how the English have 'been taught to dress our meat by nations that have no meat to dress'.[14] Fielding used the popular song again in *Don Quixote in England*, and it was frequently sung at concerts in Covent Garden, sometimes under a slightly different, if telling, title: *The Roast Beef of England, or the Antigallican*. As Félix Paknagel notes, it is 'the anti-French character of the song that pleased the audience, and not the stricture against current fashion.'[15]

Whether Hogarth had an eye on what could make his print popular, the allusions to English patriotism and superiority were bound to please his audience. The roast beef in *The Gate of Calais* as well as the loin of beef (or mutton) in *Beer Street* are signs that may be said to belong to a code that urges the observer to activate her/his knowledge of pre-established, popular attitudes to France and England. Again, one notices how the print plays with dualistic concepts, at first alluding to them in juxtapositions of good and bad, English and French, rich and poor, and then subverting them in their very presentation, or rather re-presentation. As Frederick Antal pointed out back in 1962, this is done in theatrical terms. Indeed, one can hardly ignore it, with the gateway resembling a backcloth, and the two houses on the sides serving as props and lines of perspective.[16] But the stage-like structure, like the 'realism' of modern photographs, is a rhetorical device, a means and way of (de)figuring reality. Here it means precisely that this is a play. We see a charade in which the characters act out roles rather than being real persons in themselves. This, the iconography suggests, is a comedy that reveals for our inspection what we expect to see.[17] In terms of Paulson's theory of the two audiences, one may say that there is one reading for the common people here, and another, more ironical one, for the theatre-goers.

The sirloin of roast beef is merely one polyvalent sign among a welter of related signifiers that, more often than not, establish codes in Hogarth's graphic works. Witness, for instance, the predominantly pejorative depiction of the Jew, from the cuckolded lover in plate 2 of *A Harlot's Progress* to the bloodthirsty religious fanatic in *Credulity, Superstition and Fanaticism* (illus. 92). This again is an allusion activating the observer's knowledge of texts and images figuring Jews, all the way back to Shakespeare and his sources and Christian imagery. Indeed, a close reading of the apparently marginal signifiers in Hogarth's prints will demonstrate not only the links between the plates in his series (the article about what happens *between* the scenes in Hogarth's series remains to be written) but also the existence of what might be called 'secret codes', systems of signification that need to be

94 William Hogarth, *A Harlot's Progress – 5*, 1732, etching and engraving (first state).

re-established. Take the 'Jew's-bread' hanging near the door in plate 5 of *A Harlot's Progress* (illus. 94). In terms of the Peircean triad of the sign, this object represents, on the iconic level, a flytrap; and yet it also refers to eighteenth-century customs (hence, it is indexical); and it is symbolical in that the term 'Jew's-bread' alludes to the Harlot's former wealth as the mistress of a Jewish keeper, and by implication, to one of the male predators who have exploited her (one could of course also explore the connotations of 'flytrap' in conjunction with 'Jew's-bread'). As a sign, the object near the door, then, asks us to look back in the series and, perhaps, to recall the person whose place has been taken by the object; if we do that, the Jew of plate 2 appears beside the two quacks in plate 5.[18] These signifiers and codes need to be explored; they yield fascinating insights into the workings of Hogarthian prints.

Pictures, however, also have frames – visual and verbal margins as well as larger verbal contexts. In the case of illustrations the frame is constituted by a surrounding text. In this book I have discussed some examples of such iconotextual framing, although paying less attention to the contextual setting. In a penetrating study of this issue in book illustrations, John Dixon Hunt has pointed out that, all too often, we take the text for granted and consider the imagery as a new ingredient.[19] In fact, his article proves beyond doubt that the illustration is transformed by its text rather than – as in more usual declensions of book illustration – that the words are changed by their illustrator. We need more investigations of this kind.

The consequences of such intermedial and intertextual analyses are (or should be) far-reaching. And I am not surprised that, at times, they prove frightening for traditionalists in history, art history and literature. I will sketch only a few.[20] The archaeology of texts and pictures outlined above forces us to reconsider such cherished notions as the alleged existence of, and difference between, 'popular' and 'elite' cultures as maintained by E. P. Thompson. It seems that as far as the eighteenth century is concerned, both 'cultures' had more in common in *mentalités* and discursive traditions than Thompson wanted to admit.[21] Similarly, the pursuit of the traces of *mentalités* and the power lines of discourse in visual representations eventually casts doubt on other concepts based on binary thinking. Take the theory of history as a cycle or a series of epochs 'marked' by particular enunciations or persons. In the light of intertextuality, the term 'Enlightenment', for instance, suddenly loses its persuasive power. Like the expression 'Renaissance', it proves to be a notion built on opposites (the *dark* Middle Ages as opposed to the *siècle des lumières*) that disappear as we discover the threads of verbal and visual discourse linking one 'epoch' to the other.[22]

One major problem, however, seems unsolvable. Several decades ago, Michel Foucault addressed it in *Les Mots et les choses*. Commenting on the relation of language to painting, he argued that

It is not that words are imperfect or that, when confronted by the visible, they prove insuperably inadequate. Neither can be reduced to the other's terms: it is in vain that we say what we see; what we see never resides in what we say. And it is in vain that we attempt to show, by the use of images, metaphors, or similes, what we are saying; the space where they achieve their splendor is not that deployed by our eyes but that defined by the sequential elements of syntax.[23]

Foucault's insistence on the fact that painting cannot be narrated but that we need (insufficient) language, for instance in art criticism, has continued to plague scholars dealing with images and texts. It is no exaggeration to say that in attempts to overcome the problem, the word has generally triumphed over the image. In fact, looking back at the inroads structuralism and post-structuralism have made upon hermeneutics, one can agree with W.J.T. Mitchell, E. B. Gilman, and Barbara Stafford, who have repeatedly described the relations between the arts as a history of iconoclastic oppression in which *pictura* is denounced as *fictura*.[24] Language continues to occupy a strategic and dominant position among the arts. Concepts such as the speech act theory or terms such as 'perspective' are borrowed from it to explain phenomena in visual art, with results that are fascinating if not completely persuasive.[25]

A paradox and a dilemma we have to live with reside in the contradictory nature of the image that is so powerful in our culture: Wim Wenders's film *Bis ans Ende der Welt* is a wonderful artistic and critical comment on the state and future of a world dominated by pictures, of images that are helpless and render observers as helpless as Narcissus. In a recent interview, Umberto Eco (partly echoing Barthes) paraphrased that paradox. The image, he argues, 'possesses an irresistible force. It produces an effect of reality, even when it is false. It cannot say by itself that it does not exist or that it is false, whereas the text can do that. Without text, the image lies or gives way to a multitude of interpretations'.[26]

The ambiguous and ambivalent image, then, is both powerful and helpless.[27] Commenting on this paradoxical nature of the visual work of art, Derrida has recently argued that it is distinguished by mutism (the silence of a thing that cannot speak) and by the fact that it is 'already talkative, full of virtual discourse'.[28] To a reader it will (initially) always be more attractive than a text, but in order to mean something it needs mendacious and distorting words: a title, an epigraph, a signature, an ekphrasis. Pictures without legends or similar paratexts (titles, commentaries) may indeed prove frustrating for spectators and critics, the lacking words indicating the powerlessness of the unexplicated pictorial signs. Thus the commentators on Israhel van Meckenem's *Kinderbad* (*c.* 1490), reprinted in a recent exhibition catalogue (illus. 95), complain about the absence of 'signifying words' (*deutendes Wort*) in this obviously unfinished engraving, in which the scroll above the children, had it been filled with text, would direct, confine, and exhaust our reading.[29]

I can only hope that my exemplary *interprétations d'iconotextes* here presented indicate, if not a way out of this situation, then at least a set of instruments (borrowed from deconstruction, semiotics and discourse analysis) that are applicable to both media without oppressing the image. While I agree with W.J.T. Mitchell that we 'have not gone far enough in our exploration of text-image relations' and that we need a new 'iconology' that studies the problem of perceptual, conceptual,

95 Israhel van
Meckenem,
Kinderbad, c. 1490,
engraving.

verbal and graphic images in a unified way, I do not share his
pessimism about the possibilities of critical analysis.[30] My contention is
that if there are no 'pure' images, if images always incorporate texts in
one way or another, we simply cannot sustain the assumption that there
is a line separating the visible from the readable. Derrida has recently
argued that if there is a separation between word and image, the
demarcation line does not run between painting and words, it traverses
both the pictorial and the lexical field in 'the labyrinthine way of an
idiom'.[31] Images, then, should be approached as a mixed form – as
iconotexts. Both Michel Butor and Svetlana Alpers have written
extensively about the function of words in paintings or, more precisely,
about the function of painted words or letters, Paul Klee's *Villa R* being
a famous example from the early twentieth century.[32] There is still a lot
to be explored in this area, and even more as far as graphic art is
concerned. In fact, the very word 'graphic' exposes the double nature
of that art form, referring as it does not (as Hillis Miller claims) '*either*
to writing *or* to picture' but to constructs that are graphic/spatial and
verbal *at once* (my italics).[33]

A new approach in reading images should not, therefore, be based
on purely linguistic or semiotic models that are bound to founder
because they are grounded in the notion of art works as conglomer-
ations of (linguistic) signs.[34] In the wake of Foucault's exemplary
archaeology of *mentalités* and the (post-)structuralist exploration of the
fickle nature of the sign, I suggest that we move forward with a
combination of semiotics and discourse analysis in the spirit of
Foucault. Admittedly, this will not enable us to escape the snares of

rhetoric in verbal and visual representation or those of our own critical metalanguage; but it will put us in a better position to reflect on the historical and ideological functions of representation and ekphrasis. The advantage of this position is that it allows us to cast a critical eye both at the objects of analysis and at the analysers. Given the state of what some American critics call 'art writing', with its continuing belief (in a few quarters) in the great artist and the aesthetically perfect artistic product, this new position would be no small achievement.[35]

Finally, a word about the neglected observer/reader, whose role, if we aim at such a new approach, must be reconsidered. If the conviction I voiced in the introduction holds water, namely that it is the reader who ultimately makes sense of a work of art by re-activating the *déjà vu* and *déjà lu* (one might add: and the *déjà vécu*), the traditional critical concepts of the reader hardly seem satisfactory because they exclude his/her social and ideological background. Although we have already come a long way in our understanding of the role of the reader, a way marked by the allegedly 'free' concepts ('the implied reader') developed and introduced by Iser and Eco,[36] the notion of a predetermined art work that must be re-established by the 'receiver' still prevails. Umberto Eco's seminal *The Open Work* (1989) at long last suggests a participating reader who actively formulates the meaning of a work, and not necessarily a meaning intended by the author. As Eco indicates, the open fictional text or the painting is a 'work to be completed', offering a field of interpretative possibilities, a configuration of substantially indeterminate stimuli which the recipient employs for his 'readings'.[37]

In his recent devastating attack on the 'pure' eye of the beholder and the implied (educated) reader (who turns out, more often than not, to be the educated critic), Pierre Bourdieu suggests substituting such concepts of the cultivated reader in hermeneutics and art history (as advanced, for example, by Gadamer, Panofsky and Iser) with a social history of the observer. For the eye of the beholder is not a given constant; it is the product of institutional settings and social forces constituting that which Bourdieu labels the 'habitus'.[38] It is by historicizing the categories of thinking and perceiving in the observer's experience, not by dehistoricizing them in the construction of a transhistorical ('pure') eye, that we can arrive at an adequate understanding of understanding (*comprende le comprende*).[39] Unlike Bourdieu, I do not think that only sociology or social history can achieve this aim. I would argue that we need less disciplining by traditional fields and more interdisciplinary analyis. To reconstruct the moral and spiritual eye of the observer – past and present – we have a useful tool: discourse analysis, in conjunction with a social history inspired by semiotics. All it takes to apply that tool is a little bit of courage, the courage to cross borders and to visit neighbouring fields, even if the defenders of those fields initially will be displeased with, rather than delighted about, such daredevil aliens.

As an illustration of the task that lies ahead I conclude tacitly, but visually, with Hogarth's *Tail Piece, or The Bathos* (illus. 96). It is an iconotext *par excellence*, and one that, if this book makes sense, deserves the critical, verbal space of another one.

96 William Hogarth, *Tail Piece, or The Bathos*, 1764, etching and engraving.

References

Full publication details are given in the Bibliography

1 *How to (Mis)Read Prints*

  1 See the discussion of the combination of words and images, and the ambiguous role of titles, in the works of René Magritte in Foucault's *This is Not a Pipe*, p. 38. What Foucault says about the sense-making function of titles is also true for captions, for different captions of photographs, for instance, often produce radically different or even contradictory meanings. See I. Gaskell's comments on this issue in 'History of Images', p. 187.

  2 This passage in *Life on the Mississippi* is to be found in chapter 44. Twain's remarks have served as a kick-off for, among others, J. Hillis Miller, *Illustration*, pp. 61–5, and Martin Heuser, *Word & Image Interactions*, p. 16. Hillis Miller's story of how he first came to see the painting of Jackson and Lee in a reproduction on a place-mat in a motel in Winchester, Virginia, is almost as entertaining as Twain's iconoclastic commentary.

  3 For surveys of the development and the present state of 'intertextuality', a term coined by Julia Kristeva in 1969, see H.F. Plett, ed., *Intertextuality*, pp. 3–30, and M. Worton and J. Still, eds, *Intertextuality*, pp. 1–45.

    There is now a vast body of critical literature on the function of allusions in (verbal and visual) texts. The early pioneering work of Barthes, particularly on the importance of connotations and the relations between words and pictures, remains unsurpassed. See especially his *S/Z*, pp. 9–23; the essays on the rhetoric of images and the language of pictures reassembled in *L' Obvie et l'obtus. Essais critiques III*, pp. 25–43 and 139–42, and the essays on semiotics (published between 1963–73) republished in *L'Aventure sémiologique*.

    Recent important studies of allusions include Z. Ben-Porat, 'The Poetics of Allusion', pp. 588–93, C. Perri, 'Knowing and Playing: The Literary Text and the Trope Allusion', pp. 117–28, and U. Hebel, *Romaninterpretation als Textarchäologie*, Introduction and ch. I.

  4 See the *Historical Dictionary of the French Revolution 1789–1799*, ed. S.F. Scott and B. Rothaus (Westport, CT, 1985), pp. 599–602, 635–7, and the critical literature cited there. Cf. the entry on 'Marie-Antoinette' in the *Dictionnaire de la Révolution française*, ed. F. Furet and M. Ozouf (Paris, 1988), where a slightly different view emerges.

  5 See the thoughtful, if now slightly dated, article on this issue by Max Black, 'How do Pictures Represent?'. For a fascinating and challenging collection of essays drawing on intertextual principles in deconstructive readings of art works, see P. Brunette and D. Wills, eds., *Deconstruction and the Visual Arts: Art, Media, Architecture*, especially the contributions by S. Melville, M. Bal and M.-C. Ropars-Wuilleumier.

  6 The term refers to a mingling of pictures and words in one object or within a

given framework. Coined by M. Nerlich, it has been propagated by Alain Montandon and by me in articles on Hogarth. See Nerlich's article, 'Qu'est-ce qu'un iconotexte? Réflexions sur le rapport texte-image photographique dans *La Femme se découvre*', pp. 255–303; and, also edited by Montandon, *Signe, texte, image*. Hans-Jürgen Lüsebrink also uses the term in his analysis of Foucault's handling of text-image constructs: 'Iconotextes. Über Bilder und Metaphernnetze in den Schrifttexten Michel Foucaults'.

7 Intermediality is what Norman Bryson, in a number of works, calls 'interpenetration' (of words and images): see especially his 'Intertextuality and Visual Poetics', and his chapter on 'Semiology and Visual Interpretation' in *Visual Theory*, pp. 61–74.

8 For a fuller explanation of this, see my 'How to (Mis)Read Hogarth or Ekphrasis Galore'.

9 See George's *English Political Caricature to 1792*, and *Hogarth to Cruikshank*. Jarrett's phrase implies that photographs may be used as realistic and reliable evidence. Such a view ignores the creation of realism by the viewer or reader, a process Barthes has discussed in detail.

10 See Stone's *The Family, Sex and Marriage in England*, pp. 277–8, 522, and 540. Stone assumes, for instance, that the depiction of erotica in Hogarth's works (e.g., in *Marriage A-la Mode*), reflects a social practice when, as a matter of fact, that depiction has a strategic, characterizing, and hence rhetorical, function. Similarly, he draws conclusions about sexual practices from Rowlandson's depiction of sexual acts. For a perceptive critique of Stone's suggestions for the use of such (erotic) visual material, see P. Stewart, *Engraven Desire*, pp. 359–62 nn. 32, 53, where Stewart comments on Stone's 'Sex in the West', *New Republic* (8 July 1985).

11 P. Brunette and D. Wills, *Deconstruction and the Visual Arts*, p. 4.

12 See Barthes's 'The Reality Effect', in Roland Barthes, *The Rustle of Language*, pp. 141–54, and Bal's *Reading 'Rembrandt'*, p. 69. Bal's challenging and comprehensive study is the most sophisticated attempt to date to explore from a decidedly feminist viewpoint the potential for interdisciplinary methodology between literature and visual art. On the importance of 'rhetoricality' for literary criticism, art, and other disciplines, see John Bender's essay in *The Ends of Rhetoric*, ed. Bender and Wellbery, pp. 3–43.

13 See H. White, *Metahistory*, and *idem*, *Tropics of Discourse*. A more recent analysis in this area is Hans Kellner's *Language and Historical Representation*. For recent examples of a more self-conscious and better use of visual material by historians: J. Brewer, *The Common People and Politics 1750–1790s*, S. Schama, *The Embarrassment of Riches*, K. Herding and R. Reichardt, *Die Bildpublizistik der Französischen Revolution*, and V. Carretta, *George III and the Satirists from Hogarth to Byron*.

14 For instance, P.J. de Voogd, *Henry Fielding and William Hogarth*, and M. Roston, *Changing Perspectives in Literature and the Visual Arts*, pp. 170–89. I am not arguing that such studies are not useful (the relations between Hogarth and Fielding, for instance, are too well known to be ignored). My point is merely that Hogarth's graphic art should not be seen primarily in relation to polite culture, and that the enormous influence of popular, 'low', forms of literary discourse deserves more attention in terms of structure, ideology, and even morality.

15 See P. Rogers, *Grub Street*, abridged as *Hacks and Dunces*, and *Literature and Popular Culture in Eighteenth-century England*, and R. Paulson, *Popular and Polite Art in the Age of Hogarth and Fielding*. But even these two lucid critics tend to succumb to the preference of the twentieth century for polite forms: Rogers's *Literature and Popular Culture*, for instance, is ultimately interested in 'the reaction of the purveyors of "high" art to the new leisure industry' (p. x); and

Paulson, in the introduction to his recently revised catalogue of the prints, stresses the importance for Hogarth of Shakespeare, Bunyan, Defoe, Swift and Pope – yet his commentary to the plates provides ample evidence of the importance of popular forms of writing. See Paulson, *Hogarth's Graphic Works*, p. 1, and my review of this catalogue in *Eighteenth-century Studies*, XXVI/3 (1993), pp. 499–503.

16 The background of this print is discussed in Paulson, *Hogarth's Graphic Works*, p. 70 (no. 107), and in volume 1 of Paulson's revised biography, *Hogarth: The 'Modern Moral Subject', 1697–1732*, pp. 166–7. J. K. Welcher explores Hogarth's use of the *bambocciate* in 'Hogarth's Reading of *Gulliver's Travels*'. Unfortunately, Welcher (in tune with the correspondences-of-the-arts approach) misses the opportunity to demonstrate the differences between Hogarth's image (and its grotesque and obscene rhetoric) and Swift's text.

17 For detailed analysis of the entertainments alluded to in these prints, and a critique of the middle-class ideology inspiring such graphic works, see my 'Hogarth's Graphic Palimpsests'.

18 I have provided a survey of the issues involved in ekphrasis, that is the verbal representation of a visual representation, in the introduction to a collection of essays on *Icons – Texts – Iconotexts*. Also see the Introduction (pp. 1–9) and the case studies in J.A.W. Heffernan, *Museum of Words*.

19 For critiques of Paulson's view of Hogarth see my review of the catalogue, *Hogarth's Graphic works*, cited in n.15 above; and Bindman, 'The Nature of Satire in the Modern Moral Subjects', and Monod, 'Painters and Party Politics in England 1714–1760', where Hogarth's commercial exploitation of politics is stressed.

20 A brief critique of Hogarth commentaries can be found in Roskill, *The Interpretation of Pictures*, pp. 11–15. See also my 'How to (Mis)Read Hogarth'. Important studies within the three approaches indicated are (first) Paulson's revised biography cum analysis, *Hogarth*, (second) Shesgreen's 'Hogarth's *Industry and Idleness*: A Reading', and his *Hogarth and the Times-of-the-Day Tradition*, and (third) W. Busch, *Nachahmung als bürgerliches Kunstprinzip*, and B. Krysmanski's dissertation, 'Hogarth's "Enthusiasm Delineated" '.

21 The term is Gaskell's ('History of Images', p. 182), denoting the 'attempt to interpret visual material as it might have been when it was first made, whether by the maker, his contemporaries, or both'.

22 See Behrendt's 'Hogarth, Dualistic Thinking, and the Open Culture' and Busch's 'Lektüreprobleme bei Hogarth'. Paradoxically, Behrendt (after discussing the relevance of Umberto Eco's seminal work on open structures for explications of Hogarth's prints) even suggests that we 'leave our critical egos at the door with our intellectual side-arms' in order to 'free ourselves for a far more productive encounter with the art of William Hogarth'. It seems to me that such fear of theory is exactly what stands in the way of an insightful reading of Hogarth's *œuvre*.

23 See also Stafford's *Voyage into Substance*. However, one might hold against Stafford that, although she is painfully aware of the domination of language over images, she uses her impressive, massive, visual material all too often as (accompanying) 'illustration' in the traditional sense of historical writing I have criticized above. This is unfortunately also true of her *Artful Science*, where Stafford argues convincingly (p. xxii) that images in critical studies 'tend to serve as illustrations of changes in the meaning of writing, not as vibrant shapers of knowledge'. While Stafford manages to uncover 'the lost epistemological dimension of the informed and performative gaze' (p. xxii), one would have appreciated more information on the rhetoric of the numerous images that accompany the text of *Artful Science*.

An interesting study that goes beyond disciplinary limits is Martin Kemp, *The Science of Art*; see, especially, ch. 3, on the development of perspective from Rubens to Turner, which includes Hogarth.

24 The phrasing is Stanley Fish's in a recent extension of his much debated and persuasive study of the way 'group pressures' determine how we read and interpret texts: *Doing What Comes Naturally*.

25 For a collection of articles by New Historicists, see H.A. Veeser, ed., *The New Historicism*.

Bryson argues for a new semiotic analysis of images that is to replace Gombrich's subjective perceptualism: see his edition of critical essays in semiotics spanning the period from Jan Mukarovsky to Jean Baudrillard and Julia Kristeva: *Calligram*, pp. xiii–xxix. A challenging collection of critical essays is assembled in *Visual Theory*, ed. Bryson, M.A. Holly and K. Moxey, but see, too, G. Mermoz, 'Rhetoric and Episteme'. Stephen Bann, in *The True Vine*, is also critical of Gadamer's hermeneutics and welcomes the New Art History.

Unfortunately, French art historians have been working in the shadow of their Anglo-American colleagues. Bryson and Bal, however, occasionally refer to important works written in French. See particularly H. Damisch's *Théorie du nuage*, which tries to ground art-historical writing in linguistics and semiotics, and Damisch's *L'Origine de la perspective*, a thoughtful study integrating poststructural theories while remaining conscious of the 'unspeakable' and the 'silences' in works of art. Similarly, G. Didi-Huberman's *Devant l'image*, highly critical of Panofsky, uses post-structural theories (e.g., Lacan's writings) to suggest new ways of art-historical inquiry.

26 J. Hart, 'Erwin Panofsky and Karl Mannheim', p. 566.

27 See Foucault's essay, first published in French in 1969, 'What is an Author?'. Foucault suggests that once the author function disappears we can ask more interesting questions: 'What are the modes of existence of this discourse? Where has it been used, how can it circulate, and who can appropriate it for himself? What are the places in it where there is room for possible subjects? Who can assume these various subject functions?' (p. 275).

More recently, P. Bourdieu has criticized the continuing use, in literary criticism and art history, of the myth of the author/artist as genius (replacing God) who is in command of the production and meaning of his/her work; see 'Le "projet originel", mythe fondateur' in Bourdieu, *Les Règles de l'art*, pp. 263–9.

28 Cited in F.H. Mautner, *Lichtenberg*, p. 421.

29 See J. Kristeva, *Sémeiotiké*, pp. 194 and 225, *idem*, *La Révolution du langage poétique*, pp. 388–9; and R. Barthes, *S/Z*, pp. 27–8.

30 See, especially, the publications of John Searle and Louis Marin, and the recent critique of their works by Mieke Bal, *Reading 'Rembrandt'*, pp. 270–1.

31 Introduction in P. Brunette and D. Wills, *Deconstruction and the Visual Arts*, p. 3.

32 See Walpole's *Anecdotes of Painting*, p. 1, quoted in William Hogarth, *The Analysis of Beauty*, p. xlvi.

Lichtenberg's extremely clever and deliberately 'anarchic' commentary remains unsurpassed. Although he still championed the idea of the genial artistic creator, his comments take cognizance of both indeterminacy and ambiguity in Hogarth's graphic art. It is hardly suprising that his method has been misunderstood as 'erratic' by his modern and postmodern followers who read for central and hierarchic meaning. For a discussion see my 'How to (Mis)Read Hogarth'. Also J.A. McCarthy, 'Lichtenberg as Post-structuralist', *Transactions of the Eighth International Congress on the Enlightenment* (Oxford, 1992), pp. 1567–71.

33 See Behrendt's essay, 'Hogarth, Dualistic Thinking, and the Open Culture'. But

Behrendt leaves Hogarth's work there, arguing implicity and explicitly with and for a genial author always in charge of the ambiguity he creates.

34 A. Guillerm was one of the first to suggest an analysis of French erotic engravings in terms of semiotics, providing a few tentative case studies in his 'Le Système de l'iconographie galante'. For a persuasive study of book illustrations, and their intertextual relations with each other and the verbal texts in which they are embedded, see P. Stewart's *Engraven Desire*. In his extensive bibliography (pp. 363–71) Stewart quotes additional critical works published since 1980.

For some lucid comments on Hogarth's handling of language and literature in the prints see M. Baridon, 'Hogarth et le langage'.

35 On 'différance' and logocentric/hierarchic meaning see Derrida, *Of Grammatology*, *Writing and Difference*, *Dissemination*, and the article on 'différance' in *A Derrida Reader*, ed. P. Kamuf, pp. 59–80. Derek Attridge clarifies Derrida's formulation 'il n'y a pas de hors-texte' in the introduction to his edition of Derrida essays and interviews entitled *Jacques Derrida: Acts of Literature*, pp. 16–17. See also Derrida's '. . . That Dangerous Supplement . . .' in this volume, p. 102. Derrida's latest views on visual art can be glimpsed in 'The Spatial Arts: An Interview with Jacques Derrida', in P. Brunette and D. Wills, eds, *Deconstruction and the Visual Arts*, pp. 9–33, where he comments on the importance of spacing, the mutism and intertextual nature of artworks, and the issue of presence (authorial signature).

36 The art-historical references, mostly parodic in kind, in this scene and in the series as such are the subject of studies by F. Antal, *Hogarth and His Place in European Art*, and W. Busch, *Hogarth in Context*. Paulson in particular has made the Choice of Hercules his favourite subject of discussion. I am indebted to his detailed commentary in *Hogarth's Graphic Works*, pp. 75–9; and in *Hogarth: The 'Modern Moral Subject'*, pp. 237–337.

37 See, for instance, Georgette de Montenay, *Emblemata Christiana* (Lyon, 1571; reprd. Frankfurt, 1619), Andrea Alciati, *Emblemata cum commentariis* (Padua, 1621; reprd New York, 1976), and Gérard de Lairesse, *The Art of Painting in all its Branches* (Amsterdam, 1701; trans. and pubd in English in 1738).

38 See my article on 'Eroticism in Graphic Art: The Case of William Hogarth'.

39 On this system, which Lichtenberg compared to flagpoles, see P. Georgel, ' "The Most Contemptible Meanness that Lines can be Formed into": Hogarth et les arts "autres" '.

40 See J. Trusler, *Hogarth Moralized*, p. 111. The visual and verbal layering of the signifiers in *The Sleeping Congregation*, with particular consideration of the allusions to art, has been explored in B. Krysmanski's dissertation, 'Hogarth's "Enthusiasm Delineated" ', especially ch. 2 (pp. 42–60). My discussion of the fan relies on Krysmanski's detailed research.

41 Here, and throughout his commentaries on Hogarth, Paulson seems to be unaware of (and does not really care about) what Mieke Bal, drawing on Van Alphen, has described as two 'moments of meaning production': the text or engraving as produced by its author brings order into the collection of possible meanings couched in the pre-text(s); the second moment of meaning production occurs when the critic or spectator articulates an ordering or reworking of the collection of possible meanings. See Bal's insightful essay, 'Light in Painting: Dis-Seminating Art History', p. 58. Paulson, it seems to me, consistently denies that he too makes meaning, attributing his own, secondary, production to Hogarth.

42 See Paulson's *Breaking and Remaking*, p. 151, *Hogarth's Graphic Works*, p. 99, and *Hogarth: High Art and Low*, pp. 97–103, 407 n.28. On the long history of the triangle as a polysemous sign, see G. Stuhlfaut, *Das Dreieck*, and M. Corbett and R. Lightbown, *The Comely Frontispiece*, pp. 40–1.

43 When, in 1993, Richard Dorment reviewed Ronald Paulson's revised study (in three volumes) of *Hogarth*, a stormy battle broke out between author and reviewer, mainly because of their differing views of Hogarth's 'intention'. I find their critical animosities completely superfluous, for Paulson's reconstruction of Hogarth's personality is as fictional and personal as Dorment's more 'primitive' view of the author. See their acrimonious exchanges in *The New York Review of Books* between July and October 1993.

44 See Busch's essay, 'Lektüreprobleme bei Hogarth'. Busch provides fine case studies of the interplay of traditional artistic codes and their subversion, of such sign systems as clothes and gestures, and – most importantly – of the syntax of the Hogarthian 'language' that he sees marked by the discrepancy between content and form. The only problem I have with this informative essay is its author's continuing belief in the fundamental importance of Hogarth's intention. In fact, Busch could easily have replaced the name Hogarth with 'Hogarth's work' or (following the example of Mieke Bal's study of Rembrandt's art) at least put it in inverted commas: he would thus have achieved the same result without implying that the intermediality of Hogarth's engravings is the work of the artist.

45 On the pros and cons of deconstructive readings, see J. Derrida in 'The Spatial Arts: An Interview with Jacques Derrida', in Brunette and Wills, *Deconstruction and the Visual Arts*, pp. 30–2. Derrida argues (p. 31): 'I don't believe that deconstruction is essentially or solely that which . . . destroys the production of knowledge. No. Or rather, it does and it doesn't. On the one hand it can in fact disturb or block a certain type of work; on the other hand it indirectly produces knowledge – indirectly it provokes work.'

2 *Captain Gulliver and the Pictures*

1 For discussions of the problems discussed in this paragraph (the genres of the *Travels*; its intertextual aspects; the role of the reader) see especially G. Holly, 'Travel and Translation: Textuality in *Gulliver's Travels*', H.J. Real and H.J. Vienken, *Jonathan Swift: Gulliver's Travels*, M.E. Novak, '*Gulliver's Travels* and the Picaresque Voyage', L.K. Barnett, 'Deconstructing *Gulliver's Travels*: Modern Readers and the Problematic of Genre', F.N. Smith, 'The Danger of Reading Swift: The Double Binds of *Gulliver's Travels*', and N. Frye, *The Anatomy of Criticism*. Genette voices his critique of traditional genres in *Introduction à l 'architexte*, trans. as *The Architext: An Introduction*.

2 See Genette's studies: *The Architext, Palimpsestes. La littérature au second degré*, and *Seuils*. Also see J. Derrida, 'The Law of Genre'. For recent assessments of the *Travels* in the light of its intertextual allusions, see especially Paul Turner's edition (1986), J.P. Hunter, '*Gulliver's Travels* and the Novel', L.K. Barnett, 'Deconstructing *Gulliver's Travels*', and F.N. Smith, 'The Danger of Reading Swift.'

3 Turner, ed., *Gulliver's Travels*, p. xvi.

4 *The Genres of Gulliver's Travels*, p. 253. See Brean Hammond, *Gulliver's Travels*, p. 105, Paul Goetsch, 'Linguistic Colonialism and Primitivism: the Discovery of Native Languages and Oral Traditions in Eighteenth-century Travel Books and Novels', p. 351, D.F. Paßmann, '*Full of Probable Lies': Gulliver's Travels und die Reiseliteratur vor 1726*, p. 352.

5 As Jacques Derrida explains (adopting the term from Kant and Heidegger), *parergon* denotes an accessory, a supplement, and, for him, an 'hors d'oeuvre' in *all* its French meanings (e.g., outside of a work, but also the marginal part of a work). The 'clothes' of statues as well as the decorative columns at the entrance of a building are thus examples of the *parergon*. The frame of paintings is another one; it is at the focus, if focus there is, of Derrida's *La Vérité en peinture*, pp. 21–

169. I will return to this seminal study in my chapter on framing.

6 A short excerpt from *Seuils*, translated by Marie Maclean, was published in *New Literary History*, XXII (1991): 'Introduction to the Paratext', pp. 261–73.

7 See Genette's *Palimpsestes*, pp. 7–12; and *Seuils*, pp. 10–15.

8 On these editorial problems see H.J. Real and H.J. Vienken, *Jonathan Swift*, pp. 16–18 and 140–41. See also H. Hunfeld's 'Gullivers fünfte Insel' in his *Literatur als Sprachlehre*, pp. 179–212.

9 In *The Correspondence of Jonathan Swift*, III, pp. 152–3.

10 See *The Correspondence*, V, pp. 152–81; and *Gulliver's Travels*, ed. H. Davis, pp. xxiv–xxviii.

11 See *Gulliver's Travels*, 2nd edn, ed. R.A. Greenberg (New York, 1970), p. 271.

12 On these irritations see C. Rawson, *Gulliver and the Gentle Reader*, p. 6; H.J. Schnackertz, '*Gulliver's Travels*: Swifts aufklärerisches Spiel mit der Fiktion', and J. Mezciems, 'Utopia and "the Thing which is not"': More, Swift, and Other Lying Idealists'.

13 This is R. Halsband's argument in his article, 'Eighteenth-century Illustrations of *Gulliver's Travels*', p. 83.

14 Mezciems, 'Utopia and "the Thing which is not" ', p. 49.

15 See A.E. Newton, quoted in P. Rogers, ed., *Robinson Crusoe* (London, 1979), p. 5.

16 On Swift's knowledge of travel literature, see Real and Vienken, *Jonathan Swift*, p. 35, and D.F. Passmann, '*Full of Improbable Lies*', pp. 473–8.

17 For information about the various illustrations in the works of John Smith, including the portraits and maps, see his *The Complete Works*, ed. P.L. Barbour, I, p. 322; II, p. 97; III, p. 244. Barbour provides no illustration of Pocahontas, noting only that it must have been in circulation in February 1717. It appears in Smith's *General History*, facing p. 104, in his *Travels*.

18 For a detailed analysis of this frontispiece see M. Corbett and R. Lightbown, *The Comely Frontispiece*, pp. 172–82.
    On the change that took place in the Renaissance and early eighteenth century in making and studying maps, see E. Reeves, 'Reading Maps'. Also see D. Woodward, ed., *Art and Cartography*, which contains two important essays by S.Y. Edgerton and S. Alpers, pp. 10–96; and the special issue of *Word & Image* (IV/2, 1988) devoted to the relationship of cartography and graphic systems.

19 On the meaning and importance of the Latin passage see especially W. Barr, 'Introduction and Commentary' in *The Satires of Persius*, trans. G. Lee (Liverpool, 1987), pp. 4, 99; J.R. Jenkinson, *Persius: The Satires* (Warminster, 1980), pp. 7, 27; M. Morford, *Persius*, pp. 1–25, 43; and J. Mezciems, 'Utopia and "the Thing which is not" ', p. 50.

20 Holly, 'Travel and Translation: Textuality in *Gulliver's Travels*', pp. 149–50.

21 See the recent studies by A. Wilton, *The Swagger Portrait*, and M. Pointon, *Hanging the Head*.

22 On the importance of 'iconic epigraphs' see A. Compagnon, *La Seconde main ou le travail de la citation* (Paris, 1979), p. 337; and D. Scott, 'Epigraphic Structure in the Nineteenth-century French Prose Poem' in *Word & Image Interactions*, ed. M. Heuser, pp.53–60, esp. p. 53.

23 See Corbett and Lightbown, *The Comely Frontispiece*, p. 5.

24 See B.M. Stafford, *Body Criticism*, pp. 362–5. In her vastly instructive chapter on 'magnifying' and 'visual quackery' (pp. 362–78) Stafford analyses the importance of optical innovations for Enlightenment understanding and thinking. *Gulliver's Travels* should perhaps be read with the information in mind that, as Stafford argues, 'empiricism, as a form of skeptical iconoclasm, continually harped on the difficulty of distinguishing the fictional from the factual. Cartesian rationalism, equally implacable toward the lie, the feint, the trick, de-realised the world into a

dream metaphysics. This double-barreled assault left the visual arts in the precarious position in which they find themselves today' (p. 378). In many respects, the *Travels* joins this attack on visuality.

25 For a detailed analysis of the importance of the mirror as image and metaphor between 1300 and 1700 see H. Grabes, *The Mutable Glass: Mirror-Imagery in Titles and Texts of the Middle Ages and the English Renaissance*, trans. G. Collier (Cambridge, 1982).

26 On the meaning and context of the quotation from Horace see the *Odes and Epodes*, trans. C.E. Bennett, p. 218. The importance for Swift of this Roman author has been discussed by M.E. Dolan Brown, 'The Poet's Mask', and W.B. Ewald, *The Masks of Jonathan Swift*, pp. 1–12.

27 J. Derrida, *La Vérité en peinture*, pp. 63–94.

28 On the history of framing paintings, especially portraits, see C. Grimm, 'Histoire du cadre: un panorama', and my chapter Three below. Also see Derrida, *La Vérité en peinture*, p. 67.

29 Welcher, 'Hogarth's Reading of *Gulliver's Travels*', forthcoming. For a very perceptive discussion of these relations between the visual and the verbal in the discourse of travel literature, in a case study of Jean-François Lafitau's *Moeurs des sauvages amériquains comparées aux moeurs des premiers temps* (Paris, 1724), see M. de Certeau, 'Writing vs. Time', pp. 37–65. See also Stafford, *Voyage into Substance*, pp. 33–59, 437–70.

30 On the importance of titles for the understanding and interpretation of literary works see especially Genette, *Seuils*, p. 88ff.; M. Di Fazio Alberti, *Il titolo et la funzione paraletteraria* (Turin, 1984); and A. Rothe, *Der literarische Titel. Funktionen, Formen, Geschichte* (Frankfurt, 1986).

31 On this generic aspect see Mezciems, 'Utopia and "the Thing which is not" ', p. 46; P. Adams, *Travel Literature and the Evolution of the Novel*, p. 38; M. Novak, '*Gulliver's Travels* and The Picaresque Voyage', pp. 26–31, and D.F. Passmann, '*Full of Improbable Lies*', pp. 14, 340–6.

32 See F. Dietz, 'The Image of Medicine in Utopian and Dystopian Fiction' in *The Body and the Text*, ed. B. Clarke and W. Aycock (Lubbock, 1990), p. 117. Dietz reads Hythlodaeus's first name literally, arguing that 'Raphael' is derived from Hebrew 'rafael – God has healed'. See also U. Seeber, *Wandlungen der Form der literarischen Utopie*, pp. 51–3.

33 For a fuller treatment see my *Eros Revived*, pp. 8–47, and my 'The Satire on Doctors in Hogarth's Graphic Works' in *Literature and Medicine During the Eighteenth Century*, ed. M.M. Roberts and R. Porter, pp. 200–26.

34 See P. Adams, *Travelers and Travel Liars 1660–1800*, and D.F. Passmann, '*Full of Improbable Lies*', pp. 97–101, 333–9.

35 On the cultural and ideological implications of simulation see J. Baudrillard, *Simulacres et simulation*, especially pp. 12–14. On Swift's rhetorical strategy in his satires see M.J. Croghan, 'Savage Indignation: An Introduction to the Philosophy of Language and Semiotics in Jonathan Swift'. The Dean's iconoclasm is treated by R. Paulson, *Breaking and Remaking*, pp. 35–48; and in my 'Swift and the Female Idol: The Dean as Iconoclast'.

36 See H.J. Real and H.J. Vienken, *Jonathan Swift*, pp. 20, 56–8.

37 See Stafford, *Voyage into Substance*, p. 438. See also D. Reynaud, 'Pour une théorie de la description au 18e siècle'.

38 This is F. Krey's argument in 'Interpretationskommentar zu *Gulliver's Travels*: Vorspann und Buch I', PhD diss. (Berlin, 1969), p. 39.

39 See *The Prose Writings of Jonathan Swift*, ed. H. Davis *et al.* (Oxford, 1939–74), IX, p. 338. On the authenticity of this piece, signed 'E.F.', see ibid., pp. xxiv–xxvii, and L.T. Milic, *A Quantitative Approach to the Style of Jonathan Swift*, p. 237ff.

40 Genette, *Seuils*, pp. 137–49.
41 See Titus Lucretius Carus, *De rerum natura*, ed. M.F. Smith, pp. ix–liv,1,79.
42 *Seuils*, p. 150.
43 On this aspect of the (fictional) preface see Genette, *Seuils*, pp. 192–267; and J.-P. Forster, 'Swift: The Satirical Use of Framing Fictions', especially p. 179.
44 *Gulliver's Travels*, ed. P. Turner, p. 307. n.2.
45 See Genette, *Seuils*, pp. 192–3.
46 For a perceptive discussion of simulation in this context see R.H. Rodino, ' "Splendide Mendax": Authors, Characters, and Readers in *Gulliver's Travels*'.
47 *Seuils*, p. 269.
48 For a detailed discussion see C. Fox, 'The Myth of Narcissus in Swift's *Travels*'.
49 For a discussion of the maps in the editions of *Utopia* published in 1516 and 1518 in terms of semiotics see Louis Marin, 'Frontiers of Utopia', and also his earlier *Utopics: Spatial Play*. Bibliographical information can be found in Thomas More, *The Complete Works*, IV, pp. clxxxviii, 277–8.
50 *Seuils*, p. 376. On the isssue of entrapment in Swift's works see R. Nash, 'Entrapment and Ironic Modes in *Tale of a Tub*', pp. 415 and 431.

3 Frame-work: The Margin(al) as Supplement and Countertext

1 See N. Paquin, 'Le "cadre" comme lieu de paradoxe au dix-huitième siècle', p. 1486.
2 For a detailed commentary to this plate, see *Die Très Riches Heures des Jean Duc de Berry im Musée Condé Chantilly*, intro. by M. Meiss (Munich, 1973), plate 33.
3 M. Camille, *Image on the Edge*, p. 41. Further examples of such 'fantastic' and oppositional framing can be found in the catalogue of the recent exhibition at the Bibliothèque Nationale in Paris: see F. Avril and N. Reynaud, eds., *Les Manuscrits à peintures en France 1440–1520*: on p. 217, for instance, one finds a reproduction of a double page from the *Chansonnier de Jean de Montchenu* (*c.* 1475) showing an amorous couple surrounded by musical notes. The pages themselves are held in the form of a heart. Another example that comes to mind is the famous border imagery of the Bayeux Tapestry, which burlesques the heroic central narrative.
4 I have borrowed this example from J.-C. Lebensztejn who discusses it as an illustration of the 'windows' tradition in Baroque painting. See Lebensztejn, 'Framing Classical Space', p. 38. In a revised and extended version of this piece the author explores the multiple meanings and figurations of the physical frame as it appears throughout the whole of the history of art: 'Starting Out from the Frame (Vignettes)'.
5 See Fantuzzi's *Panneau d'ornement avec ovale vide* (1542–43) and *Cartouche rectangulaire vide* (1544–45), both reproduced in J. Derrida, *La Vérité en peinture*, pp. 75–6. The phrase, 'cadre pour cadre', echoing 'l'art pour l'art', is N. Paquin's in her 'Le "cadre" comme lieu de paradoxe', p. 1486.
    For additional examples of *trompe-l'oeil* frames in early Renaissance book illumination see Gaspare Visconti's *De Paulo et Daria amanti* (1494/5); and *Epistolae Hieronymi* (Venice, 1480), reproduced in A. Dückers, ed., *Das Berliner Kupferstichkabinett*, pp. 56–7, 59.
6 See Lebensztejn, 'Framing Classical Space', pp. 37–9. For other artistic opinions on the importance of the frame, from the Renaissance to the twentieth century, *idem*, 'Starting Out from the Frame (Vignettes)', pp. 120 and 128.
7 See Lebensztejn's discussion ('Framing Classical Space', p. 38) of Ingres's *Mademoiselle Rivière* in its original frame in the Louvre and in its 'normalized' form as a slide issued by the National Museums in Paris. The original frame stresses the rectangular shape and also contains an arch.

On the re-framing, around 1920, of Dutch Old Masters in the Rijksmuseum, see P.J.J. van Thiel, 'Eloge du cadre: la pratique hollandaise'. Van Thiel rightly calls the Dutch masterworks in French frames a 'monstruosité hybride' (p. 32).

Such interferences prove that museums are of course also sites where framing and meaning-making occurs; they frame 'history, memory, and meaning' and, ultimately, also art history. For an insightful study of the museum as a framing device and powerful institution see D. Preziosi, 'Modernity Again: The Museum as Trompe l'Oeil' (quotation from p. 141).

8 For studies in this area see the articles by N. Paquin, J.-C. Lebensztejn, and C. Grimm cited above. Also B. Pons, 'Les cadres français du XVIIIe siècle et leurs ornements', C. Grimm, *The Book of Picture Frames* (New York, 1981), W. Ehlich, *Bilderrahmen von der Antike bis zur Romantik* (Dresden, 1979), and L. Marin, 'Du cadre au décor ou la question de l'ornement dans la peinture', *Rivista di estetica*, XII (1982), pp. 16–35. Also helpful are the earlier studies by E. Goffman, *Frame Analysis* (Cambridge, 1974) and M. Shapiro, 'On Some Problems in the Semiotics of Visual Art: Field and Vehicle in Image Signs', *Semiotica*, I (1969), pp. 223–42. Further analyses up to 1986 are listed in Jacques Foucart's 'Bibliographie du cadre', *Revue de l'art*, LXXVI (1987), pp. 60–2.

There are challenging essays by M.-C. Ropars-Wuilleumier, D.N Rodowick, D. Preziosi and C. Altieri, all addressing variations on the *parergon*, in Brunette and Wills, *Deconstruction and the Visual Arts*.

9 Such an exploration would require a monograph of its own. Suffice it to say here that painters and critics commenting on the use and function of picture frames, from the seventeenth to the nineteenth centuries, like to compare the 'bordure' of a painting to the finery of a woman. See the sources cited in J.-C. Lebensztejn, 'Starting Out from the Frame', pp. 120 and 128. In his study of ekphrasis, J.A.W. Heffernan discusses the powerfully gendered contest between 'the voice of male speech striving to control a female image'; see *Museum of Words*, p. 1. For a lucid analysis of this contest in art, art history and literature, which usually ends with the female body reduced to an object controlled by a male artist or critic, see E. Bronfen, *Over Her Dead Body*.

10 See Derrida's critique of these traditions, including formalism, in *La Vérité en peinture*, pp. 71–3. Specifically, he argues that no theory and no critical practice can really do without a consideration of the frame as the area where such issues as inside/outside and the establishment of meaning emerge as problems to be faced and not to be left aside (p. 71). On p. 73 Derrida argues that, 'I do not know what is essential and accessory in a work . . . for instance, the frame. Where does the frame take place? Does it take place? Where does it begin? Where does it stop? What is its internal limit? What its external one?' (my trans.).

It is Derrida's suspicion that the much neglected frame, and framing as such, is the very site of paradoxical sense-making in art (and not the 'truth inside' any given work) which leads him to write 'four times around painting' in a refusal to answer the question, 'what is art', precisely because that question implies a certain notion and existence of art as such and because critical analyses of art have always made a difference between the 'inside' and the 'outside'. Convinced that it is high time to 'approach/enter [the art work] in a different manner' (*il faut aborder autrement*), he focuses on what allegedly constitutes the surroundings of a work of art – the frame, the title, the signature, the museum, the archive, reproduction, discourse and the market. See the introductory section, ironically entitled 'passe-partout', in *La Vérité en peinture*, pp. 5–18.

11 On the publishing history and the background of Scheuchzer's *Physica Sacra* see the abbreviated edition, with a commentary by Hans Krauss, pp. 8–12; and M. Lanckoronska and R. Öhler, *Die Buchillustration des 18. Jahrhunderts in Deutschland, Österreich und der Schweiz* (Leipzig, 1932–4), I; and two studies by

K. Nissen: *Die botanische Buchillustration. Ihre Geschichte und Bibliographie*, 2 vols (Stuttgart, 1951–66), and *Die zoologische Buchillustration*, 2 vols (Stuttgart, 1951–66).

12 B.M. Stafford has shown how the medical and general scientific background (optics, physics) of the time invades both the illustrations and the commentary of Scheuchzer's *Physica Sacra*; see her *Body Criticism*, especially the chapters on 'Conceiving', 'Dis-secting', and 'Magnifying', where many illustrations have been reproduced.

While I am also interested in the traces of contemporary science, my concern is chiefly with the intra/intermedial relations between verbal and poetic commentary and illustration, and between the frame-work and the pictures themselves.

13 In the following passage I have drawn on the introduction in the abbreviated edition of the *Physica Sacra*, ed. H. Krauss, pp. 9–12.

14 For an explanation of the details see *Physica Sacra*, ed. H. Krauss, p. 220.

15 Stafford, for instance, makes extensive use of the plates (from a French edition of the *Physica Sacra*) in her *Body Criticism*, revealing how the changes in Enlightenment science affected verbal and visual ways of seeing and representing. But she considers the heteroclite plates, made (as we have seen above) by at least two artists supervised by at least two writers, as entities that, although not necessarily harmonious (she does comment on the fantastic framework), express Scheuchzer's opinion. I am arguing that the plates have their own contradictory messages, inscribed as traces in the border and in the centre, and that Scheuchzer's commentary is another level to be considered apart.

16 The phrase is Krauss's in the commentary to the plate. See his edition of *Physica Sacra*, 1984, on which I have drawn in this instance and for some of the other illustrations discussed in this chapter.

17 The biblical text reads as follows: 'And Jacob was left alone, and there wrestled a man with him until the breaking of the day. And when he saw that he prevailed not against him, he touched the hollow of his thigh; and the hollow of Jacob's thigh was out of joint, as he wrestled with him . . . And as he passed over Penuel the sun rose upon him, and he halted upon his thigh'.

18 To a certain extent, this art is of course also a trace of the *mentalité* of the creators and engravers (who were of Swiss and south German origin), of the world of Catholic Church decorations in which they had grown up (Augsburg and Nuremberg having special traditions again).

19 See Krauss's commentary on these plates, *Physica Sacra*, pp. 60–2.

20 One textual/visual thread I cannot trace within the confines of this chapter concerns the emblematical history of such representations. As even a brief glance at a handbook of emblems will show, the eighteenth century was heir to a tradition (in visual representations) that associated herbs and plants with emblematical (transferred) meanings. See, for instance, *Emblemata – Handbuch zur Sinnbildkunst des XVI. und XVII. Jahrhunderts*, ed. A. Henkel and A. Schöne, including the 'Supplement'.

21 For details see Krauss, *Physica Sacra*, p. 240.

22 For collections of such mildly erotic prints see E. Dacier, *La Gravure en France au XVIIIe siècle*, B.L. Dighton and H.W. Lawrence, *French Line Engravings of the Late Eighteenth Century*, and plates 1–57 in my *Lust and Love in the Rococo*.

23 See the discussion of French Rococo frames by Pons, 'Les cadres français du XVIIIe siècle et leurs ornements', who points out that the royal portraits always received the richest decoration in the frame. Since *Le Carquois épuisé* is dedicated to a prince, its *parergon* must be elaborate, but not as sophisticated as that of a king. See Pons, p. 48, and the discussion of similar engravings in my *Lust and*

Love in the Rococo Period.

24 See J. Derrida, 'Signature événement contexte', in his *Marges de la philosophie*, especially pp. 390–3. Specifically, Derrida criticizes the logocentric function of writing (and signatures), which always pretends to provide a 'hermeneutic decoding' (un déchiffrement herméneutique) of a sense that is never transported but deferred (p. 392).

On the engraving see E. Dacier, *La Gravure en France*, p. 89: the picture was first exhibited at the Salon of 1787.

25 See C. Grimm, 'Histoire du cadre: un panorama', p. 20; and J.C. Lebensztejn, 'Framing Classical Space', p. 38.

26 On the notion of 'centre' and decentering in this context, see J. Derrida, 'La Structure, le signe et le jeu dans le discours des sciences humaines' in *L'Ecriture et la différence* especially pp. 410–12.

27 For details see Dacier, *La Gravure en France*, p. 78.

28 On the presence and signature of the artist, Derrida has recently remarked that the artist 'signs while painting' and that 'the signature of the author isn't limited to the name of the author' who ultimately, in the case of the painter, is blind. See 'The Spatial Arts: An Interview with Jacques Derrida', in Brunette and Wills, *Deconstruction and the Visual Arts*, pp. 16–17, 24. Obviously, my treatment of the artist's signature works at a more concrete level.

29 For more information on this print, see Dacier, *La Gravure en France*, pp. 87–8.

30 For that background, see M. Sheriff, *Fragonard: Art and Eroticism*.

31 On the importance of the signature, the rebus, and the seigns, vis-a-vis art, see B. Fraenkel, 'La Signature et le rébus du nom propre' in *Word & Image Interactions*, ed. M. Heuser, pp. 35–40; J.-C. Lebensztejn, 'Esquisse d'une typologie', *Revue de l'art*, XXVI (1974), pp. 48–57; and M. Butor's excellent study, *Les Mots dans la peinture*.

32 See Swift, *The Complete Poems*, ed. P. Rogers, ll.81–96 (p. 338) and notes.

33 See the chapter on 'Marginal Characters' in my forthcoming study of Hogarth's graphic art published by Cambridge University Press, and Paulson's discussion of the figures in the frame of plate 2 of *The Analysis of Beauty*, in *Hogarth's Graphic Works*, pp. 160–61.

34 Paulson briefly discusses the ambiguity of the framework and the entire series in his recent *Hogarth: High Art and Low*, pp. 289–323, especially pp. 291–3. See also M. Baridon's apposite remarks about language (and discourse) as a framing device in Hogarth's graphic art in 'Hogarth et le langage'.

35 See *A New and Complete Collection of Trials for Adultery: or A General History of Modern Gallantry and Divorces* (London, 1796), I, pp. 3–6. I have analysed this collection and earlier examples in 'The Pornographer in the Courtroom'.

36 On the curtain in front of paintings see C. Grimm, 'Histoire du cadre: un panorama', p. 18 (fig. 5), where such a frame (from sixteenth-century Spain) is reproduced.

A history of the curtain covering paintings would, of course, reach back all the way to Apelles and Protogenes, two almost legendary Greek painters from the fourth century BC. They tried to outdo each other in the representation of reality: the winner, Pliny reminds us, painted a curtain over his picture so true to life that his competitor believed it was real. The point for my subject is that the story implies the existence of covers for (sacred) works of art. The 'sanctum' or 'arcanum' in Greek and Jewish temples was traditionally hidden by a curtain or similar device. This parergetical notion was then adopted by decorative religious art and has remained as a trace on the margin or in the margin in works since the transition from the religious to the secular.

For an illustration in *Physica Sacra*, with a curtain, see B.M. Stafford, *Body Criticism*, p. 30. For a discussion of Hogarth's seemingly odd erotic picture in a series of religious paintings (showing the Evangelists) in plate 2 of *Marriage A-la-Mode*, see R. Simon, 'Wits About Him: Hogarth, Pope, and Burlington'. It is perhaps telling that in the first version of the painting, Hogarth depicted a seated Madonna and Child; but then apparently he changed his mind. The later version, Simon argues, is a typical Augustan ironic juxtaposing of the ill-fitting as one also finds it in Pope's mock-heroic verse.

As late as the nineteenth century, Robert Browning makes ambiguous use of the Renaissance custom of covering paintings with curtains in an allusion by his Duke, in 'My Last Duchess', who controls the image of his late wife with the help of a curtain. For a recent discussion of the poem, see J.A.W. Heffernan, *Museum of Words*, pp. 139–46.

37 For a discussion of this interesting problem in travel literature see M. de Certeau, 'Writing vs. Time', especially pp. 58–60.

38 On the history and meaning of the Medusa head see J. Clair, *Méduse*. Also see A. Alciati, *Emblemata cum commentariis*, pp. 663–5.

Louis Marin discusses the iconography and the semiotics of the Medusa paintings by Poussin and Caravaggio, and the texts behind them, in his wonderfully inventive and intelligent *Détruire la peinture*; see especially pp. 134–7.

39 The phrase is J. Hillis Miller's, in *The Linguistic Moment: From Wordsworth to Stevens*, p. xiii, where he discusses the 'thresholds' or 'gates' of texts with reference to Derrida's analysis of the *parergon* in *La Vérité en peinture*, pp.21–168 and in *La Dissémination*, pp. 9–67.

40 This problem is intrinsically raised by what could be termed internal frames (e.g., the circle of putti at left) in Watteau's *Embarkation for Cythera*. See Catherine Cusset's discussion of this aspect of the painting in 'Watteau: The Aesthetics of Pleasure', in my *Icons – Texts – Iconotexts*.

For a discussion that takes the issue into postmodern times, see C. Altieri, 'Frank Stella and Jacques Derrida: Toward A Postmodern Ethics of Singularity' in Brunette and Wills, *Deconstruction and the Visual Arts*, pp. 177–82.

4 'Official Discourse' in Hogarth's Prints

1 See Hogarth's *Autobiographical Notes*, in his *The Analysis of Beauty*, p. 205. For detailed discussions of the engravings see Paulson's catalogue, *Hogarth's Graphic Works*, pp. 47–9, 55–7; and the more biographically orientated *Hogarth*, vol. I: *The 'Modern Moral Subject', 1697–1732*, pp. 76–90, 119–22.

2 On the importance of these popular forms of entertainment and their treatment by Hogarth see my 'Hogarth's Graphic Palimpsests'.

3 See U. Böker, 'John Gay's *The Beggar's Opera* und die Kommerzialisierung der Kunst', p. 136.

4 See R. Barthes, 'L'Effet de réel', and G. Genette, 'Vraisemblance et motivation' in *Figures II*, pp. 71–100.

5 On this process in which periodicals played an important role by establishing aesthetic (exclusive) norms, see U. Böker, 'Die Institutionalisierung literarischer Produktions- und Rezeptionsnormen'.

6 See P. Bourdieu, *Distinction: A Social Critique of the Judgment of Taste*. Although Bourdieu is mainly concerned with the attempts of the Parisian upper middle class to cordon themselves off with the help of aesthetic canons that serve to achieve difference from neighbouring social groups, his study can be usefully applied (*cum grano salis*) to other countries and periods.

Persuasive studies of the process of suppression of popular entertainments during the establishment of new aesthetic norms can be found in P. Stallybrass and A. White, *The Politics and Poetics of Transgression*, pp. 80–175; I. Pears, *The*

Discovery of Painting, and in the two essays by U. Böker cited above.

7 For an evaluation of the print see Paulson, *Hogarth's Graphic Works*, pp. 110–11; and his *Hogarth*, vol. II, pp. 113–6.

8 On the phenomenon of commercialization within eighteen-century cultural consumption, see J.H. Plumb, *The Commercialization of Leisure in Eighteenth-century England*, N. McKendrick, J. Brewer and J.H. Plumb, eds, *The Birth of a Consumer Society: The Commercialization of Eighteenth-Century England* (Bloomington, 1982), U. Böker, 'John Gay's *The Beggar's Opera*', pp. 140–5, and J. Brewer and R. Porter, eds, *Consumption and the World of Goods*.

9 See especially Foucault's *The Order of Things*, and *The History of Sexuality*, 3 vols.

10 This is the view of mentality that governs the insightful study of N. Simms, *The Humming Tree: A Study in the History of Mentalities*. Simms argues that mentalities 'are only partly textualizable' and that their textual form 'includes both the things that are unspeakable, unimaginable, and inconceivable and the tension that exists between them' and what can be expressed (p. 14).

11 See my articles listed in the Bibliography.

12 On the publicity of Pastoral Letters see Paulson, *Hogarth*, vol. I, p. 283 n.49; and p. 376 n.48; and N. Sykes, *Edmund Gibson, Bishop of London, 1669–1748: A Study in Politics and Religion in the Eighteenth Century* (Oxford, 1926).

13 My account here is indebted to Paulson, *Hogarth*, vol. I, pp. 288–92; and II, pp. 88–9.

14 This is David Dabydeen's persuasive argument in *Hogarth, Walpole and Commercial Britain*, pp. 104–5. Lichtenberg also stresses the general unpopularity of the Letter, arguing that it began to sell well when the merchants supported the 'sender' by distributing it at their expense. But given his dislike of clergymen (which he shared with Hogarth), he may be confirming a stereotype, for the high sales of the Letter tell a different story – but then again very little about the actual reception. See G.C. Lichtenberg, *Ausführliche Erklärung der Hogarthschen Kupferstiche*, p. 117.

15 See Paulson, *Hogarth*, vol. I, pp. 1–2, 290.

16 My reading is indebted to the information provided by Paulson, *Hogarth*, vol. I, pp. 288–90; II, pp. 88–9, and *Hogarth's Graphic Works*, pp. 79–80. Paulson, again following his interest in author-intention, also develops a reading that relates this scene to the fact that Hogarth was a Deist and probably also a freemason.

17 On the role of paintings as part of the furniture in the seventeenth and eighteenth centuries, see the articles by C. Grimm and P.J.J. van Thiel cited above.

18 I discuss the series in the context of Hogarth's treatment of conduct books, and prescribed behaviour, in an article in a forthcoming collection of essays edited by Jacques Carré (Université de Clermont-Ferrand).

 For detailed discussions of *Industry and Idleness* see Paulson, *Hogarth's Graphic Works*, pp. 129–39, and *Hogarth*, vol. II, pp. 289–322.

19 See R. Hume, *Henry Fielding and the London Theatre, 1728–1737*, and L.W. Conolly, *The Censorship of English Drama, 1737–1824*.

20 For details of the print see Paulson, *Hogarth's Graphic Works*, pp. 108–9.

21 My discussion is indebted to the information provided by Paulson, *Hogarth's Graphic Works*, pp. 146–7, and B. Hinz, *William Hogarth: Beer Street and Gin Lane*. Also see the recent evaluation of *Beer Street* and *Gin Lane* in the art-historical context of the 'Last Judgment', by Werner Busch, *Das sentimentalische Bild*, pp. 264–94, where Busch provides useful information about the sociological and iconographic background for his new, interesting, reading of the series.

22 See *G.C. Lichtenberg's* [sic] *Erklärung der Hogarthischen Kupferstiche*, 10. Lieferung (Göttingen, 1808), p. 51.

23 Cf., for instance, the views advanced by Barry Wind and Ronald Paulson. Wind,

in an author-oriented reading, sees Hogarth and his print as part of the establishment, sympathizing with Hanoverian ideas and brewer interests. Paulson believes that the print (in conjunction with *Gin Lane*) offers two possibilities of reading: one for the prosperous middle class (good *versus* evil) and one for the poor (prosperity causes evil). See Wind's essay, '*Gin Lane* and *Beer Street*: A Fresh Draught', and Paulson's latest discussion of *Beer Street* in *Hogarth*, vol. III, pp. 23–6. Unfortunately, Wind's 'fresh draught' produces some rather stale ale, for it is basically a study of visual and verbal sources that served Hogarth as pre-texts; Wind never questions the dualistic frame(work), including the relation between the accompanying verses and the image, and rejects the possibility that there might be irony (either intended by the author or produced by the reader) at work in Hogarth's iconotext.

24 Perhaps Paulson has this common feature in mind when he argues in *Hogarth*, vol. III, p. 23, that the fishwives are '*reading* the king's speech'. They have come all the way from Billingsgate to Westminster in order to sell their fish – but they are clearly reading the ballad, not the speech.

25 This is the persuasive argument of Stephen Behrendt's essay, in which he maintains that in *Beer Street* and *Gin Lane* 'an *implied* dualism is in fact not supported but instead exploded'. See Behrendt, 'Hogarth, Dualistic Thinking and the Open Culture'.

26 See Wind, '*Gin Lane* and *Beer Street*: A Fresh Draught', and Paulson, *Hogarth*, vol. III, pp. 23–4. Also see Paulson's *Hogarth's Graphic Works*, pp. 145–8.

27 See Hogarth, *The Analysis of Beauty*, p. 226.

28 See Bal's *Reading 'Rembrandt'*, pp. 235–6 and passim; and Damisch, *Théorie du nuage*, pp. 106–59, *idem*, *L'Origine de la perspective*.

29 See F. Ogée, 'L'œil erre: les parcours sériels de Hogarth'. On the meaning of *Beer Street* that emerges from its serial aspect (*Gin Lane* being both its counterpart and its complement), see also D. Kunzle, *The Early Comic Strip: Narrative Strips and Picture Stories in the European Broadsheet from c. 1450 to 1825* (Berkeley, 1973), pp. 298–340, and H.J. Schnackertz, *Form und Funktion medialen Erzählens. Narrativität in Bildsequenz und Comicstrip* (Munich, 1980), pp. 35–86. See also Paulson, *Hogarth's Graphic Works*, p. 148.

30 Paulson, *Hogarth's Graphic Works*, p. 148.

31 See, for instance, Barry Wind, '*Gin Lane* and *Beer Street*', who believes that the verses 'make the message patent' and that Hogarth's personal commentary 're-enforced the admonitory message'.

32 Paulson, *Hogarth*, vol. III, pp. 25–6.

33 Paulson's argument echoes the theories of Wittgenstein and Nelson Goodman, who both assert that the codes in images are essentially richer and denser than those of verbal texts. See Wittgenstein's suggestion that density is by definition visual in *Tractatus Logicus-Philosophicus* (1921; New York, 1961). However, in his later writings he changed his mind, maintaining that language is no less dense than pictures: see *Philosophical Investigations* (1953; New York, 1958). Also see Nelson Goodman, *Languages of Art*. But the issue is far from resolved – witness Mieke Bal's statement, in *Reading 'Rembrandt'* (p. 401) that the density of codes is *not* a hallmark of the visual, which contradicts Paulson's underlying belief.

34 Paulson, *Hogarth*, vol. III, pp. 26.

35 This point, which I entirely endorse, is made by Behrendt in 'Hogarth, Dualistic Thinking, and the Open Culture'.

36 See Paulson, *Hogarth's Graphic Works*, pp. 146–7; and Wind, '*Gin Lane* and *Beer Street*'. Berthold Hinz, in his detailed study of the series, follows Paulson and takes the meat to be a loin of mutton: *William Hogarth: Beer Street and Gin Lane*, p. 18. Werner Busch thinks the blacksmith is holding up pork: see *Das*

sentimentalische Bild, p. 280.

37 See the *Collected Papers of Charles Sanders Peirce*, ed. C. Hartshorne *et al.*, vol. II.

38 In his commentary to this scene, Lichtenberg, always perspicacious, finds a telling term – politics – for the speech and the papers, while stressing the relations between the beer, the mutton, and the interests of the King and the burghers. (*G.C. Lichtenberg's Erklärung der Hogarthischen Kupferstiche*, p. 50).

39 On the newspaper background of the *Harlot* series, see Paulson, *Hogarth*, vol. I, pp. 241–56; see also Paulson's *Emblem and Expression*, p. 37; and the commentary to *The Stage-Coach, or the Country Inn Yard* (1747), in *Hogarth's Graphic Works*, pp. 126–7.

40 For a recent perceptive discussion of the print see F. Ogée, 'L'Onction extrême: une lecture de *A Midnight Modern Conversation* (1733) de William Hogarth'.

41 Lichtenberg, *Ausführliche Erklärung*, pp. 47–8.

42 Lichtenberg bases his own punning ekphrasis of the central scene (he uses the German term *Denkzettel*, signifying memorandum, reminder and a lesson taught by physical means such as beating or thrashing) on the full title of the journal: *The Remembrancer or Weekly Slab* [Lichtenberg writes, 'Stab'] *on the Face for the Ministry*, which obviously inspired Hogarth for his pictoral playing. See *G.C. Lichtenberg's Erklärung*, pp. 19–20. On the contemporary background see Paulson, *Hogarth's Graphic Works*, pp. 142–5.

43 Lichtenberg, *Ausführliche Erklärung*, pp. 236–8.

44 For a discussion of the possible allusions see Paulson, *Hogarth's Graphic Works*, pp. 94–5, and the critical works by Dabydeen and others cited there.

45 The term is Lichtenberg's, in *Ausführliche Erklärung*, p. 239.

46 Culler, *The Pursuit of Signs*, p. 111.

47 Bernd Krysmanski, in his attempt (dissertation, 1994) to provide a comprehensive reading of Hogarth's *Enthusiasm Delineated*, has written more than 1000 pages – and there are still many open questions.

48 'Signature, Event, Context', pp. 185–6, reprd in *A Derrida Reader*, p. 97.

49 See D. Eilon, *Factions' Fiction: Ideological Closure in Swift's Satire*, pp. 65–94, and my 'Swift and the Female Idol'.

50 See Althusser's essay 'Ideology and Ideological State Apparatuses' in *Lenin and Philosophy and Other Essays*, and the critical discussion of Althusser's thesis in *Visual Theory*, ed. N. Bryson, pp. 3–4. Among the 'Ideological State Apparatuses' identified by Althusser (and to be distinguished from the repressive apparatuses, such as the Government, the Administration, the Police, the Army, the Courts, and the Prisons) and applicable to Hogarth's day and age one could name: the religious ISA; the educational ISA; the family ISA; the legal ISA; the political ISA; the communications ISA; and the cultural ISA (Literature, the Arts). See the reprint of the major sections of Althusser's seminal essay in *Art in Theory, 1900–1990: An Anthology of Changing Ideas*, ed. C. Harrison and P. Wood, pp. 928–36. For a critique of Althusser's view of the individual, which is partly based on Lacan's 'imaginary consciousness' and would seem to leave little room for personal ideological rebellion, see T. Eagleton, *Literary Theory*, pp. 171–3.

51 See especially Foucault's *Surveiller et punir. Naissance de la prison*, and the three volumes of his *Histoire de la sexualité*. For a discussion of the role of discourse as seen by Althusser and Foucault, and of their influence on 'New Historicism', see M. Sarup, *An Introductory Guide to Post-structuralism and Postmodernism* (London, 1988), pp. 63–95; and R. Selden and P. Widdowson, *A Reader's Guide to Contemporary Literary Theory*, 3rd edn (London, 1993), ch. 4 and 6.

52 See R. Barthes, 'De l'oeuvre au texte', p. 229, *Le Plaisir du texte*, pp. 100–01, and J. Kristeva, *Sémeiotiké*, pp. 145–6.

53 For a discussion, and application to art-historical studies, of Lacan's theory of the gaze, see Bryson's *Vision and Painting: The Logic of the Gaze*, the essays

collected in his *Visual Theory: Painting and Interpretation*, and David Clarke's 'The Gaze and the Glance: Competing Understandings of Visuality in the Theory and Practice of Late Modernist Art', *Art History*, XV/11 (1992), pp. 80–99. Also my 'Learning to Read the Female Body'.

Reacting to my article on eroticism in Hogarth's prints, in which I outline the discursive effects of Puritan moralism, Paulson finds such a view 'wholly untenable'; see his comments to my discussion of *Before* and *After* in *Hogarth*, vol. III, p. 461 n.66. Also see his negative response to my reading of *The Sleeping Congregation*, in *Hogarth*, vol. II, p. 407 n.28.

As my chapter above shows, it may be vastly more interesting to consider Hogarth not as a genial artist, but as a Derridean blind artist who masters neither space nor discourse. Hogarth, I have tried to show, was also written by the discursive fields and the *mentalités* of his age: some of them he manipulated, others, however, overpowered him. Paulson does not like the idea of a powerless Hogarth; I am not afraid of such a common sight (in art and literature), since we are all to some extent victims of the power lines of writing that have been the subject of Foucault's analyses.

5 *Obscenity and Body Language in the French Revolution*

1 See B. Fort's lucid survey and critique of 'The French Revolution and the Making of Fictions' in Fort, ed., *Fictions of the French Revolution*, pp. 3–33. An equally interesting and challenging collection of essays is edited by J.A.W. Heffernan: *Representing the French Revolution: Literature, Historiography and Art*. On the merits of these two volumes see Suzanne Desan's review in *Eighteenth-century Studies*, XXVII/2 (1993), pp. 296–9.

   Behind the arguments put forward by the schools represented by Albert Soboul and François Furet respectively, to name just two giants of recent French historiography, one recognizes political attitudes. In their recent *Dictionnaire de la Révolution française* (Paris, 1988), Furet and Mona Ozouf prefer to ignore the arguments of their adversaries.

2 See R. Darnton, *The Literary Underground of the Old Regime*, p. 1, and J. Revel, 'Marie-Antoinette in Her Fictions: The Staging of Hatred' in Fort, ed., *Fictions of the French Revolution*, p. 111. Also see A. de Baecque, 'Pamphlets: Libel and Political Mythology' in R. Darnton and D. Roche, eds, *Revolution in Print: The Press in France 1775–1800*, p. 168, where de Baecque measures the pamphlets ('second-rate literature' with 'few literary graces') by the standards of 'the glorious libertine literature of the second half of the eighteenth century'. For critiques of Darnton's model see, for instance, E. Eisenstein, *Grub Street Abroad*, pp. 131–63 and passim, and J. Popkin's 'Pamphlet Journalism at the End of the Old Regime'.

3 *Revolution in Print*, ed. Darnton and Roche, p. 48.

4 For a discussion of the 'chronique scandaleuse', including references to critical studies, see my *Eros Revived: Erotica of the Enlightenment in England and America*, ch. 3.

5 See especially R. Darnton's recent essay, 'Philosophy under the Cloak' in *Revolution in Print*, ed. Darnton and Roche, pp.27–49, in which he revises some of the conclusions offered in chapters 1 and 6 of *The Literary Underground*; J. Popkin, 'Pamphlet Journalism', pp. 351–68, who (unlike Darnton) does not see the writers as disgruntled outsiders; and A. de Baecque, 'The "Livres remplis d'horreur": Pornographic Literature and Politics at the Beginning of the French Revolution'.

6 See J. Revel, 'Marie-Antoinette in Her Fictions', pp. 113–14. Revel strongly believes in the effectiveness of the *libelles*, but he provides no proof for his thesis, apart from the fact that 'the Parisian mob (especially on 5 and 6 October 1789,

during the march on Versailles) appropriated themes and formulas that were already those of the pamphlets denouncing the Queen' (p. 117). A. de Baecque, in 'The "Livres remplis d'horreur" ', is more careful, stressing (like Darnton) the economic-financial aspect of selling such writings; and Chantal Thomas, in her useful introduction to 'La Foutromanie révolutionnaire', credits the obscene pamphlets less with the creation of a political consciousness than with the destruction of the holy aura surrounding aristocratic bodies in a literature that generally lacks didactic dimensions and art: see *Oeuvres anonymes du XVIIIe siècle. L'Enfer de la Bibliothèque Nationale*, vol. VI (Paris, 1987), pp. 267–79.

7 To date, the best study of this phenomenon is Jean-Pierre Dubost's post-doctoral thesis (a German Habilitationsschrift) published in an abbreviated form as *Eros und Vernunft: Literatur und Libertinage*. The book deserves to be translated into English. See also Dubost's forthcoming article on a similar subject in Wagner, ed., *Icons – Texts – Iconotexts*.

8 In this passage I draw on A. de Baecque, 'The "Livres remplis d'horreur" '. A good survey of prosecutions of obscene libel, with details about the various 'procès-verbaux de saisies' in Paris, can be found in Alexandre Tuetey, ed., *Répertoire général des sources manuscrites de l'histoire de Paris pendant la Révolution française*, vol. II (Paris, 1892).

9 Tuetey, *Répertoire général*, no. 1434.

10 For studies of libertine fiction, including novels, and their erotic illustrations, see especially R. Darnton, 'Philosophy Under the Cloak', and P. Stewart, *Engraven Desire*, pp. 271–335. Whereas Darnton focuses on the relations between politics, ideology and literature, Stewart is interested mainly in the semiotics of prints as a part of literary texts.

11 See E.-M. Benabou, *La Prostitution et la police des moeurs au XVIIIe siècle*.

12 See *Archives de la préfecture de Police. Minutes des Procès-verbaux des commissaires de police de la section du Palais Royal*, AA81, pièce 299, cited in A. de Baecque, 'The "Livres remplis d'horreur" ', p. 132.

13 See, for instance, M. C. Cook, 'Politics in the Fiction of the French Revolution 1789–1794', pp. 264–5, and A. de Baecque, 'Pamphlets: Libel and Political Mythology', p. 172. Chantal Thomas even argues (convincingly) that the pamphlet literature is self-centred and rarely has a didactic message to tell: 'La Foutromanie révolutionnaire', p. 279. Despite their doubts about definite meanings or readings of the *libelles*, these critics explain them within a political context and discourse.

14 De Baecque, 'Pamphlets', p. 167; Revel, 'Marie-Antoinette', p. 116.

15 B. Fort, *Fictions of the French Revolution*, p. 11.

16 Revel, 'Marie-Antoinette', p. 116.

17 For perceptive studies of this book and its consquences, see J. M. Goulemot, 'Fureurs utérines'; and G. Rousseau, *Perilous Enlightenment*, pp. 44–65.

18 See the copies in the Bibliothèque Nationale, Enfer nr. 653 and 654.

19 In addition to the pieces cited above, see *Vie de Marie-Antoinette . . . depuis la perte de son pucelage jusqu'au premier Mai 1791* (1793), *Vie privée libertine et scandaleuse de Marie-Antoinette* (1791–3), and *La Journée amoureuse, ou les derniers plaisirs de M . . . Ant . . .* (1792).

20 Revel, 'Marie-Antoinette', p. 126.

21 Ibid.

22 On the etymology, the definition, and the rise of pornography see the introduction in my *Eros Revived*. In *The Invention of Pornography*, the editor, Lynn Hunt, and some of the contributors to the volume start from my definition and demarcation of the term for the eighteenth century.

23 See the articles by these historians cited above. Revel discusses 'two obscene prints with Marie-Antoinette as the central figure' (pp. 126–7) in a pamphlet

entitled *Les Embarras de Marie-Antoinette* (*c.* 1790). Also see Claude Langlois, *La Caricature contre-révolutionnaire*, and A. de Baecque, *La Caricature révolutionnaire*; both authors reproduce one obscene illustration showing Marie-Antoinette. Similarly, Vivian Cameron abstains from the reproduction of the obscene visual material she discusses (with one exception) while referring the reader to my *Lust and Love in the Rococo Period*, whereas Lynn Hunt includes one obscene engraving in the chapter on Marie-Antoinette in her anthology *Eroticism and the Body Politic*, which includes Cameron's insightful article.

   For collections of such controversial prints contained in libertine and popular writings published during the Revolutionary period, see A. Borel, *Cent vignettes érotiques gravées par Elluin*, L. von Brunn, *Ars erotica: Die erotische Buchillustration im Frankreich des 18. Jahrhunderts*, and my *Lust and Love in the Rococo Period*.

24 The apposite description is Cameron's in Hunt, ed., *Eroticism and the Body Politic*, p. 91.

25 See Brunn, *Ars erotica*, p. 319. The best-known engravers of erotica were Antoine Borel and François Elluin, although the engravers of most of the illustrations in the *libelles* cannot be identified.

26 On this body of erotica see chapters 1 and 5 in my *Eros Revived*.

27 For a discussion of these representational codes (that continue into the Victorian age) in the light of feminist theories, see H. Michie, *The Flesh Made Word*, ch. 5.

28 For discussions of the erotic code in these engravings see A. Guillerm, 'Le Système de l'iconographie galante', pp. 177–95; my *Lust and Love in the Rococo Period*, pp. 9–32; and P. Stewart, *Engraven Desire*, pp. 103–33, and 271–335. For a discussion of the importance of the framework (with which de Launay's engraving first appeared) vis-à-vis the content see my chapter above on framing.

29 See, for instance, the illustrations depicting penes, vulvae, and sexual intercourse, in Pierre-François Hugues d'Hancarville, *Antiquitées étrusques, grecques et romaines*, *Monumens du culte secret des douze Césars* and *Monumens du culte secret des dames romaines* ('A Caprrées', 1784), allegedly based on genuine source material. For a discussion of these erotica, see my *Eros Revived*, pp. 264–9.

30 See, for instance, the pieces mocking the members of the Assemblée Nationale: *Les Enfants de Sodome à l'Assemblée Nationale* (1790), and *Requète et décret en faveur des putains, des fouteuses, des macquerelles et des branleuses: contre les bougres, les bardaches et les brûleurs de paillasse* (*c.* 1791).

31 Another such explosion apparently occurred during the 1960s. For a discussion of the functions of the representations of sex in the literature of that decade, which shows some interesting parallels with the discourse of the French Revolution (e.g., carnivalization and the levelling of high and low genres), see W. Wolf, 'The Flame of Sex'.

32 See C. Thomas's introduction in *Oeuvres anonymes*, vol. 4, p. 277; also see the articles by J. Popkin and H.J. Lüsebrink in R. Koselleck and R. Reichardt, eds, *Die Französische Revolution*, pp. 182, 311–12.

   In the wake of the seminal studies of M. Bakhtin, the carnivalization of eighteenth-century culture has been studied by T. Castle, *Masquerade and Civilization*, and B. Fort, 'Voice of the Public: The Carnivalization of Salon Art in Pre-Revolutionary France'.

33 See H.J. Lüsebrink, 'Volksliteratur und historische Anthropologie' in R. Koselleck and R. Reichardt, eds, *Die französische Revolution*, pp. 311–12. Also see M. Slavin's meticulous study of a small area of Paris (in the 'Marais') during the Revolution: *The French Revolution in Miniature. Section Droits-de-l'Homme, 1789–1795*. Slavin shows the importance of everyday needs and the fact that the ideas of Revolutionary pamphlets were first expressed and formulated in public meeting places.

34 See J.H. Campe, *Briefe aus Paris, zur Zeit der Revolution geschrieben*, pp. 138 and

225. Also see H. Günther, ed., *Die französische Revolution. Berichte deutscher Schriftsteller und Historiker*, and M. Espagne and M. Werner, eds, *Transferts: Les relations interculturelles dans l'espace franco-allemand*.

35 See D. Roche, 'Soziokulturelle und wirtschaftliche Aspekte des Bilderhandels zwischen Ancien Régime und Revolution' in Koselleck and Reichardt, eds, *Die französische Revolution*, p. 554.

36 It is sad (but hardly surprising) to notice that even recent studies of Revolutionary art continue to ignore prints and popular satire (including its obscene variety). See, for instance, P. Bordes and M. Régis, eds, *Aux armes et aux arts! Les arts de la Révolution 1789–1799*.

37 J.M. Boyer-Brun, *Histoire des caricatures de la révolte des Français*, (Paris, 1792), I, pp. 9–10; and F.-A. Aulard, *Receuil des actes du Comité de Salut public*, VI (Paris, 1893), p. 443.

38 Darnton, *Revolution in Print*, p. 29.

39 This is H.J. Lüsebrink's persuasive argument in Koselleck and Reichardt, eds, *Die französische Revolution*, pp. 668–70. See also the self-critical assessments of historical analysis in the articles by J. Guilhaumou, R. Koselleck and D. Roche in the same volume; and R. Darton's introduction in *Revolution in Print*.

40 This is one of the problems that plague Lynn Hunt's study of 'The Many Bodies of Marie-Antoinette' in her *Eroticism and the Body Politic*. Discussing the function of obscene illustrations, for instance, she argues that 'the political effect of the pornography is apparent' (p. 120); and her use of the term 'political pornography' suppresses the multifarious levels of discourse and the codes contained in the obscene engravings.

41 See her article on 'Sexuality and Caricature in the French Revolution' in *Eroticism and the Body Politic*, pp. 103–4.

42 See J.P. Goulemot's preface ('L'Effet érotique') to *La Messaline française* in *Oeuvres anonymes du XVIIIe siècle*, III (Paris, 1986), pp. 289–94. A number of important obscene pamphlets from the Revolutionary period have been reprinted, but unfortunately badly edited, in this volume and in IV (1987).

For a critique of traditional literary canons and some excellent suggestions for a re-writing of the literary history of the Revolution, including its neglected popular forms, see the articles in *Literatur der Französischen Revolution*, ed. H. Krauss, especially those by H. Hudde on the theatre, and D. Rieger on Revolutionary fiction.

43 See C. Thomas, 'La Foutromanie révolutionnaire', p. 268.

44 On René-Jacques Hébert and his popular *Le Père Duchesne*, see the *Historical Dictionary of the French Revolution, 1789–1799*, ed. S. Scott and B. Rothaus, pp. 457–59. Also see J. Guilhaumou, 'Les mille langues du Père Duchêne. La parade de la culture populaire pendant la Révolution'. Bernadette Fort, together with Barthes and Thomas, is one of the critics to have noticed the 'signifying' power and the origins of the new obscene language: see her *Fictions of the French Revolution*, p. 11.

45 See Barthes, *Le Degré zéro de l'écriture*, p. 8: 'Hébert ne commençait jamais un numéro du *Père Duchêne* sans y mettre quelques "foutre" et quelques "bourgre". Ces grossièretés ne signifiaient rien, mais elles signalaient. Quoi? Toute une situation révolutionnaire. Voilà donc l'exemple d'une écriture dont la fonction n'est plus seulement de communiquer ou d'exprimer, mais d'imposer un au-delà du langage qui est à la fois l'Histoire et le parti qu'on y prend'.

46 See chapters 4 and 5 and the conclusion in my *Eros Revived*, and C. Thomas, 'L'héroïne du crime: Marie-Antoinette dans les pamphlets', *idem*, *La Reine scélérate. Marie-Antoinette dans les pamphlets*. Also see Lynn Hunt, 'The Many Bodies of Marie-Antoinette'. J. Revel's article ('Marie-Antoinette'), cited above, is concerned with the (inter)textual staging of the Queen as a sexual monster.

47 On the male fear of women's rights and the exclusion of women from politics see D. Outram, '*Le langage mâle de la vertu:* Women and the Discourse of the French Revolution', and *idem, The Body and the French Revolution.*

The attacks on the emancipation of women in popular and oral sources culminated in the suppression of women's political rights in France in October 1793. Important studies of the history of the representation of the female body in this context are M. Gutwirth, *The Twilight of the Goddesses*, and H. Michie, *The Flesh Made Word*, which focuses more on the 'consequences' in the nineteenth century.

48 The critical literature on the body as text or place of representation is now vast. M. Merleau-Ponty's *Phénoménologie de la perception*, especially pp. 235–81, remains a seminal study which is, unfortunately, hardly ever considered by scholars writing in English.

For surveys of the field, with particular consideration of the role of women and medicine, see R. Porter, 'History of the Body', and the introduction by M.M. Roberts and R. Porter in their *Literature and Medicine During the Eighteenth Century*, pp. 1–22 (especially n.24).

For studies of the body as and in visual representation see B.M. Stafford, *Body Criticism*, J. Bremmer and H. Roodenburg, eds, *A Cultural History of Gestures*, K. Adler and M. Pointon, eds, *The Body Imaged*, I.B. Fliedl and C. Geissmar, eds, *Die Beredsamkeit des Leibes*, and P. Brooks, *Body Work.*

6 *In Lieu of a Conclusion*

1 See Diderot, *Oeuvres complètes*, I, p. 385. For a survey of the history of the concept of the 'mutual illumination of the arts', a phrase apparently coined by Oskar Walzel in 1917 (see Walzel's 'Wechselseitige Erhellung der Künste', reprd in *Gehalt und Gestalt im Kunstwerk des Dichters*, pp. 265–81), see U. Weisstein, ed., *Literatur und Bildende Kunst*, pp. 11–34. Significantly, Weisstein and the authors in his volume continue propagating Diderot's basic assumption: one looks in vain in this 'handbook' for important studies published by post-structuralists (Derrida, Foucault, Kristeva).

2 J. Hillis Miller, *Illustration*, p. 95.

3 Fowler argues that 'the notion of a universally valid systematic correspondence between the arts must be regarded as a chimera'. See his 'Periodization and Interart Analogies' in Weisstein, ed., *Literatur und Bildende Kunst*, pp. 86–101, quotation p. 99.

4 See H.J. Lüsebrink, 'Les tambours de la mémoire', p. 186. Also see J. Le Goff, *Histoire et mémoire*, p. 162; and J. Assmann and T. Hölscher, eds, *Kultur und Gedächtnis*, pp. 9–19.

Bourdieu, in *Les Règles de l'art*, p. 423, argues that we tend to overlook the large invisible basis that informs the history of ideas ('l'immense socle invisible des grandes pensées'), precisely because the varieties of 'habitus' or doxa they display were self-evident to contemporaries and therefore never recorded in documents and chronicles. I would contend that images can serve as what Bourdieu (quoting Satie) terms 'memories of an amnesiac' ('mémoires d'un amnésique') because, for those who care to look, they display the silent codes much more obviously than writing.

5 See, for instance, my articles published in *Word & Image, Etudes anglaises*, and two essays: 'Hogarth and the English Popular Mentalité', *Mentalities/Mentalités*, VIII/1 (1992), pp. 24–44, and 'The Satire on Doctors in Hogarth's Graphic Works', in *Medicine and Literature During the Eighteenth Century*, ed. M. Roberts and R. Porter, pp. 200–26.

6 For a recent, useful, discussion of the issue see the articles by, and the lively

exchange between, David Summers, ('Intentions in the History of Art', pp. 305–21) and Steven Levine ('Moxey's Moxie and the Summers of '84: Intention and Interpretation in the History of Art – A Commentary', pp. 323–31, and Summers's reply, pp. 333–44) in *New Literary History*, XVII (1986). Summers makes a good case for the art-historical use of what we know about an artist's intention while Levine, partly relying on and discussing publications by Keith Moxey, is concerned with the interpretive disadvantages of such approaches (e.g., limitation of meaning and hence reading; the art work as a closed, predetermined system etc.).

7   In my iconoclastic reading, I apply some conclusions from J. Grigeley's perceptive critique of semiotic readings. Discussing the Peircean triad, and the traditional arrangement in hierarchies, he argues that 'semiotic values can be concomitant without having to acquiesce to a notion of dominance. That is, a sign can be described as iconic without abandoning its symbolic value; a painting could be described as symbolic without abandoning its iconic value . . . these values are determined by the strategy we bring to the process of reading'. See his essay, 'The Implosion of Iconicity', p. 247. Umberto Eco voices a similar critique of Peirce's triad, with some suggestions for more comprehensive semiotic models, in 'Producing Signs'.

8   See F. Paknadel, 'Hogarth's *Gate of Calais*: Myth and Reality', p. 13.

9   For commentaries on the engraving see Paulson, *Hogarth's Graphic Works*, pp. 139–40; and *Hogarth*, vol. II, pp. 352–6. Paknagel's article relies mainly on the sources provided by Paulson.

10 Hogarth, *Autobiographical Notes*, pp. 227–8.

11 I cite this passage not because I want to rely on Hogarth's intention for my reading of the picture, but to indicate the degree to which the artist himself was a victim of dominant *mentalités* (if his words can be taken seriously – another problem of interpretation).

12 See Paulson, *Hogarth*, vol. II, p. 354.

13 *Hogarth*, vol. III, p. 356.

14 Cited in Paulson, *Hogarth's Graphic Works*, p. 139.

15 'Hogarth's *Gate of Calais*: Myth and Reality', p. 13.

16 Frederick Antal, *Hogarth and His Place in European Art*.

17 In this instance, I borrow Stephen C. Behrendt's argument about the explosion of dualism in Hogarth's *Before* and *After* as what he terms an act of enculturation: See 'Hogarth, Dualistic Thinking, and the Open Culture'.

18 More could be said about the meaning of this apparently marginal sign, depending on how we relate its denotations and connotations to the objects and people in the room. In his commentary, Lichtenberg, perspicacious as ever, implies, for instance, that this is a reference to an entire (Jewish) sub-culture in eighteenth-century England. Typically, he leaves it up to the reader/observer to decide whether the bread indicates 'the last precious remnant of Christianity belonging to the inhabitant of the room, a bit of despise for Jews, or . . . a remnant of the former magnificence of plate 2'. Lichtenberg then launches into another, vastly interesting, exploration of the sign, based on its resemblance to the moon that shines into the conscience of the dying woman. See G.C. Lichtenberg, *Erklärung der Hogarthschen Kupferstiche*, p. 165.

19 J.D. Hunt, 'Making Vergil Look English', quotation from p. 98.

20 Keith Moxey outlines the future of a new art history drawing on semiotics in his 'Semiotics and the Social History of Art'.

21 See E.P. Thompson's *Customs in Common*, pp. 1–97, where, unperturbed by several decades of scholarship, he repeats his familiar theory of the difference between the 'plebs' and the 'patricians'. Also see my critique of this notion in my article on Hogarth in *Word & Image* (1991).

22 For a critique of the notion of history as a series of distinct epochs, with particular consideration of the eighteenth century, see J. Schlobach, *Zyklentheorie und Epochenmetaphorik*, and Schlobach's article 'Siècle des Lumières et Aufklärung: Mots, métaphores et concepts'.

23 See *The Order of Things*, p. 9. For a thoughtful analysis of Foucault's writing on 'iconotexts' see H.J. Lüsebrink's essay, 'Iconotextes'.

24 See, for instance, Mitchell's *Iconology: Image, Text, Ideology*, idem, 'Going Too Far with the Sister Arts', Gilman's 'Interart Studies and the "Imperialism of Language" ', B.M. Stafford, *Body Criticism*, pp. 465–80, idem, *Artful Science*, p. 8. Also see U. Weisstein, *Literatur und Bildende Kunst*, p. 13.
    As early as 1978 Derrida deplored the fact that plastic or musical works of art are always subject to the authority of language and the 'discursive arts' ('l'autorité de la parole et des arts "discursifs" '); see *La Vérité en peinture*, p. 26.

25 See, for instance, Hubert Damisch's challenging view that perspective is a discursive apparatus of enunciation based not on the fitting but on the mismatch between geometrical and symbolic points of origin, a mismatch that produces visual subjectivity: *L'Origine de la perspective*. For a critique of such language-centred analogies (which also mark the work of Louis Marin), see Mieke Bal's review essay 'First Person, Second Person, Same Person: Narrative as Epistemology', and C. Guillén, 'On the Concept and Metaphor of Perspective'.

26 I have translated this text from Eco's interview with Jean Daniel in *Le Nouvel Observateur*, no. 1504 (2–8 September 1993), p. 45. In this instance, Eco partly draws on Roland Barthes's *Image-Music-Text*, where Barthes posits that in combinations of texts and images (e.g., in photographs with captions) the verbal message is the primary determinant.

27 In this respect, Wittgenstein saw one of the disadvantages of the image in that it cannot represent its form of representation, it merely contains it as a trace which is frequently overlooked by the observer. See his *Tractatus Logico-Philosophicus* ([1921] Frankfurt, 1984), no. 2.172, trans. B.F. McGuinness (New York, 1961).

28 See 'The Spatial Arts', in Brunette and Wills, eds, *Deconstruction and the Visual Arts*, pp. 12–13.

29 See A. Dückers, ed., *Das Berliner Kupferstichkabinett*, p. 102, where Hans Mielke, the commentator, confesses that he does not know what the image signifies. He suggests that a proverb might be involved, since such scenes depicting merely aspects from everyday life (without some allegorical or deeper meaning) begin to appear much later (in the seventeenth century).

30 See Mitchell's 'Going Too Far with the Sister Arts', p. 2, and his *Iconology*, p. 155.

31 J. Derrida, *Psyché. Inventions de l'autre*, p. 106: 'ce partage entre le visible et le lisible je n'en suis pas sûr, je crois pas à la rigueur de ces limites, ni surtout qu'il passe entre la peinture et les mots. D'abord il traverse chacun des corps sans doute, le pictural et le lexical, selon la ligne – unique chaque fois mais labyrinthique – d'un idiome'.

32 For a recent analysis of this iconotext see K. Porter Aichele, 'Letter and Image in Paul Klee's *Villa R*'.

33 See S. Alpers, *The Art of Describing*, pp. xvii–xxvii and 169–221, M. Butor, *Les Mots dans la peinture*, and J. Hillis Miller, *Illustration*, p. 75. Also see the useful introduction to post-structuralist discussions of paintings by Lacan, Derrida, Kristeva, by Michael Payne, 'Reading Paintings' in his *Reading Theory*, pp. 212–14.

34 Thus Martin Heuser, in the introduction to his superb collection of essays about the word-image relationships, argues that 'word and image are inseparable because they are essentially the same – they are both signs, *aliquid pro aliquo*, *simulacra*'. Towards the end of his survey, however, he has to admit that 'they are

constitutionally part of one another.' See M. Heuser, ed., *Word & Image Interactions*, pp. 13 and 17. Similarly, Alan Robinson bases his recent detailed analysis of Victorian art and its reception on what he terms 'the linguistic analogy', on a method that posits the linguistic model as one appropriate for the description of the semantics of visual sign systems: see his 'Reading Victorian Paintings', pp. 211–26.

The solution to the problem lies, indeed, not in a purely linguistic model that would again assert the dominance of language over pictures (although, as Robinson justly points out, we cannot avoid using linguistic models in the critical analysis of art), but in the exploration of the common ground they cover. Deconstructionists in particular can easily fall prey to the snares of the linguistic model. Mieke Bal, for instance, in an otherwise brilliant essay (see 'Light in Painting'), argues that images 'are also texts precisely in that they constitute a network of discursive practices, albeit visually shaped' (p. 52 n.8). In this respect, M. Blonsky suggests to 'crack [semiotics] out of its present uses', while Umberto Eco (in Blonsky's volume) outlines some rather interesting escape routes from the semiotic dilemma. See M. Blonsky, ed., *On Signs*, pp. L and 157–84.

In his recent interview by Peter Brunette and David Wills, Derrida suggests a further exploration of the spatial in visual art (which he prefers to call 'spatial art'): this idea is taken up by other contributors to the volume. See *Deconstruction and the Visual Arts*, pp. 22–5, and S. Melville's essay on colour, pp. 33–49.

35 M.K. Johnson makes an exciting step in this direction in '(Re)framing the Photograph'.

36 See especially W. Iser's *The Implied Reader* and *The Act of Reading*, and Eco's *The Role of the Reader*. The trouble with these concepts (Iser and Eco differ in the range of freedom and creativity they allot the reader) is that while they do allocate a more important role to the reader in establishing meaning in a textual work of art, the implication remains that it is the author who has somehow devised a machinery in which the receiver is not more than a cog. Eco, however, occasionally goes beyond this stage, arguing (unlike Iser) that the meaning of a work of art is principally open and can thus be 'filled' by the innovative, participating, reader.

37 Eco, *The Open Work*, pp. 4 and 15; see especially the chapter on 'The Open Work in the Visual Arts'. For an exemplary and challenging case study along Derridean and feminist lines, see M. Bal, 'Light in Painting', in Brunette and Wills, eds, *Deconstruction and the Visual Arts*, pp. 49–65.

38 See P. Bourdieu, 'La genèse sociale de l'oeil' in his *Les Règles de l'art*, pp. 431–41. Bourdieu briefly defines the term 'habitus' as 'le principe de la structuration sociale de l'existence temporelle, de toutes les anticipations et les présuppositions à travers lesquelles nous construisons pratiquement le sens du monde, c'est-à-dire sa signification' [the principle of the social structuring of temporal existence, of all the expectations and presuppositions with which we practically construct the meaning of the world, that is signification] (p. 450). For an assessment of the work of Bourdieu in social theory see *Bourdieu: Critical Perspectives*, ed. Craig Calhoun *et al.* (Cambridge, 1993), pp. 1–14. Also see Stanley Fish's contention that critical judgements are determined by disciplinary settings in 'Why Literary Criticism is Like Virtue', p. 12.

39 Bourdieu, *Les Règles de l'art*, pp. 393–448. Also see Fish's persuasive critique of Iser's concepts that are partially based on the notion of 'pure perception': 'Why No One's Afraid of Wolfgang Iser', in Fish's *Doing What Comes Naturally. Change, Rhetoric, and the Practice of Theory in Literary and Legal Studies*, pp. 68–87. Specifically, Fish rejects Iser's *The Act of Reading* because it is 'a piece of literature that satisfies Iser's own criteria for an "aesthetic object" ' (p. 85).

Bibliography

Percy Adams, *Travelers and Travel Liars, 1660–1800* (Los Angeles, 1962).
—, *Travel Literature and the Evolution of the Novel* (Lexington, 1983).
Kathleen Adler and Marcia Pointon, eds, *The Body Imaged: The Human Form and Visual Culture since the Renaissance* (Cambridge, 1993).
K. Porter Aichele, 'Letter and Image in Paul Klee's *Villa R*', *Word & Image*, IX (1993), pp. 229–45.
Andrea Alciati, *Emblemata cum commentariis*, (Padua, 1621; reprd New York, 1976).
Svetlana Alpers, *The Art of Describing: Dutch Art in the Seventeenth Century* (London, 1989).
Louis Althusser, *Lenin and Philosophy and Other Essays* (London, 1971).
Charles Altieri, 'Frank Stella and Jacques Derrida: Toward a Postmodern Ethics of Singularity', in *Deconstruction and the Visual Arts: Art, Media, Architecture*, ed. P. Brunette and D. Wills (Cambridge, 1994), pp. 168–88.
A New And Complete Collection of Trials for Adultery: or A General History of Modern Gallantry and Divorces (London, 1796).
Frederick Antal, *Hogarth and His Place in European Art* (London, 1962).
Dana Arnold, ed., *Belov'd by Ev'ry Muse: Richard Boyle, 3rd Earl of Burlington & 4th Earl of Cork (1694–1753)* (London, 1994).
Jan Assmann and Tonio Hölscher, eds, *Kultur und Gedächtnis* (Frankfurt, 1988).
François Avril and Nicole Reynaud, eds, *Les Manuscrits à peintures en France 1440–1520* (Paris, 1993).
Antoine de Baecque, *La Caricature révolutionnaire* (Paris, 1988).
—, 'The "Livres remplis d'horreur": Pornographic Literature and Politics at the Beginning of the French Revolution', in *Erotica and the Enlightenment*, ed. P. Wagner (Frankfurt, 1991), pp. 123–66.
—, 'Pamphlets: Libel and Political Mythology', in *Revolution in Print*, ed. R. Darnton and D. Roche (Berkeley, 1991), pp. 165–77.
Mieke Bal, 'First Person, Second Person, Same Person: Narrative as Epistemology', *New Literary History*, XXIV/2 (1993), pp. 293–320.
—, 'Light in Painting: Dis-seminating Art' in *Deconstruction and the Visual Arts: Art, Media, Architecture*, ed. P. Brunette and D. Wills (Cambridge, 1994), pp. 49–65.
—, *Reading 'Rembrandt': Beyond the Word-Image Opposition* (Cambridge, 1991).
Stephen Bann, *The True Vine: On Visual Representation and the Western Tradition* (Cambridge, 1989).
Michel Baridon, 'Hogarth et le langage', *Interfaces. Image, Texte, Langage*, I (1991), pp. 5–21.
Louise K. Barnett, 'Deconstructing *Gulliver's Travels*: Modern Readers and the Problematic of Genre', in *The Genres of Gulliver's Travels*, ed. F.N. Smith (Newark, 1990), pp. 230–46.
Roland Barthes, 'De l'œuvre au texte', *Revue d'Esthétique*, XXIV (1971), reprd in *Le Bruissement de la langue* (Paris, 1984), pp. 69–79.

—, *L'Aventure sémiologique* (Paris, 1985).

—, *Le Degré zéro de l'écriture* [1953] (Paris, 1972).

—, 'L'Effet de réel', *Communications*, IV (1968), pp. 84–9.

—, *Image-Music-Text*, trans. S. Heath (New York, 1977).

—, 'La peinture est-elle un langage', *L'Obvie et l'obtus*, pp. 139–42.

—, *Le Plaisir du texte* (Paris, 1973).

—, *L'Obvie et l'obtus. Essais critiques* (Paris, 1982).

—, *The Rustle of Language*, trans. R. Howard (New York, 1986).

—, *Sade, Fourier, Loyola* (1980).

—, *S/Z* (Paris, 1970, reprd 1976).

Jean Baudrillard, *Simulacres et simulation* (Paris, 1981), trans. as *Simulacra and Simulations* (1988).

Stephen C. Behrendt, 'Hogarth, Dualistic Thinking and the Open Culture' in *Hogarth in Context: Ten Essays and a Bibliography*, ed. J. Möller (Marburg, forthcoming).

Erica-Marie Benabou, *La Prostitution et la police des mœurs au XVIIIe siècle* (Paris, 1987).

John Bender and David E. Wellbery, eds, *The Ends of Rhetoric: History, Theory, Practice* (Stanford, 1990).

Ziva Ben-Porat, 'The Poetics of Allusion' in *A Semiotic Landscape: Proceedings of the First Congress of the International Association for Semiotic Studies*, ed. Seymour Chatman (The Hague, 1979), pp. 588–93.

J.D.T. Bienville, *La Nymphomanie, ou traité de la fureur utérine* (Amsterdam, 1771).

David Bindman, 'The Nature of Satire in the Modern Moral Subjects', in *Image et société dans l'œuvre graphique de William Hogarth*, ed. F. Ogée (Paris, 1992), pp. 45–59.

Max Black, 'How Do Pictures Represent?' in E.H. Gombrich, Julian Hochberg and Max Black, eds, *Art, Perception, and Reality* (Baltimore, 1972), pp. 95–131.

Marshall Blonsky, ed., *On Signs* (Baltimore, 1985).

Uwe Böker, 'Die Institutionalisierung literarischer Produktions- und Rezeptionsnormen: Überlegungen zur Erforschung der Unterhaltungsliteratur um 1800', in *Unterhaltungsliteratur: Ziele und Methoden ihrer Erforschung*, ed. D. Petzold and E. Späth (Erlangen, 1990), pp. 139–61.

—, 'John Gay's *The Beggar's Opera* und die Kommerzialisierung der Kunst zu Beginn des 18. Jahrhunderts', *Schriftenreihe der Universität Regensburg*, XVII (1990), pp. 121–46.

Bordel national (c. 1790).

Bordel royal (c. 1790).

Philippe Bordes and Michel Régis, eds, *Aux armes et aux arts! Les arts de la Révolution 1789–1799* (Paris, 1988).

Antoine Borel, *Cent vignettes érotiques gravées par Elluin* (Lyon, 1978).

Paul-Gabriel Boucé, ed., *Sexuality in Eighteenth-century England* (Manchester, 1982).

Pierre Bourdieu, *Distinction: A Social Critique of the Judgment of Taste*, trans. R. Nice (Cambridge, MA, 1987).

—, *Les Règles de l'art. Genèse et structure du champ littéraire* (Paris, 1992).

Jan Bremmer and Herman Roodenburg, eds, *A Cultural History of Gestures: From Antiquity to the Present* (Cambridge, 1991).

John Brewer, *The Common People and Politics 1750–1790s* (Cambridge, 1986).

— and Roy Porter, eds, *Consumption and the World of Goods* (London, 1993).

Elisabeth Bronfen, *Over Her Dead Body: Death, Femininity and the Aesthetic* (Manchester, 1992).

Peter Brooks, *Body Work: Objects of Desire in Modern Narrative* (London, 1993).

M.E. Dolan Brown, 'The Poet's Mask: Swift, Horace, Steele in "The First Ode of the Second Book of Horace Paraphrased" ', *Swift Studies*, V (1990), pp. 3–10.

Peter Brunette and David Wills, eds, *Deconstruction and the Visual Arts: Art, Media, Architecture* (Cambridge, 1994).

—, 'The Spatial Arts: An Interview with Jacques Derrida', in *Deconstruction and the Visual Arts*, ed. P. Brunette and D. Wills (Cambridge, 1994), pp. 9–33.

Ludwig von Brunn, *Ars erotica: Die erotische Buchillustration im Frankreich des 18. Jahrhunderts*, 3 vols (Dortmund, 1983).

Norman Bryson, *Vision and Painting: The Logic of the Gaze* (London, 1983).

—, ed., *Calligram: Essays in the New Art History from France* (Cambridge, 1988).

—, 'Intertextuality and Visual Poetics', *Style*, XXII (1988), pp. 183–93.

—, Michael A. Holly and Keith Moxey, eds, *Visual Theory: Painting and Interpretation* (Cambridge, 1991).

Peter Burke, ed., *Perspectives on Historical Writing* (Cambridge, 1991).

— and Roy Porter, eds, *The Social History of Language* (Cambridge, 1987).

Werner Busch, *Das sentimentalische Bild. Die Krise der Kunst im 18. Jahrhundert und die Geburt der Moderne* (Munich, 1993).

—, 'Lektüreprobleme bei Hogarth: Zur Mehrdeutigkeit realistischer Kunst', in *Hogarth in Context. Ten Essays and a Bibliography*, ed. J. Möller (Marburg, forthcoming).

—, *Nachahmung als bürgerliches Kunstprinzip. Ikonographische Zitate bei Hogarth und in seiner Nachfolge* (Hildesheim and New York, 1977).

Michel Butor, *Les Mots dans la peinture* (Geneva, 1969).

Craig Calhoun *et al.*, eds, *Bourdieu: Critical Perspectives* (Cambridge, 1993).

Vivian Cameron, 'Political Exposures: Sexuality and Caricature in the French Revolution', in *Eroticism and the Body Politic*, ed. L. Hunt (Baltimore, 1991), pp. 90–108.

Michael Camille, *Image on the Edge: The Margins of Medieval Art* (London, 1992).

Johann H. Campe, *Brief aus Paris, zur Zeit der Revolution geschrieben* [1790] (Hildesheim, 1977).

Vincent Carretta, *George III and the Satirists from Hogarth to Byron* (Athens, GA, 1990).

Terry Castle, *Masquerade and Civilization: The Carnivalesque in Eighteenth-century English Culture and Fiction* (Stanford, 1986).

Michel de Certeau, 'Writing vs. Time: History and Anthropology in the Works of Lafitau', trans. J. Hovde, *Yale French Studies*, LIX (1980), pp. 37–65.

Seymour Chatman, ed., *A Semiotic Landscape: Proceedings of the First Congress of the International Association for Semiotic Studies* (The Hague, 1979).

Jean Clair, *Méduse. Contribution à une anthropologie des arts du visuel* (Paris, 1989).

L.W. Conolly, *The Censorship of English Drama 1737–1824* (San Marino, CA, 1976).

Malcolm C. Cook, 'Politics in the Fiction of the French Revolution 1789–1794', *Studies on Voltaire and the Eighteenth Century* CCI (1982).

Margery Corbett and Ronald Lightbown, *The Comely Frontispiece: The Emblematic Title-Page in England, 1550–1660* (London, 1979).

Martin J. Croghan, 'Savage Indignation: An Introduction to the Philosophy of Language and Semiotics in Jonathan Swift', *Swift Studies*, V (1990), pp. 11–37.

Jonathan Culler, *The Pursuit of Signs: Semiotics, Literature, Deconstruction* (London, 1981).

David Dabydeen, *Hogarth, Walpole and Commercial Britain* (London, 1987).

Emile Dacier, *La Gravure en France au XVIIIe siècle. La gravure de genre et de mœurs* (Paris, 1925).

Hubert Damisch, *L'Origine de la perspective* (Paris, 1987).

—, *Théorie du nuage. Pour une histoire de la peinture* (Paris, 1972).

Robert Darnton, *The Great Cat Massacre and Other Episodes in French Cultural History* (London, 1984).

—, *The Literary Underground of the Old Regime* (London, 1982).

— and Daniel Roche, eds, *Revolution in Print: The Press in France 1775–1800* (Los Angeles, 1989).

Robert C. Davis and Ronald Schleifer, eds, *Contemporary Literary Criticism*, 2nd edn (New York, 1989).

Jacques Derrida, *A Derrida Reader: Between the Blinds*, ed. P. Kamuf (New York, 1991).

—, *Dissemination*, trans. B. Johnson (Chicago, 1981).

—, *La Vérité en peinture* (Paris, 1978), trans. as *The Truth in Painting* (1987).

—, *L'Ecriture et la différence* (Paris, 1967); trans. A. Bass as *Writing and Difference* (Chicago, 1978).

—, *Marges de la philosophie* (Paris, 1972).

—, *Of Grammatology*, trans. G. Spivak (Baltimore, 1976).

—, *Psyché. Inventions de l'autre* (Paris, 1987).

—, 'Signature, Event, Context', *Glyph*, 1 (1977), trans. A. Bass, reprd in *A Derrida Reader*, ed. P. Kamuf (New York, 1991), pp. 82–111.

—, 'The Law of Genre', trans. A. Ronell in *Critical Inquiry*, (special number: 'On Narrative', ed. W.J.T. Mitchell), VII/1 (1980), pp. 55–81.

Dictionnaire de la Révolution française, ed. François Furet and Mona Ozouf (Paris, 1988).

Denis Diderot, *Oeuvres complètes*, ed. J. Assézat and M. Tourneux, 1 (Paris, 1875).

Georges Didi-Huberman, *Devant l'image. Question posée aux fins d'une histoire de l'art* (Paris, 1990).

Basil L. Dighton and H.W. Lawrence, *French Line Engravings of the Late Eighteenth Century* (London, 1910).

Klaus Dirscherl, ed., *Bild und Text im Dialog* (Passau, 1993).

Jean-Pierre Dubost, *Eros und Vernunft: Literatur und Libertinage* (Frankfurt, 1988).

Alexander Dückers, ed., *Das Berliner Kupferstichkabinett. Ein Handbuch zur Sammlung* (Berlin, 1994).

Terry Eagleton, *Literary Theory* (Oxford, 1983).

Umberto Eco, 'How Culture Conditions the Signs We See', in *On Signs*, ed. Marshall Blonsky (Baltimore, 1985), pp. 157–76.

—, *The Open Work* (Cambridge, MA, 1989).

—, 'Producing Signs', in *On Signs*, ed. Marshall Blonsky (Baltimore, 1985), pp. 176–84.

—, *The Role of the Reader: Explorations in the Semiotics of Texts* (Bloomington, 1979).

David Eilon, *Factions' Fiction: Ideological Closure in Swift's Satire* (Newark, 1991).

Elizabeth Eisenstein, *Grub Street Abroad: Aspects of the French Cosmopolitan Press from the Age of Louis XIV to the French Revolution* (Oxford, 1992).

Michel Espagne and Michael Werner, eds, *Transferts: Les relations interculturelles dans l'espace franco-allemand (XVIIIe–XIXe siècles)* (Paris, 1988).

William B. Ewald, *The Masks of Jonathan Swift* (New York, 1967).

Stanley Fish, *Doing What Comes Naturally: Change, Rhetoric, and the Practice of Theory in Legal and Literary Studies* (Durham, NC, 1989).

—, 'Why Literary Criticism is Like Virtue', *The London Review of Books* (10 June 1993), pp. 11–16.

Ilsebill Barta Fliedl and Christoph Geissmar, eds, *Die Beredsamkeit des Leibes. Zur Körpersprache in der Kunst* (Vienna, 1992).

Jean-Paul Forster, 'Swift: The Satirical Use of Framing Fictions', in *The Structure of Texts*, ed. U. Fries (Tübingen, 1987), pp. 177–93.

Bernadette Fort, ed., *Fictions of the French Revolution* (Evanston, 1991).

—, 'Voice of the Public: The Carnivalization of Salon Art in Pre-Revolutionary France', *Eighteenth-century Studies*, XXII (1989), pp. 368–95.

Michel Foucault, *Surveiller et punir. Naissance de la prison* (Paris, 1975); trans. as *Discipline and Punish* (New York, 1977).

—, *The History of Sexuality*, 3 vols, trans. R. Hurley (New York, 1978–87).

—, *Les Mots et les choses* (Paris, 1966), trans. A. Sheridan as *The Order of Things* (New York, 1973).

—, *This is Not a Pipe*, trans. and ed. J. Harkness (Los Angeles, 1983).

—, 'What Is an Author', trans. D.F. Bouchard and S. Simon, in *Contemporary Literary Criticism*, 2nd edn, ed. R.C. Davis and R. Schleifer (New York, 1989), pp. 263–75.

Alastair Fowler, 'Periodization and Interart Analogies', in *Literatur und Bildende Kunst*, ed. U. Weisstein (Berlin, 1992), pp. 86–101.

Christopher Fox, 'The Myth of Narcissus in Swift's *Travels*', *Eighteenth-century Studies*, XX (1986), pp. 17–33.

Udo Fries, ed., *The Structure of Texts* (Tübingen, 1987).

Northrop Frye, *The Anatomy of Criticism* (Princeton, 1957).

Fureurs utérines de Marie-Antoinette, femme de Louis XVI (c. 1791).

Ivan Gaskell, 'History of Images', in *New Perspectives on Historical Writing*, ed. P. Burke (Cambridge, 1991) pp. 168–93.

Gérard Genette, *Figures II* (Paris, 1969).

—, *Introduction à l'architexte* (Paris, 1979); trans. J.E. Lewin as *The Architext: An Introduction* (Berkeley, 1992).

—, *Palimpsestes. La littérature au second degré* (Paris, 1982).

—, *Seuils* (Paris, 1987); part trans. by Marie Maclean ('Introduction to the Paratext') in *New Literary History*, XXII (1991), pp. 261–73.

M. Dorothy George, *English Political Caricature to 1792: A Study of Opinion and Propaganda* (Oxford, 1959).

—, *Hogarth to Cruikshank: Social Change in Graphic Satire* (London, 1967).

Pierre Georgel, ' "The Most Contemptible Meanness that Lines can be Formed into": Hogarth et les arts "autres" ' in *Image et société dans l'œuvre graphique de William Hogarth*, ed. F. Ogée (Paris, 1992), pp. 91–113.

Ernest B. Gilman, 'Interart Studies and the "Imperialism of Language" ', *Poetics Today*, X (1989), pp. 5–30.

Paul Goetsch, 'Linguistic Colonialism and Primitivism: The Discovery of Native Languages and Oral Traditions in Eighteenth-century Travel Books and Novels', *Anglia*, CVI (1988), pp. 338–59.

Nelson Goodman, *Languages of Art: An Approach to a Theory of Symbols* (Indianapolis, 1976).

Jean-Marie Goulemot, 'Fureurs utérines', *Dix-huitième siècle*, XII (1980), pp. 97–113.

Joseph Grigeley, 'The Implosion of Iconity', in *Word & Image Interactions. A Selection of Papers Given at the Second International Conference on Word and Image. Universität Zürich*, ed. M. Heuser *et al.* (Basle, 1993), pp. 243–51.

Claus Grimm, 'Histoire du cadre: un panorama', *Revue de l'art*, LXXVI (1987), pp. 15–20.

Jacques Guilhamou, 'Les mille langues du Père Duchène. La parade de la culture populaire pendant la Révolution', *Dix-huitième Siècle*, XVIII (1986), pp. 143–54.

Claudio Guillén, 'On the Concept and Metaphor of Perspective', in *Literatur und Bildende Kunst*, ed. U. Weisstein (Berlin, 1992), pp. 196–209.

Alain Guillerm, 'Le Système de l'iconographie galante', *Dix-huitième Siècle*, XII (1980), pp. 17–94.

Horst Günther, ed., *Die französische Revolution. Berichte deutscher Schriftsteller und Historiker* (Frankfurt, 1985).

Madelyn Gutwirth, *The Twilight of the Goddesses: Women and Representation in the French Revolutionary Era* (New Brunswick, NJ, 1992).

Robert Halsband, 'Eighteenth-century Illustrations of *Gulliver's Travels*', in *Proceedings of the First Münster Symposium on Jonathan Swift*, ed. H.J. Real and H.J. Vienken (Munich, 1985), pp. 83–112.

Brean Hammond, *Gulliver's Travels* (Milton Keynes, 1988).

Pierre-François Hugues d'Hancarville, *Antiquitées étrusques, grecques et romaines*, 4 vols (Naples, 1766–7).

—, *Monumens du culte secret des dames romaines* (1784).

—, *Monumens du culte secret des douze Césars* (Nancy, 1780–84).

Charles Harrison and Paul Wood, eds, *Art in Theory, 1900–1990: An Anthology of Changing Ideas* (Oxford, 1992).

Joan Hart, 'Erwin Panofsky and Karl Mannheim: A Dialogue on Interpretation', *Critical Inquiry*, XIX (1993), pp. 534–66.

Udo Hebel, *Romaninterpretation als Textarchäologie* (Frankfurt, 1989).

James A.W. Heffernan, *Museum of Words: The Poetics of Ekphrasis from Homer to Ashbery* (Chicago, 1993).

—, ed., *Representing the French Revolution: Literature, Historiography and Art* (Hanover, NH, 1992).

—, ed., *Space, Time, Image, Sign: Essays on Literature and the Visual Arts* (New York, 1987).

Arthur Henkel and Albrecht Schöne, eds, *Emblemata – Handbuch zur Sinnbildkunst des XVI. und XVII. Jahrhunderts* (Stuttgart, revd edn, 1976, including a supplement).

Klaus Herding and Rolf Reichardt, *Die Bildpublizistik der Französischen Revolution* (Frankfurt, 1989).

Martin Heuser, ed., *Word & Image Interactions: A Selection of Papers Given at the Second International Conference on Word and Image. Universität Zürich* (Basle, 1993).

Berthold Hinz, *William Hogarth: Beer Street and Gin Lane. Lehrtafeln zur britischen Volkswohlfahrt* (Frankfurt, 1984).

Historical Dictionary of the French Revolution 1789–1799, ed. Samuel F. Scott and Barry Rothaus (Westport, CT, 1985).

William Hogarth, *The Analysis of Beauty: With the Rejected Passages from the Manuscript Drafts and Autobiographical Notes*, ed. J. Burke (Oxford, 1955).

Grant Holly, 'Travel and Translation: Textuality in *Gulliver's Travels*', *Criticism*, XXI (1979), pp. 134–53.

Horace, *Odes and Epodes*, trans. C.E. Bennett (Cambridge, MA, 1914).

Robert Hume, *Henry Fielding and the London Theatre, 1728–1737* (Oxford, 1988).

Hans Hunfeld, *Literatur als Sprachlehre* (Berlin, 1990).

John Dixon Hunt, 'Making Vergil Look English', in *Word & Image Interactions*, ed. M. Heuser, (Basle, 1993), pp. 97–109.

Lynn Hunt, ed., *Eroticism and the Body Politic* (Baltimore, 1991).

—, 'The Many Bodies of Marie-Antoinette: Political Pornography and the Problem of the Feminine in the French Revolution', in *Eroticism and the Body Politic*, ed. L. Hunt (Baltimore, 1991), pp. 108–31.

—, ed., *The Invention of Pornography* (New York, 1993).

J. Paul Hunter, '*Gulliver's Travels* and the Novel', in *The Genres of Gulliver's Travels*, ed. F.N. Smith (Newark, 1990), pp. 56–75.

Wolfgang Iser, *The Act of Reading* (Baltimore, 1978).

—, *The Implied Reader: Patterns of Communication in Prose Fiction from Bunyan to Beckett* (Baltimore, 1974).

Derek Jarrett, *England in the Age of Hogarth* (London, 1976).

M.K. Johnson, '(Re)framing the Photograph', *Word & Image*, IX (1993), pp. 245–51.

Hans Kellner, *Language and Historical Representation: Getting the Story Crooked* (Madison, WN, 1990).

Martin J. Kemp, *The Science of Art: Optical Themes in Western Art from Brunelleschi to Seurat* (London, 1990).

Reinhart Koselleck and Rolf Reichardt, eds, *Die französische Revolution* (Munich, 1988).

Henning Krauss, ed., *Literatur der Französischen Revolution* (Stuttgart, 1988).

Julia Kristeva, *Sémeiotiké. Recherches pour une sémanalyse* (Paris, 1969, reprd 1978).

—, *La Révolution du langage poétique* (Paris, 1974).

Carl R. Kropf, ed., *Reader Entrapment in Eighteenth-century Literature* (New York, 1992).

Bernd Krysmanski, 'Hogarth's "Enthusiasm Delineated". Nachahmung als Kritik am Kennertum', PhD diss., 2 vols (Ruhr Universität Bochum, 1994).

Jacques Lacan, *The Four Fundamental Concepts of Psycho-Analysis*, trans. A. Sheridan (London, 1977).

Jean-François Lafitau, *Mœurs des sauvages amériquains comparées aux mœurs des premiers temps* (Paris, 1724).

Gérard Lairesse, *The Art of Painting in All its Branches* (Amsterdam, 1701, trans. 1738).

La Journée amoureuse, ou les derniers plaisirs de M . . . Ant . . . (1792).

La Liberté, ou Mlle Raucour à toute la secte anandrine, assemblée au foyer de la Comédie Française (c. 1791).

Claude Langlois, *La Caricature contre-révolutionnaire* (Paris, 1988).

L'Autrichienne en goguettes, ou l'orgie royale (1789).

Jean-Claude Lebensztejn, 'Framing Classical Space', *Art Forum*, XLVII (1988), pp. 37–41.

—, 'Starting Out from the Frame (Vignettes)', in *Deconstruction and the Visual Arts*, ed. P. Brunette and D. Wills (Cambridge, 1994), pp. 118–41.

Jacques Le Goff, *Histoire et mémoire* (Paris, 1988).

Les Amours de Charlot et Toinette (c. 1789).

Les Embarras de Marie-Antoinette (c. 1790).

Les Enfants de Sodome à l'Assemblée Nationale (1790).

Les Petits bougres au manège (c. 1791).

Le Triomphe de la fouterie, ou les apparences sauvées: comédie en deux actes et en vers (1791).

Steven Z. Levine, 'Moxey's Moxie and the Summers of '84: Intention and Interpretation in the History of Art – A Commentary', *New Literary History*, XVII (1986), pp. 323–31.

Georg Christoph Lichtenberg, *Ausführliche Erklärung der Hogarthschen Kupferstiche*, ed. F.H. Mautner (Frankfurt, 1991).

—, *G.C. Lichtenberg's* [sic] *Erklärung der Hogarthischen Kupferstiche, mit verkleinerten aber vollständigen Copien derselben von E. Riepenhausen*, 13 issues (Göttingen, 1794–1835).

Lucretius, *De rerum natura*, ed. and trans. M.F. Smith (Cambridge, 1982).

Hans-Jürgen Lüsebrink, 'Iconotextes. Über Bilder und Metaphernnetze in den Schrifttexten Michel Foucaults', in *Bild und Text im Dialog*, ed. Klaus Dirscherl (Passau, 1993), pp. 467–87.

—, 'Les Tambours de la mémoire. Mémoire collective et conscience historique des cultures orales aux sociétées modernes', in *Oralités – Polyphonix 16*, ed. R. Chamberland and R. Martel (Quebec City, 1992), pp. 183–95.

Louis Marin, *Détruire la peinture* (Paris, 1977).

—, *Etudes sémiologiques* (Paris, 1971).

—, 'Frontiers of Utopia', *Critical Inquiry*, XIX (1993), pp. 397–420.

—, *Utopics: Spatial Play*, trans. R.A. Vollrath (Atlantic Highlands, NJ, 1984).

Franz H. Mautner, *Lichtenberg. Geschichte seines Geistes* (Berlin, 1968).

Stephen Melville, 'Color Has Not Yet Been Named: Objectivity in Deconstruction', in *Deconstruction and the Visual Arts*, ed. P. Brunette and D. Wills (Cambridge, 1994), pp. 33–49.

Maurice Merleau-Ponty, *Phénoménologie de la perception* [1945] (Paris, 1971).

Gérard Mermoz, 'Rhetoric and Episteme: Writing About "Art" in The Wake of

Post-Structuralism', *Art History*, XII/4 (1989), pp. 497–509.

Jenny Mezciems, 'Utopia and "the Thing which is not": More, Swift, and Other Lying Idealists', *University of Toronto Quarterly*, LII (1982), pp. 49–53.

Helena Michie, *The Flesh Made Word: Female Figures and Women's Bodies* (Oxford, 1987).

Louis T. Milic, *A Quantitative Approach to the Style of Jonathan Swift* (The Hague, 1967).

J. Hillis Miller, *Illustration* (London, 1992).

—, *The Linguistic Moment: From Wordsworth to Stevens* (Princeton, 1985).

W.J.T. Mitchell, 'Going Too Far with the Sister Arts', in *Space, Time, Image, Sign: Essays on Literature and the Visual Arts*, ed. J.A.W. Heffernan (New York, 1987), pp. 1–11.

—, *Iconology: Image, Text, Ideology* (Chicago, 1986).

Joachim Möller, ed., *Hogarth in Context: Ten Essays and a Bibliography* (Marburg, forthcoming).

Paul Monod, 'Painters and Party Politics in England, 1714–1760', *Eighteenth-century Studies*, XXVI/3 (1993), pp. 367–99.

Alain Montandon, ed., *Iconotextes* (Paris, 1990).

—, ed., *Signe, texte, image* (Meyzieu, 1990).

Thomas More, *Utopia* [1516], in *The Complete Works of St. Thomas More*, IV, ed. E. Surtz, S.J., and J.H. Hexter (New Haven, 1965).

M. Morford, *Persius* (Boston, 1984).

Keith Moxey, 'Semiotics and the Social History of Art', *New Literary History*, XXII/4 (1991), pp. 985–1001.

Richard Nash, 'Entrapment and Ironic Modes in *Tale of a Tub*', *Eighteenth-century Studies*, XXIV/4 (1991), pp. 414–32.

Michael Nerlich, 'Qu'est-ce qu'un iconotexte? Réflexions sur le rapport texte-image photographique dans *La Femme se découvre*', in *Iconotextes*, ed. A. Montandon (Paris, 1990), pp. 255–303.

Jean Baptiste Nougaret, *Les Progrès du libertinage* (c. 1791).

Maximillian E. Novak, '*Gulliver's Travels* and the Picaresque Voyage: Some Reflections on the Hazards of Genre Criticism', in *The Genres of Gulliver's Travels*, ed. F.N. Smith (Newark, 1990), pp. 23–39.

Oeuvres anonymes du XVIIIe siècle. L'Enfer de la Bibliothèque Nationale, 7 vols, ed. Michel Camus (Paris, 1984–7).

Frédéric Ogée, ed., *Image et société dans l'œuvre graphique de William Hogarth* (Paris, 1992).

—, 'L'œil erre: les parcours sériels de Hogarth', *Tropismes*, V (1991), pp. 39–106.

—, 'L'Onction extrême: une lecture de *A Midnight Modern Conversation* (1733) de William Hogarth', *Etudes anglaises*, XLV/1 (1992), pp. 56–65.

Dorinda Outram, *Le langage mâle de la vertus*: Women and the Discourse of the French Revolution', in *The Social History of Language*, ed. P. Burke and R. Porter (Cambridge, 1987), pp. 120–35.

—, *The Body and the French Revolution: Sex, Class and Political Culture* (New Haven, 1989).

Félix Paknadel, 'Hogarth's *Gate of Calais*: Myth and Reality', *Studies on Voltaire and the Eighteenth Century*, CCXCII (1991), pp. 7–13.

Nycole Paquin, 'Le "cadre" comme lieu de paradoxe au dix-huitième siècle', in *Transactions of the Eighth International Congress on the Enlightenment* (Oxford, 1992), pp. 1485–9.

Dirk F. Passmann, *'Full of Improbable Lies': Gulliver's Travels und die Reiseliteratur vor 1726* (Frankfurt, 1987).

Ronald Paulson, *Breaking and Remaking: Aesthetic Practice in England, 1700–1820* (New Brunswick, NJ, and London, 1989).

—, *Hogarth*, in 3 vols: I *The 'Modern Moral Subject', 1697–1732*; II *High Art and Low, 1732–1750*; III *Art and Politics, 1750–1764* (New Brunswick, NJ, and Cambridge, 1991–3).

— ed. and comp., *Hogarth's Graphic Works*, 3rd revd edn (London, 1989).

—, *Popular and Polite Art in the Age of Hogarth and Fielding* (Notre Dame, 1979).

Michael Payne, *Reading Theory: An Introduction to Lacan, Derrida, and Kristeva* (Oxford, 1993).

Iain Pears, *The Discovery of Painting: The Growth of Interest in the Arts in England, 1680–1768* (London, 1988).

Charles Sanders Peirce, *Collected Papers*, ed. C. Hartshorne *et al.*, 8 vols. (Cambridge, MA, 1931–60).

Carmela Perri, 'Knowing and Playing: The Literary Text and the Trope Allusion', *American Imago*, XLI (1984), pp. 117–28.

Persius, *The Satires*, trans. G. Lee (Liverpool, 1987).

Heinrich F. Plett, ed., *Intertextuality* (New York, 1991).

John H. Plumb, *The Commercialization of Leisure in Eighteenth-century England* (Reading, 1974).

Marcia Pointon, *Hanging the Head: Portraiture and Social Formation in Eighteenth-century England* (London, 1993).

Bruno Pons, 'Les Cadres français du XVIIIe siècle et leurs ornements', *Revue de l'art*, LXXVI (1987), pp. 41–50.

Jeremy Popkin, 'Pamphlet Journalism at the End of the Old Regime', *Eighteenth-century Studies*, XXII (1989), pp. 351–68.

Roy Porter, 'History of the Body', in *New Perspectives on Historical Writing*, ed. P. Burke (Cambridge, 1991), pp. 206–33.

Donald Preziosi, 'Modernity Again: The Museum as Trompe l'œil', in *Deconstruction and the Visual Arts*, ed. P. Brunette and D. Wills (Cambridge, 1994), pp. 141–51.

Claude Rawson, *Gulliver and the Gentle Reader: Studies in Swift and Our Time* (London, 1973).

Hermann J. Real and Heinz J. Vienken, *Jonathan Swift: Gulliver's Travels* (Munich, 1984).

—, eds, *Proceedings of the First Münster Symposium on Jonathan Swift* (Munich, 1985).

Eileen Reeves, 'Reading Maps', *Word & Image*, IX/1 (1993), pp. 51–65.

Requète et décret en faveur des putains, des fouteuses, des macquerelles et des branleuses: contre les bougres, les bardaches et les brûleurs de paillasse (c.1791).

Jacques Revel, 'Marie-Antoinette in Her Fictions: The Staging of Hatred', in *Fictions of the French Revolution*, ed. B. Fort (Evanston, 1991), pp. 111–31.

Denis Reynaud, 'Pour une théorie de la description au 18e siècle', *Dix-huitième Siècle*, XXII (1990), pp. 347–67.

Marie M. Roberts and Roy Porter, eds, *Literature and Medicine During the Eighteenth Century* (London, 1993).

Alan Robinson, 'Reading Victorian Paintings', in *Bild und Text im Dialog*, ed. Klaus Dirscherl (Passau, 1993), pp. 211–27.

Richard H. Rodino, ' "Splendide mendax": Authors, Characters, and Readers in *Gulliver's Travels*', in *Reading Swift: Papers from the Second Münster Symposium on Jonathan Swift*, ed. R.H. Rodino and H.J. Real (Munich, 1993), pp. 167–85.

Pat Rogers, *Grub Street: Studies in a Subculture* (London, 1972).

—, *Hacks and Dunces* (London, 1980).

—, *Literature and Popular Culture in Eighteenth-century England* (Brighton, 1985).

Marie-Claire Ropars-Wuilleumier, 'The Dissimulation of Painting', in *Deconstruction and the Visual Arts*, ed. P. Brunette and D. Wills (Cambridge, 1994), pp. 65–80.

Mark Roskill, *The Interpretation of Pictures* (Amherst, 1989).

Murray Roston, *Changing Perspectives in Literature and the Visual Arts, 1650–1820* (Princeton, 1990).

George S. Rousseau, *Perilous Enlightenment: Pre- and Post-Modern Discourse, Sexual, Historical* (Manchester, 1991).

Simon Schama, *The Embarrassment of Riches: An Interpretation of Dutch Culture in the Golden Age* (Cambridge, MA, 1987).

Johann Jakob Scheuchzer, *Kupfer-Bibel, in welcher die Physica sacra oder geheiligte Naturwissenschaft derer in Heil. Schrift vorkommenden natürlichen Sachen deutlich erklärt und bewährt von Joh. Jakob Scheuchzer . . . verlegt durch Johann Andreas Pfeffel*, 4 vols (Augsburg and Ulm, 1731–5; reprd and abbrev., with an introduction by H. Krauss, Konstanz, 1984).

Jochen Schlobach, 'Siècle des Lumières et Aufklärung: Mots, métaphores et concepts', *Interfaces. Image, Texte, Langage*, IV (1993), pp. 109–29.

—, *Zyklentheorie und Epochenmetaphorik* (Munich, 1980).

Hermann Josef Schnackertz, '*Gulliver's Travels*: Swifts aufklärerisches Spiel mit der Fiktion', *Poetica*, XIV (1982), pp. 45–69.

Ulrich Seeber, *Wandlungen der Form der literarischen Utopie* (Göppingen, 1970).

Mary Sheriff, *Fragonard: Art and Eroticism* (Chicago, 1990).

Sean Shesgreen, *Hogarth and the Times-of-the-Day Tradition* (Ithaca, 1983).

—, 'Hogarth's *Industry and Idleness*: A Reading', *Eighteenth-century Studies*, IX (1976), pp. 569–98.

Norman Simms, *The Humming Tree: A Study in the History of Mentalities* (Chicago, 1992).

Robin Simon, 'Wits About Him: Hogarth, Pope, and Burlington', in *Belov'd By Ev'ry Muse: Richard Boyle, 3rd Earl of Burlington & 4th Earl of Cork (1694–1753)*, ed. D. Arnold (London, 1994), pp. 45–50.

Morris Slavin, *The French Revolution in Miniature: Section Droits-de-l'Homme, 1789– 1795* (Princeton, 1984).

Frederick N. Smith, 'The Danger of Reading Swift: The Double Binds of *Gulliver's Travels*', in *Reader Entrapment in Eighteenth-century Literature*, ed. R.C. Kropf (New York), 1992, pp. 109–31.

John Smith, *The Complete Works of Captain John Smith*, 3 vols, ed. P.L. Barbour (London, 1986).

—, *The Travels of Captain John Smith* (New York, 1907).

Barbara Maria Stafford, *Artful Science: Enlightenment Entertainment and the Eclipse of Visual Education* (Cambridge, MA, 1994).

—, *Body Criticism: Imaging the Unseen in Enlightenment Art and Medicine* (Cambridge, MA, 1991).

—, *Voyage Into Substance: Art, Science, Nature, and the Illustrated Travel Account, 1760– 1840* (London, 1984).

Peter Stallybrass and Allon White, *The Politics and Poetics of Transgression* (London, 1986).

Philip Stewart, *Engraven Desire: Eros, Image, and Text in the French Eighteenth Century* (London, 1992).

Laurence Sterne, *The Life and Opinions of Tristram Shandy, Gentleman* (London, 1759–66).

Lawrence Stone, *The Family, Sex and Marriage in England 1500–1800* (London, 1977; abridged and revd edn, Harmondsworth, 1979).

Georg Stuhlfaut, *Das Dreieck. Die Geschichte eines religiösen Symbols* (Stuttgart, 1937).

David Summers, 'Intentions in the History of Art', *New Literary History*, XVII (1986), pp. 305–22, 333–44.

Jonathan Swift, *Gulliver's Travels*, ed. P. Turner (Oxford, 1986).

—, *Gulliver's Travels*, ed. R.A. Greenberg (New York, 2nd edn, 1970).

—, *Gulliver's Travels*, ed. H. Davis (Oxford, 1965).

—, *The Complete Poems*, ed. P. Rogers (London, 1983).

—, *The Correspondence of Jonathan Swift*, ed. H. Williams, 5 vols (Oxford, 1963–5).

Chantal Thomas, 'L'héroïne du crime: Marie-Antoinette dans les pamphlets', in *La Carmagnole des Muses. L'homme de lettres et l'artiste dans la Révolution*, ed. J.C. Bonnet (Paris, 1988), pp. 245–60.

—, *La Reine scélérate. Marie-Antoinette dans les pamphlets* (Paris, 1989).

Edward P. Thompson, *Customs in Common* (London, 1991).

Rodolphe Toepffer, *Essai de physiognomonie* (Paris, 1845; reprd in French and German, trans. W. and D. Drost, ed. W. Drost and K. Riha, Siegen, 1982).

John Trusler, *Hogarth Moralized* (London, 1768).

P.J.J. Van Thiel, 'Eloge du cadre: la pratique hollandaise', *Revue de l'art*, LXXVI (1987), pp. 32–6.

H. Aram Veeser, ed., *The New Historicism* (London, 1989).

Vie de Marie-Antoinette . . . depuis la perte de son pucelage jusqu'au premier mai 1791 (1793).

Vie privée libertine et scandaleuse de Marie-Antoinette (1791–3).

Peter J. de Voogd, *Henry Fielding and William Hogarth: The Correspondences of the Arts* (Amsterdam, 1981).

Peter Wagner, *Eros Revived: Erotica of the Enlightenment in England and America* (London, 1990).

—, ed., *Erotica and the Enlightenment* (Frankfurt and New York, 1991).

—, 'Eroticism in Graphic Art: The Case of William Hogarth', *Studies in Eighteenth-century Culture*, XXI (1991), pp. 53–75.

—, 'Hogarth, Eighteenth-century Literature and the Modern Canon', in *Anglistentag Marburg 1990: Proceedings*, ed. C. Uhlig and R. Zimmermann (Tübingen, 1991), pp. 456–81.

—, 'Hogarth's Graphic Palimpsests': Intermedial Adaptation of Popular Literature', *Word & Image*, VII (1991), pp. 329–47.

—, 'How to (Mis)Read Hogarth or Ekphrasis Galore', *1650–1850: Ideas, Aesthetics, and Inquiries in the Early Modern Era*, II (1994), pp. 99–135.

—, ed., *Icons – Texts – Iconotexts: Essays on Ekphrasis and Intermediality* (Berlin and New York, 1995).

—, 'Learning to Read the Female Body: On the Function of Manet's *Olympia* in John Braine's *Room at the Top*', *Zeitschrift für Anglistik und Amerikanistik*, XLII/1 (1994), pp. 38–54.

—, *Lust und Liebe im Rokoko / Lust and Love in the Rococo Period* (Nördlingen, 1986).

—, 'Satirical Functions of the Bible in Hogarth's Graphic Art', *Etudes Anglaises*, XLVI/2 (1993), pp. 141–67.

—, 'Swift and the Female Idol: The Dean as Iconoclast', *Anglia*, CX/3–4 (1992), pp. 347–67.

—, 'The Discourse on Crime in Hogarth's Graphic Works', in *Image et société dans l'œuvre graphique de William Hogarth*, ed. F. Ogée (Paris, 1992), pp. 29–45.

—, 'The Pornographer in the Court Room: Trial Reports About Cases of Sexual Crimes and Delinquencies as a Genre of Eighteenth-century Erotica', in *Sexuality in Eighteenth-century England*, ed. P.-G. Boucé (Manchester, 1982), pp. 120–41.

Horace Walpole, *Anecdotes of Painting* (London, 1888).

Oskar Walzel, *Gehalt und Gestalt im Kunstwerk des Dichters* (Berlin, 1924).

Ian Watt, *The Rise of the Novel* (Harmondsworth, 1957, reprd 1963).

Ulrich Weisstein, ed., *Literatur und Bildende Kunst* (Berlin, 1992).

Jeanne K. Welcher, 'Hogarth's Reading of *Gulliver's Travels*', in *Hogarth in Context. Ten Essays and a Bibliography*, ed. J. Möller (Marburg, forthcoming).

Hayden White, *Metahistory: The Historical Imagination in Nineteenth-century Europe* (London, 1973).

—, *Tropics of Discourse* (London, 1978).

Andrew Wilton, *The Swagger Portrait: Grand Manner Portraiture in Britain from Van Dyck to Augustus John, 1630–1930* (London, 1992).

Barry Wind, '*Gin Lane* and *Beer Street*: A Fresh Draught', in *Hogarth in Context: Ten Essays and a Bibliography*, ed. J. Möller (Marburg, forthcoming).

Ludwig Wittgenstein, *Philosophical Investigations* [1953], trans. G.E.M. Anscombe (New York, 1958).

—, *Tractatus Logico-Philosophicus* ([1921] Frankfurt, 1984), trans. B.F. McGuinness (New York, 1961).

Werner Wolf, ' "The Flame of Sex". Neue Funktionen dargestellter Sexualität in englischsprachigem Erzählen der Postmoderne', *Arbeiten aus Anglistik und Amerikanisitk*, XVII/2 (1992), pp. 269–302.

David Woodward, ed., *Art and Cartography* (Chicago, 1987).

Michael Worton and Judith Still, eds, *Intertextuality* (Manchester, 1990).

Index

italic numerals refer to illustrations